Reading

grade by grade &

Writing

Primary literacy standards
for kindergarten through third grade

New Standards

Primary Literacy Committee

Illustrated by Garin Baker

NEW
STANDARDS®

In this book are excerpts from *Ramona Quimby, Age 8* by Beverly Cleary. Copyright © 1981 by Beverly Cleary. By permission of Morrow Junior Books, a division of William Morrow and Company, Inc.

In this book are excerpts from *Animal Habitats* by Peter Sloan and Sheryl Sloan. Copyright © 1995 by Sundance Publishing. By permission of Sundance Publishing.

In this book are excerpts from *Cam Jansen and the Mystery of the Stolen Diamonds* by David Adler, illustrated by Susanna Natti. Copyright © 1981 by Susanna Natti on Illustrations. Used by permission of Viking Penguin, a division of Penguin Putnam Inc.

The information about leveled text lists is reprinted by permission of Irene Fountas and Gay Su Pinnell: *Guided Reading: Good First Teaching for All Children* (Heinemann, a division of Reed Elsevier Inc., Portsmouth, NH, 1996).

Editorial and Design by KSA-Plus Communications, Inc.

Printed in the United States of America by Peake Printers.

ISBN 1-889630-90-X

e-mail: info@ncee.org

To America's teachers

There is no educational matter as urgent as seeing to it that every American child becomes a competent reader and writer. Your commitment to meeting this challenge — day by day, child by child — is important, noble and inspiring.

In this book, we hope to inspire *you*. Here, the path to literacy is clear and sure: Children learn to read and write with a judicious mix of attention to the print-sound code and extensive engagement with literature and writing. Here, the best ideas from the best minds are gathered in one place to illuminate the way to literacy.

Enjoy the journey.

In addition to the generous funding of the **U.S. Department of Education's Office of Educational Research and Improvement,** initial support for the development of these standards was provided by the **Noyce Foundation.** These standards build on the original work of New Standards supported by **The Pew Charitable Trusts** and the **John D. and Catherine T. MacArthur Foundation.**

Table of Contents

Preface

Imagine what it would be like to be unable to read — to be denied Shakespeare's soaring English, Faulkner's serpentine sentences, Maya Angelou's cadences, Hemingway's spare prose, the observations of *New York Times* columnists on the news of the day, the luminous creations of Gabriel Garcia Marquez, the brilliant explanations of Stephen Jay Gould, Julia Child's recipes, the calculus text that is the entry point for a budding engineer, and the travel book that explains what is most worth seeing in a new city. Imagine what it must be like to know that you will never get beyond an entry-level job and to have to hide your inability to read as if it were a hideous deformity. Think about the rage and frustration that would be yours every day if you knew that almost all ordinary opportunities were beyond your reach because you had trouble reading ordinary things.

Reading — and increasingly, writing — is the keyhole through which we all must pass to have a chance at the good life. Many don't make it. Many of those who do are only marginally literate and consequently have only marginal opportunities. Reading and writing are, without doubt, the two most important skills that we can transmit to our children. And the primary school years are an absolutely critical time in this process. The evidence is strong that young people who are not fluent readers and writers by the end of third grade may never catch up to their peers. So citizens, school boards and educators everywhere have called for students to become fluent readers and competent writers by the end of the third grade.

What, exactly, does it mean to be a competent reader and writer at the age of eight or nine? What kinds of books should children be able to read fluently and with comprehension? How much reading should they be doing? What kinds of writing should we expect of them? And — most important of all for teachers and parents — what are the steps along the way? What does a child who is developing well as a reader and writer look like? What are warning signs that some special help or more intensive teaching may be needed?

The book you are holding in your hands answers these questions and more. *Reading & Writing Grade by Grade* adds clear performance targets to the National Research Council's call for a balanced approach to reading instruction in the early years. Grade by grade, beginning with kindergarten, specific expectations are laid out for the skills and habits of reading and writing. These expectations are illustrated — with examples of children's writing, samples of their oral reading, and even videos of children discussing books and following written directions. Drawn from real classrooms, these work samples make clear just how good is good enough in primary reading and writing. The CD-ROMs that accompany this book contain all of these illustrations, plus a summary version of the standards themselves.

It has taken nearly two years of work by a distinguished group of educators and researchers to produce these standards. Many of the nation's most eminent experts on reading and writing joined our New Standards® Primary Literacy Committee in the endeavor. Five of the panelists also served on the National Research Council committee that produced the book *Preventing Reading Difficulties in Young Children*. The members of the New Standards Primary Literacy Committee (see pages 10–16 for brief biographies) came to the task of devising a set of practical standards for early literacy achievement with differing views — especially on the vexing question of "phonics" versus "whole language" as a basis for children's earliest reading instruction. They joined together in this effort because they were tired of the wars that had divided them and believed that by focusing squarely on what children needed to know and be able to do — rather than on ideologies of how to organize teaching — they could provide a unified set of guidelines for teachers and parents.

The result is this set of standards and benchmark examples that do not paper over differences with vague words but instead lay out clearly the full range of skills, knowledge and literacy habits that primary children need to learn if they are to succeed in later schooling and in life. These New Standards Primary Literacy Standards make clear that children must learn:

◆ Both the print-sound code ("phonics," "phonemic awareness") *and* the ability to comprehend and interpret what they read, right from the start. Children's progress in reading can be tracked by their ability to read benchmark books of graduated levels of difficulty.

◆ Writing *and* reading. The New Standards Primary Literacy Standards give equal weight to learning reading and writing, linking the skills in one to the other. They show how children's earliest spelling attempts are linked to their efforts to master phonics. And they illustrate how attending carefully to the language in books that they read can help children give personality and "voice" to their own writing.

◆ Specific purposes and genres of writing, including narratives, reports, functional writing and literature. Children are expected to read and write in each of these genres.

◆ Habits of literacy, including daily writing and reading, the ability to discuss with others what they read, and strategies for evaluating and revising their written work. The standards provide benchmarks for daily practice of reading and writing. Beginning in kindergarten, children should read or have read to them four to six books a day. By third grade, they should read independently each year 30 books of prescribed difficulty from different genres.

◆ Conventional spelling and the correct uses of punctuation, along with careful choice of vocabulary, style and syntax in their writing.

The New Standards Primary Literacy Standards ask much of children and, therefore, of their teachers and parents. If one visited an "average" school in America today, few children would be able to meet all of the standards laid out here. But we know that children can *learn* to perform at the levels called for by the standards. We know this because we based our expectations on the performances of children in good literacy programs of various kinds throughout the country. These are the performances that appear in our reading and writing illustrations. The standards set out realistic

Coming Soon:

Primary Literacy Standards in Speaking and Listening

Beyond reading and writing, literate Americans in the 21st century need to be able to speak effectively and listen actively to other people. A New Standards committee of researchers and practitioners is working now on recommendations for Primary Literacy Standards in speaking and listening.

expectations for children who are taught well. They are demanding because nothing less will prepare children for their futures.

Many states and districts already have standards for the early grades. These standards are intended not as a replacement for those official documents, but as an extension and companion to them, an indispensable tool for analyzing children's literacy skills and setting specific targets for their learning. The New Standards Primary Literacy Standards are designed to serve as a detailed guide for teachers and parents. They go beyond general statements about what students should be able to do to provide explicit examples of expected performance. The New Standards Primary Literacy Standards make it easy for parents and teachers to know whether children are meeting rigorous and reasonable expectations and to identify the areas in which students need more work.

We are very pleased to be able to share these standards with you. We hope they will be of great value to teachers and will make a big difference in the lives of countless children who will grow up to be adults who read well and write well, people whose opportunities are boundless.

Lauren Resnick
Co-director
New Standards

Marc Tucker
Co-director
New Standards

Committee Members

Marilyn Jager Adams is a visiting scholar at the Harvard University Graduate School of Education. She was vice president of the American Educational Research Council from 1996–98. In 1995, she received the American Educational Research Association's Sylvia Scribner Award for Outstanding Contribution to Education through Research.

A member of several national advisory boards, she chaired the Planning Committee and was a member of the National Academy of Sciences' Committee on the Prevention of Reading Difficulties in Young Children. She also has written several classroom resources and many chapters and journal articles on cognition and education issues.

Rosalinda B. Barrera is a professor of curriculum and instruction at the University of Illinois at Urbana–Champaign. A former elementary classroom teacher, she also has held a variety of positions in the curriculum and instruction department for New Mexico State University and worked as director of curriculum and instruction for K–12 in the Socorro School District in El Paso, Texas. A member of numerous committees, she is on the National Council of Teachers of English (NCTE) Commission on Curriculum and has served as chair of NCTE's Multicultural Booklist Committee as well as of the New Mexico Professional Standards Commission.

Lucy Calkins is a professor of education at Teachers College, Columbia University, and is founding director of the Teachers College Writing Project. She has taught at the elementary, middle and high school levels and now works side-by-side with teachers, conducting collaborative research on children as readers and writers. Her books include *The Art of Teaching Writing* and *A Teacher's Guide to Standardized Reading Tests: Knowledge is Power,* which she co-authored with Kate Montgomery and Donna Santman. *The Art of Teaching Reading* will be published in 2000.

These illustrations are the work of students who attend Alice Carlson Applied Learning Center in Fort Worth, Texas. Even though the children never met the committee members they were illustrating, the drawings capture the dedication — and joy — the adults bring to their work.

Courtney B. Cazden is the Charles William Eliot Professor of Education Emerita at Harvard University. A former primary-grade teacher, her research and teaching have focused for more than 30 years on the oral language and literacy of young children, especially children from language and cultural minorities. Her most recent book is *Whole Language Plus: Essays on Literacy in the United States and New Zealand*.

Phil Daro is the executive director of New Standards and the director of research and development for the National Center on Education and the Economy. His career has included tenures as the director of the Office of Project Development with the California Department of Education, the executive director of the American Mathematics Project and the executive director of the California Mathematics Project. He received his bachelor of arts in English from the University of California, Berkeley, with a minor in mathematics.

Susan Fitzgerald is a senior literacy associate for the National Center on Education and the Economy, where she serves in the research and development division, coordinates and conducts literacy institutes for America's Choice School Design, and conducts core assignment workshops in English language arts in Chicago, Pennsylvania and New York City. She received her master of science in education at Texas Wesleyan University in Fort Worth, Texas, with a specialization in early childhood education.

Barbara R. Foorman, professor of pediatrics and director of the Center for Academic and Reading Skills at the University of Texas–Houston Medical School, is principal investigator of a long-term grant funded by the National Institute of Child Health and Human Development, "Early Interventions for Children With Reading Problems." From 1978 to 1997, she was a professor of educational psychology at the University of Houston. She is on the editorial board of *Journal of Learning Disabilities* and on the board of the Society for the Scientific Study of Reading. She was a member of the National Academy of Sciences' Committee on the Prevention of Reading Difficulties in Young Children.

Mary Ellen Giacobbe is an educational consultant who works in school districts in the United States and Canada. She leads workshops on the teaching of reading and writing and frequently speaks on these topics to groups around the country. She also has contributed chapters to numerous books and published several articles. She is a member of the National Council of Teachers of English, International Reading Association and Whole Language Umbrella.

Sally Hampton is the director of research on curriculum and instruction and English language arts for the National Center on Education and the Economy. Since 1991, she has been involved with New Standards, developing both performance standards and a reference exam in English language arts. She worked as a classroom teacher for nearly 16 years before coming to the Fort Worth Independent School District in 1984 to develop a research-based writing program. She has spoken and published widely on the subject of student writing.

Angela M. Jaggar is a professor of education at New York University, where she specializes in early childhood and elementary education and directs an in-service master's degree program. Her research and teaching interests include oral language development, the role of talk in literacy development and learning, emergent and early literacy, Reading Recovery, the teaching of reading and writing, and language across the curriculum. She has written and spoken extensively on these topics.

Currently, she is a member of the National Data Evaluation Committee of the Reading Recovery Council of North America. In this capacity, she evaluates, writes and speaks about the results of Reading Recovery programs.

P. David Pearson has been the John A. Hannah Distinguished Professor of Education since 1995 at the College of Education at Michigan State University, where he holds appointments in the department of teacher education and the department of counseling, educational psychology and special education. At Michigan State, he also serves as a principal investigator and co-director of the Center for the Improvement of Early Reading Achievement (CIERA). Within CIERA, he pursues a line of research related to reading instruction and reading assessment policies and practices at the local, state and national levels.

He has written and edited several books about research and practice, most notably the *Handbook of Reading Research,* now in its second volume.

Charles Perfetti is a professor of psychology and linguistics and senior scientist at the University of Pittsburgh's Learning Research and Development Center. He was formerly chair of psychology. His research on reading processes, reading ability and learning to read has been published in over 120 journal articles and several books. A graduate of the University of Michigan, he has been a visiting professor at the Max Planck Institute for Psycholinguistics and the Netherlands Institute for Advanced Studies.

In addition to memberships on numerous editorial boards, he is a member of the National Academy of Sciences' Committee on the Prevention of Reading Difficulties in Young Children and president-elect of the Society for the Scientific Study of Reading.

Gay Su Pinnell is a professor of educational theory and practice at The Ohio State University. In 1999, she was awarded membership in the International Reading Association's Reading Hall of Fame for her contributions to literacy education. She also has received a variety of other awards, including the 1996 Ohio State University Distinguished Teaching Award and the 1993 Charles A. Dana Award for Pioneering Achievement in Health and Education.

A member of numerous national associations, she is on the editorial board of *Reading Research Quarterly, The Reading Teacher* and *Language Arts.* She also was an investigator on several research projects studying both Reading Recovery programs and early literacy in at-risk students.

Lauren B. Resnick is co-founder and co-director of New Standards, and she also founded and directs the Institute for Learning, which focuses on professional development based on cognitive learning principles and the development of effort-oriented educational programs. A professor of psychology at the University of Pittsburgh, she directs the university's Learning Research and Development Center. Her research has focused on standards and assessment, effort-based education, the nature and development of thinking abilities, and socializing intelligence, with special attention to literacy and mathematics. She has written or edited 10 books and more than 125 articles and book chapters. She has served as president of the American Educational Research Association and as a member of the Harvard Board of Overseers and the Smithsonian Council, along with several boards and committees of the National Research Council.

Dorothy S. Strickland is the State of New Jersey Professor of Reading at Rutgers University. She previously was the Arthur I. Gates Professor of Education at Teachers College, Columbia University. A former classroom teacher, reading consultant and learning disabilities specialist, she also is a former president of the International Reading Association (IRA) and the IRA Reading Hall of Fame. In 1985, she received IRA's Outstanding Teacher Educator of Reading Award. She was the recipient of the 1998 National Council of Teachers of English (NCTE) Award as Outstanding Educator in the Language Arts and the 1994 NCTE Rewey Belle Inglis Award as Outstanding Woman in the Teaching of English. She has numerous publications in the field of reading/language arts.

Elizabeth Sulzby has published extensively in the field of early and emergent literacy, and she has done research about the integration of computers as multimedia literacy teaching tools. Her research covers issues of in-home, mother-child interaction with books, emergent reading and writing, early language impairment, and the transitions into conventional reading and writing. She is a professor in the School of Education at the University of Michigan and recently was a visiting professor at Leiden University in the Netherlands. At Michigan, she is affiliated with the Combined Program in Education and Psychology and serves in the literacy and early childhood program areas. She currently is involved in research with Sally Lubeck looking at parent-teacher-researcher collaboration in Head Start programs.

Sharon Taberski teaches combination first- and second-grade classes at the Manhattan New School. This public school in the heart of New York City was opened in 1991 by Shelley Harwayne and colleagues from the Teachers College Writing Project to create a learning environment with literacy at its core.

She speaks widely on issues such as balanced literacy, writing workshops, classroom organization and management, and guided reading. Her book on the teaching of reading, *Standing on Solid Ground,* will be published in 2000.

William Teale is a professor of education at the University of Illinois (UIC) at Chicago, where he also serves as director of the UIC Reading Clinic. He received his doctorate in reading education and English education from the University of Virginia. His research of the past 20 years has focused mainly on early reading and writing development. A number of his studies have addressed family and classroom storybook reading and the home literacy environments of poor children from a variety of cultural and linguistic backgrounds. While his current work continues to address issues of early literacy, he also is engaged in school reform evaluations in Chicago Public Schools.

Josefina Tinajero is the assistant dean of the College of Education and professor of bilingual education at the University of Texas at El Paso, where she also directs the nationally acclaimed Mother-Daughter/ Father-Son programs. She is director of two Title VII grants from the U.S. Office of Education, which are focused on enhancing the skills of teachers in math and science. She is a noted author and featured speaker in the field of bilingual education and in the recruitment and retention of Hispanic students in higher education. She is the author of several comprehensive, multicomponent reading/language arts and English as a Second Language programs.

Maria Utevsky is the director of reading interventions for New York City's Community School District 2. Her work includes supervising the Reading Recovery program, Project Read and prekindergarten literacy professional development. She has written the curriculum for two courses taught to District 2 teachers, one in assessment-driven instruction and another in small-group literacy models for kindergarten through third grade, as well as contributed to the District 2 Staff Development Handbook. She began her career in the district in 1990 as a Reading Recovery teacher. Two years later, she trained as teacher leader and worked in that capacity until 1998, when she assumed her current position.

Gordon Wells, known for his expertise in oral language studies, is a professor at the Ontario Institute for Studies in Education at the University of Toronto. Since moving to Toronto, he has collaborated on research projects with teachers and professors to increase understanding of different modes of discourse in learning and teaching. At the University of Toronto, he is a member of the department of curriculum, teaching and learning with a cross-appointment to the Centre for Teacher Development and the Centre for Applied Cognitive Science. Before moving to Canada in 1984, he was director of the Longitudinal Study of Language Development at the University of Bristol in England.

Learning to Read

Learning to Read

Reading, fundamentally, is the process of understanding written language. Less clinically, reading is a joyful experience that illuminates whole worlds of knowledge, perspective, wisdom and wit from other people, times and places. These are the treasures embedded in letter shapes and printed texts. Learning to read is, arguably, the most important academic achievement of a child's life.

Reading is a complex skill that involves strategies for puzzling out meaning and gauging understanding. It requires students to recognize words on a page, comprehend what they mean and say them aloud in ways that clearly convey their meaning. The ultimate goal of reading is getting the meaning.

On the path toward that goal, learning the "code" that relates printed words to spoken language is a critical early step. Children who are exposed to printed language discover very early — even before they can speak intelligibly — that little squiggles marching across the pages of books cause adults to say certain familiar words. As early as age two, with encouragement, toddlers can begin learning the alphabet, singing the ABC song and reciting letter strings like the old favorite, *ella-menopee*. Before long, they can recognize the printed shapes that stand for the letter names they are learning to say.

Cracking the Print-Sound Code

English, like other languages that use alphabets, provides a systematic code that allows readers to recognize words efficiently. Simply put, letters and spelling patterns stand for sounds in a systematic way.

To understand this print-sound code, students must develop phonemic awareness, or the ability to perceive that streams of speech are made up of separate sounds, called *phonemes*. Phonemic awareness is a matter of perceptual coordination. Children learn to:

◆ *hear* the different sound segments at the beginning, middle and end of words; and

◆ *say,* or *blend,* separate phonemes to make meaningful utterances.

When young children begin to notice and correct speech errors or play at mixing up sounds — "pancakes, cancakes, canpakes" — or when they show an appreciation for alliteration and rhymes, they are becoming aware of phonemes.

The leap from phonemic awareness to understanding the print-sound code comes when children make the mental connection that the visual symbols of letters and spelling represent particular sounds. Children do not need to be drilled endlessly on every spelling-sound pattern in English to learn the print-sound code. Research, in fact, makes clear that once children catch on to the systematic way that spellings stand for sounds, they search on their own for spelling regularities. When they encounter the same spelling patterns again and again in their reading, they are able to learn quickly the most frequently used patterns in English.

In some ways, learning the print-sound code is like putting together a jigsaw puzzle: The task is difficult at first because there are so many options, but it gets easier and goes faster as the pattern becomes more clear and the options become fewer. To begin a jigsaw puzzle, it helps to put the straight-edged pieces together first; they're easy to spot and form a neat frame. This is comparable to students first learning the basic idea that letters stand for sounds and that sounds can be combined to make words, a primary task for kindergarten. Once the frame is completed, the next step is filling in the middle. This takes more time because there are more options, and it takes a while to work through the possibilities. This is comparable to students learning many new spelling-sound correspondences and, at the same time, developing the skill of recognizing the words they make, the primary work of first grade. Finally, once many pieces of the jigsaw puzzle are in place, the pattern provides more clues, and the options diminish. At this point, the puzzle practically finishes itself. Likewise, for primary school students, the more they learn of the print-sound code, the easier and faster it is to learn more.

The puzzle metaphor is useful in understanding the task children face in learning to read. But it also can mislead, for two reasons. First, learning to read is not a single-solution process. Beginning readers actually work puzzle after puzzle on their way to mastery. Second, how fast people put together the puzzle matters not at all to the quality of the finished product. But the speed at which children recognize words matters significantly. Children, like adults, have limited attention spans. They can attend consciously to only a few things at a time. If their attention is concentrated on puzzling out individual spellings and sounds, they can't attend to figuring out what the words and sentences mean. And meaning, of course, is the goal; that is why people read.

Grasping the meaning requires *automaticity,* or the ability to recognize individual words quickly and without much conscious attention. In this way, students can focus on the meaning of sentences and stories. Children need to learn the print-sound code, to be sure, but they also need to learn how to apply the system automatically to increasingly wider ranges of spelling patterns and words. And they need to recognize automatically high-frequency words like *the, have* and *two.* Even though these words

are spelled irregularly, they occur so frequently in texts that students must learn them early.

Getting the Meaning

The ultimate goal of reading is understanding the meaning of written language. But getting the meaning is a complex task that doesn't happen just by reading individual words. Readers also must use a variety of skills and strategies, drawing on what they know about words and their concepts, to build a sense of what the author means to say.

These standards divide the complex task of getting the meaning into four interrelated dimensions of competence:

◆ Accuracy

◆ Fluency

◆ Self-Monitoring and Self-Correcting Strategies

◆ Comprehension

In practice, some of these skills are easier to isolate and assess than others. In fact, accuracy and fluency are combined in kindergarten because the two are virtually indistinguishable in early student reading performances.

What is accuracy?

Accuracy is the ability to recognize words correctly. If children see the letters *c-a-t* printed on a page and know the word is *cat* — not *coat* or *sat* or *can* or *dog* — they accurately recognize the word. If children read a book with 100 words and accurately recognize 90 of them, they are reading with 90 percent accuracy. Sometimes children identify words incorrectly at first glance — as even the most accomplished readers occasionally do. If they notice the error without prompting and correct themselves fairly quickly, it usually means they accurately recognize the word.

Accuracy reflects two important concepts: knowledge of the print-sound code and an understanding of meaning. For example, a child who encounters the word *kin* in a text

Running Records:
A Tool to Assess Accuracy

Running records are a coding system that teachers can use to assess students' accuracy in word recognition when they read. As a student reads aloud, the teacher marks the text on a separate sheet of paper to indicate whether each word is read accurately. The teacher also adds details that indicate where the student corrects mistakes while reading, what types of errors are made and whether the teacher provides any assistance. These notations serve as a diagnosis of the kinds of problems the student encounters when reading. The teacher then calculates the percentage of total words the student reads accurately.

To learn more about running records, refer to the publications list in the Selected Committee Bibliography on page 294.

may easily pronounce it correctly without knowing what it means. When asked to use the word in a sentence, the student may say, "I kin do that!" On the next page, the child may be stumped by *Dalmatian* — an unrecognizable letter string that, when pronounced, turns out to have a familiar meaning. In these standards, accuracy reflects recognizing *both* the sounds and the meanings of words.

What is fluency?

Fluency is the ability to read aloud with appropriate intonations and pauses indicating that students understand the meaning, with only an occasional need to stop to figure out words or sentence structures. These standards expect students to be able to read fluently texts that are at an appropriate level. When students are learning to read, oral reading provides an important, though incomplete, window into the extent of their understanding. Fluent oral reading also is a valuable social skill that students can use throughout their lives.

Fluent reading requires knowledge of syntax and punctuation, which work like stage directions in a play. They are cues that tell readers how the text should sound and how the meaning should be expressed. Fluent readers need to know how sentences are structured, how sentence structure signals meaning and how punctuation is used systematically to convey meaning.

Capital letters and periods, for example, indicate where sentences begin and end, signaling to readers places to pause and words to emphasize. These structural features cue readers to raise or lower their voices to convey meaning. In stories, quotation marks usually signal dialogue, which may call for students to read in different voices for different characters. Commas give cues about which words and clauses go together. Through intonation and pauses, fluent readers use their understanding of commas to attach strings of modifiers to the right noun or verb.

Self-monitoring and self-correcting strategies: Why are they important?

Both accuracy and fluency are related directly to the self-monitoring strategies that readers develop. When beginning readers figure out unfamiliar words, they ask themselves: *Does this word match the letters? Does it make sense here? Do my answers to both of these questions confirm each other?*

Beginning readers use what they know about the print-sound code to check their understanding of the meaning of words. And they use contextual clues, such as illustrations, and their own background knowledge to check their application of the print-sound code. In other words, self-monitoring, or *metacognitive,* strategies hook the print-sound code and meaning together.

Metacognitive and word recognition strategies are central to reading comprehension. Skilled readers continually track their understanding, asking themselves: *Do I understand what I'm reading? Am I getting the words right?* When their answer is "no," they figure out how to get back on track. Strong readers insist on getting the words and the meaning right. In effect, they set their own standard for understanding what they read. They monitor themselves to make sure they are meeting this internal standard — and they will not read on until they are sure they understand. On their own, they develop strategies such as asking themselves questions, summarizing what they've read and predicting what will happen next.

While skilled readers use these self-monitoring strategies naturally, struggling or novice readers can master them as well — with explicit instruction. When students use self-monitoring or self-correcting strategies to tackle challenging texts, their fluency naturally will be disrupted. They may read aloud haltingly, stopping to sound out a word, correct a pronunciation, or puzzle over the beginning or end of a sentence. This is fine. Even fluent readers, who have a good enough command of vocabulary and syntax to read aloud smoothly, sometimes stop to think about the meaning of the text. This does not necessarily mean they lack fluency, only that they are pausing with good reason to monitor their comprehension.

Comprehension: The ultimate aim

Comprehension is the ability to understand written language. In these standards, comprehension includes both getting the gist of the meaning and interpreting the meaning by relating it to other ideas, drawing inferences, making comparisons and asking questions about it.

Students' ability to understand texts varies, depending on three factors:

◆ The complexity of the words and sentences, including spelling, vocabulary and syntax. Features such as single-syllable words or multisyllable words; common, high-frequency words or unusual words; and short, simple sentences or long sentences with clauses affect comprehension.

◆ The conceptual complexity. The simplicity or complexity of the information in the text affects comprehension. Conceptual density, or the number of ideas packed into a few words, and the accessibility of the conceptual references also impact comprehension.

◆ Students' background knowledge about the topic. The knowledge and experience students bring to their reading affects comprehension.

Writing, discussing and rereading books enhance comprehension. All three activities require readers to think more deeply about words and meaning, thus extending understanding and revealing new insights.

Reading Habits

Mastering the print-sound code and learning strategies for comprehension are the essential *skills* for reading. To be true readers, however, primary students also must develop the *habit* of reading — a lot. Students must read, read and read still more to discover the thrill of well-crafted language and well-told tales. Early immersion in books helps students develop a sense of themselves and their place in worlds both real and imaginary. Reading helps primary students discover who they are — and who they can become.

Parents and teachers play a vital role in this journey of discovery. Young children copy the reading habits of adults and older children. If adults read aloud to them, young children will follow suit, pretend-reading and mimicking the intonations and cadences they hear. If children see adults read on their own, they will pick up books and turn the pages as well.

Reading widely and deeply is a way for students to master reading skills and to acquire background knowledge that helps them construct meaning. Frequent and varied reading also helps students build rich vocabularies — words that students can use because they spring from a personal context — and understanding of story structures, syntax, spelling and punctuation.

Reading widely from good literature and other texts also is an educational goal in its own right. People get smarter when they read; they learn the words, references and concepts that are the foundation for the *next* ideas they will encounter and learn. The more you know, the more you can learn. And of course, a rich body of research shows in no uncertain terms that students who read a lot do better in school by many measures — test scores, math and science achievement, and school and post-secondary attendance, to name a few — than students who do not.

Reading habits are easier to instill in classrooms that are filled with books, magazines, signs, instructions and word walls. Taken together, this is known as a print-rich environment.

Primary students should read a variety of texts and authors, in a variety of ways, every day. In good primary literacy programs, students read and write in many fiction and nonfiction genres, including narratives, biographies, memoirs, literature, poetry and plays. They also read and write informational texts used to teach others and functional texts used to get things done. Students learn to recognize and discuss literary qualities and genre features and to compare and contrast books and authors. They learn to notice the particulars of the author's craft, such as beginnings and endings, word choice, plot, and character portrayal. Students also read throughout the school day and across the curriculum to learn about science, art, math and history.

These standards lay out several different and important ways for students to read and engage with texts:

◆ Independent Reading

◆ Assisted Reading

◆ Being Read To

◆ Discussing Books

All of these interactions with texts help children to acquire:

◆ Vocabulary

For the youngest students, hearing books read aloud is the way they most often engage in reading. But as they begin to crack the print-sound code, they also can read independently or, for harder texts, with assistance.

Still, being able to read independently does not diminish the importance of other ways of reading. On the contrary, when students read leveled books that are within their range for accuracy and fluency, they use only a fraction of the words and ideas they know. Through assisted reading and hearing books read aloud, they are exposed to new vocabulary and

Read, Read and Read Still More

Reading habits are as important as reading skills. Beginning in kindergarten, students need to read a lot — independently and with assistance — from the fiction, nonfiction, poetry and prose genres. In the standards, "a lot" is quantified in these terms:

Kindergarten: Read or reread — independently or with another student or adult — **two to four familiar books** each day. Listen to **one or two books** read aloud each day at school and at home.

First Grade: Read — independently or with assistance — **four or more books** a day. Hear **two to four books or other texts** read aloud every day.

Second Grade: Read **one or two short books or long chapters** every day. Listen to and discuss every day **one text** that is longer and more difficult than what can be read independently.

Third Grade: Read **30 chapter books** a year. Listen to and discuss **at least one chapter** read aloud every day.

concepts that serve as a springboard to the next levels of competence.

Independent reading: On their own

Students read independently when they read on their own. For beginning readers, some independent reading may be done aloud, so the teacher can observe the quality of students' reading. Specifically, the teacher may monitor which words students read correctly, whether they recognize or amend incorrect word pronunciations, which strategies they use to figure out word sounds or meanings, indications of confidence and fluency, intonation patterns, and other evidence that students get the gist of what they are reading.

Once students are beginning to read, a great deal of their independent reading will be done silently. All the teacher actually can observe is whether students appear to be engaged and attentive to the text. Whether students truly are reading can be determined only by questioning them about the text, for example, and checking their understanding.

Assisted reading: With instruction and support

To read a lot — a crucial factor for learning to read — beginning readers need plenty of help. Assisted reading comes in many formats.

For example, the teacher may guide students either in one-on-one tutorial settings or with a group of children, teaching particular strategies for reading. In these sessions, the teacher directs attention to specific elements of the text, including words, literary devices, syntactic characteristics and spelling patterns. The teacher may engage students in a discussion of text features and strategies for figuring out words or meanings. In these ways, students can learn self-monitoring and self-correcting strategies, either by learning from the teacher's direct instruction or by imitating the teacher.

Or, two or three students may read a book together, taking joint responsibility for figuring out both what the words "say" and what they "mean." In partner reading, students can take turns, checking and monitoring each other's reading. They can help each other on challenging words or sentences by asking and answering questions. Partner reading is an important way to learn to read; students play the role the teacher plays in guided reading.

Being read to: Listening to learn

Even after students can read independently, hearing good literature and other texts read aloud to them is important. Like being able to read aloud, knowing how to listen is a valuable social skill. Listening helps students develop comprehension skills that they need to advance as independent readers. When adults read to them, students learn that reading is an engaging social and learning experience. They learn that the flow of written language differs from that of conversational language.

Most importantly, reading to students gives them a way to work beyond their independent or assisted reading capacities to focus on deeper levels of meaning, more complex language structures and more sophisticated vocabulary. Third graders need this comfortable scaffold to climb to higher reading levels as much as kindergartners do.

Discussing books: Sharpening thinking with accountable talk

Independent, assisted and read-aloud reading draw on familiar traditions of primary literacy instruction. Discussing books as a habit of reading that is built into the standards departs from that tradition — justifiably so. Recent research concludes that discussing books and other texts is an effective way of understanding them — the ultimate goal of reading.

Talking to other people about ideas, an activity known as *accountable talk,* is fundamental to learning. One-on-one, in small groups or with the whole class, students understand new knowledge and make meaning in social situations. For classroom talk to promote learning, it must have certain characteristics that make it accountable, researchers and practitioners believe. Accountable talk is not empty chatter; it seriously responds to and further develops what others in the group say. Students introduce and ask for knowledge that is accurate and relevant to the text under discussion. They use evidence from the text in ways that are appropriate and follow established norms of good reasoning.

Accountable talk sharpens students' thinking by reinforcing their ability to reason with knowledge. Teachers play a vital role in shaping meaningful conversations in their classrooms. They create the norms and skills of accountable talk by modeling appropriate forms of discussion and by questioning, probing and directing conversations. They nudge students to "say why" they believe an author chooses certain words, creates particular characters or describes specific settings, for example.

When students participate in book discussions under these circumstances, they can comprehend more and grapple with complexities that otherwise may elude or never occur to them. The more students discuss particular theme, genre or craft features, the more they can understand, remember and apply what they learn. Indeed, book talks are a way of modeling or talking through good writing skills. Students learn to examine texts thoughtfully, draw evidence from them to make assertions and substantiate arguments, and double-check their facts by rereading — crossover skills that work just as well in crafting written pieces.

Through discussion, students also can demonstrate comprehension. Indeed, test questions that ask students to "discuss" a character's motive or an author's choice of words, for instance, really expect a solo performance that indicates how much students have gleaned from their reading. While such assessments are important, discussing books in these standards is a social process in which students build understanding through group talk.

> Accountable talk is not empty chatter; it seriously responds to and further develops what others in the group say. Students introduce and ask for knowledge that is accurate and relevant to the text under discussion. They use evidence from the text in ways that are appropriate and follow established norms of good reasoning.

Acquiring vocabulary: Encountering new words

In the primary grades, learning what words mean and how to use them is a huge and vital undertaking. Words help students read, learn and understand their world; the larger their vocabularies, the better able they are to learn and do.

Even on the first day of kindergarten, of course, students already know a lot of words that they have acquired through listening and speaking. Emerging readers and writers puzzle out the sounds and shapes of words that, for the most part, they already know and understand.

Read-alouds are riveting because students may encounter words they have *not* heard in conversation. If they follow along when an adult reads aloud, they can see the new words as well as hear them. With stories, pictures and the adult's voice to assist them, students' eager minds map out the meanings of increasingly difficult words. Their already impressive vocabularies grow even larger.

How quickly does this happen? Seemingly by leaps and bounds. Estimates range from three to seven words a day, although measuring the exact rate of vocabulary acquisition is impossible. Some researchers qualify that rate, saying that, while schoolchildren may

> Reading widely from good literature and other texts is an educational goal in its own right. People get smarter when they read; they learn the words, references and concepts that are the foundation for the *next* ideas they will encounter and learn. The more you know, the more you can learn.

become *aware* of seven new words a day, they still have a long way to go to *learn* the words. There are large discrepancies among the number of words students can understand when adults read to them, words they can use in conversations, words they can read and words they can write. Generally, students' *receptive vocabularies,* or words they understand if someone else uses them, exceed their *expressive vocabularies,* or words they use on their own. This gap shrinks as students mature.

In any case, a rapid rate of acquiring new vocabulary is critical for K–3 students; deficiencies in vocabulary accumulate into reading comprehension problems. If students do not recognize and understand words, they cannot read or write them either.

Mastering knowledge and use of vocabulary words comes from oral language, reading, teaching and studying. Hearing spoken language, especially books read aloud, is the primary source of vocabulary acquisition at least throughout kindergarten and first grade. By the time they reach second or third grade, students also learn new words through independent and assisted reading.

The New Standards Primary Literacy Standards classify vocabulary building as a reading habit because the key to robust vocabulary is reading a lot. As students grow older, they pay conscious attention to words and meanings, noticing and collecting new words.

What Children Should Be Reading to Meet the Standards

These reading standards are pegged to *text levels,* which indicate the level of difficulty of texts. The power of leveled texts is that even the youngest students can truly read them, right from the start. And students who are struggling to read simply can drop back to a text level that is easier for them — *but they keep on reading,* learning through practice rather than through monotonous skill drills. Leveled texts pull together the best thinking on how children learn to read.

As students progress through school, the reading skills they work on remain essentially the same. Text difficulty is the variable. Through independent, assisted and read-aloud reading, students work with books that are both easy and challenging for them.

Notably, text difficulty depends on more than the internal features of a book — the words, print size and illustrations, for example. Many external factors — such as students' familiarity with the text and background knowledge about the subject — contribute to text difficulty as well. These external factors meld with the internal text difficulty, usually expressed in terms of readability and predictability. Both factors determine which books are within a student's reading range and which require some stretching.

Not surprisingly, then, choosing appropriate texts for independent, assisted and read-aloud reading is an enormous challenge for teachers. The New Standards Primary Literacy Standards help. Here and in the grade-by-grade sections, there is useful information about the variety of texts students should be reading.

For novice readers, texts with regularly spelled words, familiar high-frequency words and simple sentence structures support them as they make the transition to independent reading. Patterns of repetition bolster students' ability to read and understand texts as well. Some texts, for example, are carefully written and designed to introduce only one new word per page, allowing the youngest students to read along rhythmically and stop only once to figure out the newest word. Some texts include only one sentence on a page or begin and end each sentence on the same line, so beginning readers don't have to tackle the skill of moving their eyes down the page. Others introduce spelling patterns systematically. Illustrations matter. Sometimes they help students understand words and meaning, sometimes they are related only loosely to the text, and sometimes they extend the text, suggesting meaning that is not written in the words.

Appropriate text levels for independent, assisted and read-aloud reading

Precisely because there are so many variables not only in texts but also in the people reading them, text leveling is still more an art than a science. Although expert opinions differ on the criteria for determining readability, the basic logic of leveling is fairly simple. Books students are expected to read independently, with accuracy and fluency, are easier than books the same students should read for assisted reading. With a partner, more sophisticated self-monitoring and comprehension skills come into play. And again, books students hear read aloud are longer and even more difficult than books read with a partner. These texts are both more interesting and more rich in vocabulary, concepts, language use and genres.

For each grade, these standards include both descriptions of text levels and lists of book titles that exemplify the kinds of books students are expected to read. The expectations for accuracy and fluency, under **Reading Standard 2: Getting the Meaning,** are expressed in terms of end-of-year text levels. Between kindergarten and the end of first grade, students move through six text levels. In second and third grade, even though their reading continues its speedy development, students move through only two or three text levels. Leveled texts for the youngest readers are divided into finer gradients than texts for older readers.

For example, a first grader who can read independently a Level I book such as *Henny Penny* — with at least 90 percent accuracy in word recognition and with intonation and pauses to signal understanding of the meaning — is right on target for the end of the school year. With assistance and hard work, the same student should be able to puzzle out a Level J book such as *Danny and the Dinosaur* — with less accuracy and fluency, to be sure, and with more overt use of self-monitoring and self-correcting strategies. The student also should be able to demonstrate comprehension by retelling or summarizing the text, describing something learned from the text and answering the teacher's questions.

At each grade, these standards also include both descriptions and examples of book titles appropriate for read-alouds. For this purpose, specific text levels matter less than other features, such as conceptual complexity, diversity of genres, sophistication of vocabulary and syntax, similarities and differences among themes, and author's craft. These features support meaty discussions of books and nudge students to deeper levels of comprehension.

Monitoring progress toward reading to learn

In these standards, the texts recommended for each grade level are appropriate for their purpose and accurately targeted. The end-of-year standards are rigorous, yet achievable — given enough time and instruction in a rich literacy program. Nevertheless, learning to read is a developmental process, not an all-or-nothing proposition. Standards, by their nature, focus on end-of-year targets. Teachers, by their nature, monitor progress throughout the year along a continuum of literacy. Teachers can use leveled texts to monitor students' progress along this continuum, tracking milestones and flagging problems by midyear — in time to intervene with extra time, attention and instruction.

With these standards, in good reading programs, students will learn the skills and habits of reading. The older they get, the less time they will spend learning to read and the more time they will spend actually engaged in wonderful, meaningful reading.

Learning to Write

Learning to Write

Just as reading is the process of *understanding* written language, writing is the process of *communicating* with written language. Readers work to get the writer's meaning, while writers work to make their meaning clear to readers. Like readers, writers discover new vistas and perspectives in the process of writing. Clearly, reading and writing are parallel processes. They belong together in the New Standards Primary Literacy Standards.

For adults and students alike, putting letters and words on paper is almost magical. Writing seems to unlock the mind, to organize and synthesize thinking, to excite the intelligence. By weaving together bits of information that may never have been joined before, writers discover new meaning. The way writers ultimately convey this meaning to readers pushes writers to make a variety of very sophisticated choices, including:

◆ how to structure the piece as a whole;

◆ what pitch or angle to take (serious? ironic? humorous?) and which words to choose to ensure precise meaning;

◆ which ideas will dominate and which will be subordinate;

◆ what to claim boldly rather than imply delicately; and

◆ which combination of sentence forms to use to produce desired cadences.

Writers are craftsmen, wordsmiths, people who employ language strategically to communicate with and engage readers. Writing is at times an art form, critiqued and practiced, or a medium to convey meaning or a tool to generate and order thinking. These standards require students to write in all of these ways.

Habits and Processes: Learning to Be a Writer

To some degree, writing is an idiosyncratic process. How students learn to write, the tools they prefer to use, the style they ultimately develop, the strategies they routinely use to revise and edit — all of these vary from student to student. Fortunately, however, researchers know a great deal about how many famous writers have developed their craft — the habits and processes of recognized wordsmiths.

These standards incorporate that research for K–3 students, requiring them to practice the habits and processes of successful writers. To do the kind of writing that the modern world requires, students need to build a foundation beginning in the primary grades.

For students to become good writers, they should engage in writerly habits and processes, apprenticing themselves to writers' routines and rituals. Students must write regularly, often generating topics in which they can invest their energies. They must view writing as hard work and adjust to the fact that getting ideas down on paper is only a first step. They must be willing to rethink (often, literally, to re-vision) how these ideas are organized and expressed — and examine a draft in light of how well it communicates. They must make needed changes willingly, perhaps handing the document off for a trusted "other" to read; for students, this "other" is most often a teacher, another student or a parent. They must assume responsibility for various rounds of changes until, finally, the document communicates — and is as good as they can make it, including precise word choice and correct spelling, grammar and punctuation.

When they are learning to write, students also must begin to think like writers. Writing is more than sitting down with pencil and paper, or computer and screen, and quick-scribbling or banging out words. In their everyday lives, students must make thoughtful mental notes by:

◆ listening for effective ways of saying things and expressive turns of phrase;

◆ internalizing the rhythms of language;

◆ keeping an eye (and ear) out for interesting new words;

◆ seeing scenes from everyday life that might be used in their stories;

◆ recording observations; and

◆ trying out ways of organizing information.

Like adult writers, students may draw stylistic ideas from their favorite authors, whose books (or poems) they have read and reread, mimicking particular elements to enrich their own writing. Also like adult writers, students should become familiar with the features that distinguish various genres and learn to move comfortably from one genre to another.

Knowledge of authors, authors' craft and genres influences students' reading as well as their writing. Such knowledge enables students to read like writers, appreciating how an author develops a character or embeds details to paint a picture. Students who are working to develop knowledge of craft grapple with the need to create specificity through detail, and they come to expect published authors to pay even greater attention to nuance and specificity. When students read like writers — that is, when they bring their own knowledge about craft and genre to text — they become more discriminating about written language. They also use this discrimination to guide their own writing: They write like enlightened readers.

Genres:
Why Are They Important?

Writers learn how to write in somewhat predictable stages. Most children begin "writing" by putting marks on paper that conform to some

sense that they are communicating meaning. These earliest markings may be scribbles; scribbles and pictures; or scribbles, pictures, and random letters and numbers. From such a starting point, students begin to experiment with words and word boundaries, left-to-right and top-to-bottom presentations, and phonetic representations of words. At the same time that their knowledge about what constitutes "writing" is developing, students produce work that corresponds to a variety of writing types. A full understanding of writing types, or genres, takes years to develop, of course. But even the youngest writers produce recognizable precursors of very sophisticated writing forms. They learn to write by writing, by trying out the forms.

While the literary tradition of genres allows writers to see the world (and write about it) through a particular set of lenses, such lenses can be both powerful and limiting. A particular genre will suggest an order and help students get their thoughts down on paper. As important as genre knowledge is, genre elements should not be configured into formulas that constrict writing or constrain thinking.

Still, genres are culturally appropriate and socially expected. Not to make students aware of their structures is to deny them academic access. Any student who does not know the expectations for appropriately presenting information in writing to readers is immediately disadvantaged. Students who learn about genres enjoy a tremendous advantage over students who do not. As long as students understand that genres are not rigid structures, genre knowledge enables them as writers.

Genre knowledge also enables students when they read. If students realize, for example, that the underlying structure for narrative is chronological, then as readers, they will pick up more readily on transition structures, whether they are one-word connectors or adverbial clauses, that signal movement through the text. Similarly, when students know about story, they anticipate some sort of conflict-and-resolution structure when they read — and they look for it.

Thus, readers who understand the structure of the classic mystery story expect that a crime will take place; that there will be a number of suspects, each with a plausible motive and opportunity; and that either one suspect or an outsider will assume the role of detective and solve the crime. Mystery readers also assume that the writer will provide clues that, if attended to, will allow them to solve the crime. So they read carefully, looking to identify potential clues. Readers not knowledgeable about the genre will not necessarily see the links in the plot, anticipate the events, identify the clues or draw inferences from clues.

Genres also provide teachers with a meta-language they can use to teach and evaluate writing. Genres are made up of distinctive characteristics, which teachers can make explicit to students. So, for example, if a teacher is working on narrative writing, she may address the expectation that writers orient or engage readers by setting a time, indicating a location, introducing a character or characters, or entering immediately into the story line. These expectations are easy both to teach and to use, giving students an array of possible starting points for their own writing.

> Any student who does not know the expectations for appropriately presenting information in writing to readers is immediately disadvantaged. Students who learn about genres enjoy a tremendous advantage over students who do not.

In combination, the genre-specific expectations should be the basis for evaluating and providing feedback to students. And to the extent that genre characteristics remain fairly constant, students will be working to become proficient with stable expectations up through the grades, as these standards show. Such stability provides coherence in a student writing curriculum.

Sharing events, telling stories: Narrative writing

The earliest forms of students' writings generally are pictures with one-word or one-sentence identifications. Drawings remain an important part of their writing through first grade, but children increasingly begin to focus their attention on the text. Since much that students hear read aloud in kindergarten and first grade is narrative in form, students produce narratives early on. Often their narratives are little more than a recount of a simple event or brief event sequence followed by a reaction or opinion: "I went to the zoo. It was fun."

Also common is writing made up of an observation and a comment: "I saw a dog. It was big." While many argue that writing this sparse does not imply any sense of narrative form, it is possible to argue that both examples, the recount and the observation, begin with some sort of initiating event, as in "I went/I saw." And it is easy to see how students use the initiating event as the springboard for a longer string of events, chronologically ordered. Because students in the early grades draw much of their writing from their own lives, their writings likely are personal accounts whose value is primarily expressive.

Children's narrative development grows in fits and starts, frequently passing through several predictable stages. One early stage is marked by "chaining," with one idea linked to another, so there is no center or no focus to the writing. Also common (usually at second grade) are:

◆ the bed-to-bed story, in which the narrative is made up of an undifferentiated list of events — literally everything from when "I got up" to "Then I went to bed";

◆ the dialogue-driven narrative, in which dialogue, usually between two people, carries the whole weight of the piece, as in "he said" then "she said" then "he said"; and

◆ the event-driven piece, in which events — typically ones associated with action-

adventure movies and familiar television shows — simply follow one another without any apparent cause-and-effect relationship.

All of these forms are early or not fully developed versions of narration, yet each demonstrates students' growing awareness of what constitutes the genre.

> When students read like writers — that is, when they bring their own knowledge about craft and genre to text — they become more discriminating about written language. They also use this discrimination to guide their own writing: They write like enlightened readers.

Next in the developmental sequence come pieces that do have a central focus, which imposes some sort of coherence, though these writings initially are simple in structure. As writers, young children are able to demonstrate better control and proficiency when they write about the events of their day-to-day lives. Their familiarity with real people, places and events allows this writing to have a depth and authenticity that otherwise might be missing.

When students in the early grades attempt narratives built around fictional problem/solution structures, the stories very often are improvised retellings, extensions involving favorite characters or blendings of familiar story lines. All such efforts and their borrowings constitute appropriate attempts to produce fictional narratives. With instruction and exposure to good literature, and allowing for some borrowing, first-grade writers can produce a fictional story with a planned entry point, a sense of time and place, some character development, some detail, and a sense of closure.

However, it is important to recognize that fiction is a demanding form for even the most sophisticated writers, so no one should be surprised when primary students have problems writing fiction. Such stories may disappoint because young writers can't produce a satisfying conclusion or because event may follow event without a logical cause-and-effect relationship. Nevertheless, because young writers are fascinated with fiction, it is often wiser to be forgiving when evaluating their stories or to make strategic suggestions to improve the stories than to deter students from attempting fiction.

Informing others:
Report or informational writing

As with narrative, informational writing is a form primary students can produce with some

---

Report Writing:
The Challenges for Students

Report writing poses many challenges for young students. Writing about a topic that they know well presents a different set of challenges from writing about a topic that is unfamiliar. When they know the topic, organizing the information is the task that consumes their energy. When they don't know the topic, gathering and phrasing the information are the challenges.

When students are writing about a topic they are familiar with, the main challenges are how to organize the information and, then, how much information to include and leave out. The second-grade piece on doves on page 171 is a case in point. The student knew about doves from personal experience although, no doubt, some facts were added to this existing knowledge. Perhaps the teacher passed along some facts or perhaps the student did some reading. The point is that the student had a deep understanding of the topic, so she could convey information in her own words. She clustered her information under three broad categories that made sense to her. She probably had more than enough information about doves in her head, so she decided — based on her deep understanding — which facts a classroom visitor would want to know. The headers and space requirements constrained her and helped guide her decisions.

By comparison, when students write about topics about which they know little or nothing, they likely will be unable to differentiate important from unimportant information. Clustering ideas, too, will be problematic because students will have neither the breadth nor the depth of understanding necessary to analyze and categorize the information. In these cases, young writers often seem to rely almost solely on headers, provided either by the teacher or by the reference materials themselves, to organize their writing.

Finally, when students write about an unfamiliar topic, simply phrasing the information is a daunting task. They must explain new information that they do not fully understand. So the logical thing for them to do is borrow heavily the wordings from the reference books to make sure they convey correctly the ideas they are writing about. Logically, then, the syntactic patterns that emerge under these circumstances frequently are made up of some introductory, transitional or evaluative phrasings, stringing together word-for-word borrowings from reference texts. This is called "patch" writing — and it is particularly acceptable and expected in the primary grades, where students are encouraged to mimic the language of written text, to apprentice themselves to authors and to borrow stylistic techniques they observe professional authors using.

When a student or classroom studies a topic in depth, it is reasonable to expect more sophisticated writing and, perhaps, multiple pieces of writing on the topic.

proficiency. The earliest beginnings of this genre take the form of lists, random words students know and can approximate spelling for. Later, students may expand on these lists with informational text made up entirely of one-clause units. Frequently, these are little more than repeated sentence stems except for the final word: "I like cats. I like dogs. I like TV."

As students become familiar with informational text, they create more sophisticated forms, such as attribute papers in which they write all about a topic: "all about whales" or "all about my brother," for example. These texts are actually bits of information strung together without any formal organization, but taken as a whole, the bits do communicate most of what the writer knows about the subject. By the time students reach third grade, they can produce coherent reports that introduce a topic; describe or define the attributes of the topic; describe or explain characteristic activities, events or processes related to the topic; employ a useful organizational structure; include adequate elaboration; and provide some kind of closure.

Across grade levels, there are obvious differences in how students approach informational writing. Beyond the degree of elaboration that students employ, the sharpest differences are in students' ability to establish some logical organization of content. To organize their writing, students must analyze and classify, tasks made easier when they read informational materials and when the teacher provides guidance about clustering similar ideas. Many students early on use headers, likely a borrowing from chapter titles, as a strategy for organizing and arranging information. Students also include with their text graphs, pictures, maps and other visual aids common to this genre.

Getting things done:
Functional and procedural writing

The functional writing that students do from kindergarten through third grade has its genesis in the labels that adorn kindergarten walls. "Don't touch" next to an emerging structure of blocks and "Feed the snake" next to the caged reptile are commonplace beginnings for writings that detail how to do something.

Functional writing is narrative in structure, so students who write stories easily can absorb the organizing chronological structure of this genre. Functional writing is much like informative writing because it requires some expertise or knowledge for the student to draw on. Fortunately, students at the primary level have much expertise; they know how to care for pets, how to carve pumpkins, how to play games. Usually, then, sequencing the steps in a plan of action does not pose problems for young writers.

Instead, the degree of specificity required sometimes makes functional writing difficult, as does the problem of introducing the topic in an engaging manner. Frequently, young writers will adopt the narrative stance for story — "One day I decided to bathe my dog. Here is what I did." This stance immediately throws the writer into the past tense, and the text is more of a recount than anything else. When students see good examples of functional writing and model their own text on these examples, there is less tendency to recount.

Producing and responding to literature

Responding to literature is not a type of writing usually taught or expected in the earliest grades. But it should be. When students respond to literature — that is, when they write a literary response or literary analysis paper — they make a judgment about something they have read or have heard read to them. This judgment can be evaluative ("I liked it because … " or "It is good because … "), or it can be interpretive ("I think the author is saying … "). The response can be about more than one work, a single work or even a part of a single work.

Significantly, this genre requires students to go back into the text to support their evaluation or interpretation. A good response to literature never is built on unsupported opinion, so young children must be taught how to support ideas through making reference to the text.

Because this is relatively demanding, many students develop the necessary skills by participating in book discussions, where they are expected to go back to the text for support. Making connections to text is an important and early precursor of this form of writing. "I like this book because it is about cats, and I have a cat" is to literary response as "We climbed hills and it was fun" is to narrative.

In schools where students are expected to become writers — to take writing seriously — they easily define themselves as authors and, as such, produce a variety of genres in addition to those specified here. Songs, poems and plays all are written frequently by young children. Initially, the texts likely will be abbreviated and rough approximations of the forms, but they clearly will be appropriate approximations. As students mature and practice their craft, their writing forms become more recognizable. Encouraging young writers to have favorite authors and to study what these authors do fosters writing development and craft knowledge, and this idea of students apprenticing themselves to a favorite author has merit for students as young as kindergartners. It is a strategy that can develop a lifelong habit.

> Just as children learn to talk and read, swim or jump rope by imitating people who already know how, they learn to write by mimicking the habits and strategies of real writers. Teachers play a valuable role in this process. By modeling good reading and writing habits, they show students that reading and writing are important activities deserving of their time and attention.

Using Language and Conventions

Readers' ability to make sense of text depends on more than the writer's ability to organize effectively. To understand meaning, readers must rely in no small part on the writer's appropriate use of language and conventions. Such elements as style and syntax, vocabulary and word choice, spelling, punctuation, and capitalization all support — are, indeed, essential to — conveying meaning effectively and appropriately.

Young children cannot reasonably be expected to master concepts about language use and conventions while they are still struggling to control left-to-right and top-to-bottom directionality and letter-sound correspondences and to communicate some meaning. Yet even while they are developing these basic competencies, young writers are aware of language use and conventions, and most show almost an enthusiasm for displaying their awareness. Many young writers who as yet are producing only minimal text — three or four words, usually tied to a picture — will embellish their writing with punctuation marks, most frequently periods. This embellishment does not reflect an awareness of appropriate use; many young writers even use periods to mark the space between words. It does indicate, however, that even the most fledgling writers recognize that writing involves more than just words.

Control over punctuation, capitalization and other conventions, as with style and syntax, spelling, and vocabulary and word choice, depends on students' increasing fluency. Increased familiarity with language and conventions comes from both reading and explicit instruction. The more students write, the better they master language use — with corrective feedback from the teacher.

Style and syntax

The style of young writers actually is little more than the voice, most frequently egocentric and exuberant, that they bring to their writing. Young students delight in telling "stuff" to readers — "stuff" about themselves, their world and their opinions. Frequent underlinings, multiple exclamation points, smiley faces and words written in all caps are hallmarks of novice writers' style.

Because their writing initially is short, syntax, or the arrangement of words and their different forms in sentences, is not an issue. As their ability to form words and produce sentences begins to develop, these youngest writers use the speech patterns, or the rhythms and wordings, of their oral language. Yet, the notion of varying word order and sentence length as stylistic considerations may be prompted as early as first or second grade, when

students write poetry and work with line breaks and white space or when they pattern their own work after a book or story by a favorite author.

Using one's own language. When students first attempt to write, they use their own language. That is, their writing derives from the language they have heard spoken in the world around them since birth. They understand writing as talk written down, so that is what they attempt to produce. There is much to recommend this language. In fact, many professional writers are esteemed primarily because they are able to capture the cadences of everyday language. The challenge, then, is not for young writers to forsake this language but to understand when and how to use it and when, instead, to use language more appropriate for addressing a distant audience for a specific purpose. Writers must succeed at shifting registers and using syntax and stylistic choices to support meaning. Eventually, writers must learn, for example:

◆ which ideas to highlight and which to subordinate;

◆ how to create cohesion by moving sentence by sentence, from old to new information;

◆ how to vary sentence length for pacing or emphasis or overall rhythm of the text; and

◆ when to repeat words or phrases — and which ones to repeat — for effect and meaning.

Certainly, the use of their own language can make employing many of these strategies easier for novice writers.

Taking on language of authors. Just as young children imitate the speech of adults, so too do they take on the language of authors in their writing. And often their writing reveals both their youth and their as yet incomplete or incorrect understanding of written language and forms. So, for example, a student may write "Once up on a hill" in an attempt to borrow "Once upon a time." Often their style suggests an attempt to produce "real" writing, text that sounds like what they imagine writing should sound like. As young writers take on the language of authors, their sentences become longer, they begin to embed clauses, and they use adjectives and adverbs more frequently. Young writers often will borrow heavily from favorite stories and poems, replicating the rhythm of a favorite piece, mimicking patterns of repetition and even embedding phrases that resonate for them.

Vocabulary and word choice

As students progress through the primary grades, their written vocabularies grow in size, quality and richness. As writers, they use the same basic, concrete words they encounter in their first experiences of reading. Later, they make more discrete choices that differentiate with greater precision. Writers choose words because they are the "right" words for a particular situation and audience. They provide readers very specific information about the topic or, in story, about a character or setting. Word choice also tells readers a great deal about the writer. That is, words convey the persona of the writer as much as they convey information or tell a story. And words help create the overall cadences that carry the meaning; they may, for example, slow down readers and create tension.

Using one's own language. In the primary grades, most of the words children use in writing are ones they also use regularly in speech. However, many of the words that children can use in conversation are too hard for them to spell, so often they will substitute a short, easily spelled word rather than risk using a longer one. Nonetheless, as students read and are read to, their vocabularies expand and new words — learned words — appear in their writing.

Taking on language of authors. Expanded vocabulary logically appears in writing that requires specific words to describe a concept. When students write about volcanoes or sharks or space, for example, they use words that are not necessarily part of their conversational lexicon. As students develop as readers and writers, they learn that concrete detail is very important. This knowledge helps them understand the need to expand their vocabulary so readers can understand precisely what they mean when they write.

Spelling

When young readers begin to sound out words or recognize them by sight, they gradually come to understand that the order in which letters are arranged determines how a word sounds. This discovery is part of mastering the print-sound code for reading, explained in **Learning to Read,** page 17. In writing, the equivalent of the print-sound code is spelling. The two develop together.

In students' early attempts at spelling, they use coded, almost telegraphic ways of communicating. Later, they will get the most salient sounds of the words down. They often will write just one letter to stand for all the phonemes of a word. Or they will write an initial consonant followed by a whole string of letters. For example, in kindergarten a child may spell *elephant* "LFTZBFTD," with "L" representing the initial sound of the word and a long string of more or less random letters making the word "big" (long) because elephants are "big." The length of the string corresponds to the size of the object. Sometimes, what looks like a written "word" actually might be a letter string containing the first sound of each word in a sentence. And the words and letters don't always read from left to right. They may go down the page or around a corner. They might even reverse direction and continue on the line above.

But as young writers develop an awareness of how words are broken into separate sounds, they begin trying to get all the letters. Consonants come first, and later they add the vowels. At the early stages, students write words phonetically — the way the words sound to them. Thus, *elephant* may be rendered as "LFNT." This early attempt to spell produces some strange-looking words, but these spellings indicate clearly that students are learning the print-sound code.

The more children read, the more opportunities they have to see the conventional spellings of words and the less they rely on phonetic spelling. Although reversals are common at the beginning, children usually have mastered the basic principles of English orthography and are ready for formal spelling instruction by age eight or nine. At this point they can be expected to spell correctly most of the words in their vocabularies, except for unusual words and irregular spellings. Beginning in third grade, getting conventional spellings right becomes critical. Still, from the end of first grade through the middle of third, there are constant trade-offs. Unconventional spelling, to some degree, is to be expected if children say what they really mean and if they use bigger, more difficult words.

Punctuation, capitalization and other conventions

Writers make punctuation choices as precisely as they make other stylistic choices. For example, there are commonly accepted definitions about what constitutes a sentence (these often are articulated in grammar books), but there are times when using something less than what is defined (a sentence fragment) is acceptable if not desirable.

However, unless writers understand the concept and function of punctuation, capitalization and other conventions, they cannot vary from the norm to bring readers up short or to emphasize. They cannot make their writing intelligible to readers. Conventions make writing work: Students need to know the rules before they can break them effectively and intelligently. The subtleties of punctuation play out with young writers not only in the obvious correspondence to their sense of syntax but also equally to their familiarity — literally — with seeing punctuation in their reading, using it when they read, and receiving explicit instruction in convention and punctuation rules.

Novice writers need to become increasingly competent in using conventions. It is not a matter of waiting until they can understand the underlying concepts. Full understanding will develop only with years of writing practice and conscious attention, spurred by good teaching. But by the end of third grade, students should develop an awareness of how the conventions work and be required at least to demonstrate proper usage of periods, an understanding of

> The secret to good writing in the primary grades is a rich literacy program that requires students to read a lot, write a lot, and learn about genres and literary conventions. These elements are built into the New Standards Primary Literacy Standards.

what words to capitalize, and the function of quotation marks and the apostrophe.

A New Standard for Writing

In these standards, the habits of writing are robust yet reasonable. Ordinary students who write every day can produce written work that is extraordinary, as the writing samples in this book show. The secret to good writing in the primary grades is a rich literacy program that requires students to read a lot, write a lot, and learn about genres and literary conventions. These elements are built into the New Standards Primary Literacy Standards.

Just as children learn to talk and read, swim or jump rope by imitating people who already know how, they learn to write by mimicking the habits and strategies of real writers. Teachers play a valuable role in this process. By modeling good reading and writing habits, they show students that reading and writing are important activities deserving of their time and attention. Teachers also can help students find topics that stir their interest and induce them to write carefully and thoughtfully.

Over time, with daily habits and direct instruction beginning in kindergarten, students can learn to communicate effectively, informatively, responsively and even poignantly. Knowledge of genres acquired through reading, study and discussion helps students become writers. Genres give students different frameworks in which to try out and build new skills, just as recipes give inexperienced cooks a way to build a meal. As their confidence and their accomplishments grow, students are more willing to depart from genre forms and substitute their own literary ingredients. On the literary continuum, students who experiment with their own distinctive voices are well on their way to developing writing skills they will need in school and in life.

About the New Standards Primary Literacy Standards

For most children, the heart of the primary years from kindergarten through third grade is learning to read and, then, beginning to read to learn. At the same time, students learn to write. With instruction and practice that connect reading and writing, students perform better at both.

During the primary grades, students should crack the print-sound code; learn to get meaning from texts; and establish reading habits that will be the foundation for formal education, informal learning and lifetime pleasure. In strong primary literacy programs, K–3 students write daily for a variety of purposes — to share events and tell stories, to inform and report, to get things done, and to produce and respond to literature. With instruction and practice, students develop proficiency in the English language, from learning syntax and style to improving vocabulary, word choice, spelling, punctuation and capitalization.

The New Standards Primary Literacy Standards specify the knowledge and skills students should demonstrate in reading and writing by the end of each school year, from kindergarten through third grade.

Students who meet these standards should be on target to meet high literacy standards in states and local school districts around the country. Educators and parents will find these standards an indispensable companion to their state and local standards. Here are samples of real student performances analyzed against standards; here are the answers to the question of how good is good enough.

How These Standards Are Organized

These standards are organized by grade level, with sections for kindergarten, first grade, second grade and third grade. Each section begins with a profile of students at that grade level, describing their readiness to learn and activities that will support their progress in reading and writing.

These profiles are not intended to suggest that all children and all programs are — or should be — alike. Rather, they evoke images of real children in real classrooms learning in rich literacy programs: the ultimate purpose of the standards. The profiles serve as a reminder that, despite the intentionally stark, precise and crisp language of the Primary Literacy Standards themselves, teaching children to read and write is complex work. There are as many nuances to this learning process as there are unique human beings.

Three standards in reading and three standards in writing follow the profiles.

Three Sensible Standards in Reading, Three Sensible Standards in Writing

The essential components of learning to read and write, like any complex process, can be segmented in many ways. For ease of use, these standards are organized under three broad headings:

Reading

1. Print-Sound Code
2. Getting the Meaning
3. Reading Habits

Writing

1. Habits and Processes
2. Writing Purposes and
   Resulting Genres
3. Language Use and Conventions

Four of the standards — Print-Sound Code, Getting the Meaning, Writing Purposes and Resulting Genres, and Language Use and Conventions — deal with knowledge and skills. These standards set end-of-year achievement expectations, but they also include midyear indicators of on-target progress and problems that call for intensive instructional intervention.

Two of the standards — Reading Habits and Writing Habits and Processes — deal with the daily practice of literacy. For these standards, the expectations apply throughout the school year. At each grade level, the standards include guidance about appropriate books for students to read.

Students meet a standard when their overall performance satisfies the expectations often enough and well enough to indicate mastery. Generally, assessing whether students meet a standard requires evaluating a *number of performances* rather than an isolated test performance.

Student Work and Companion CD-ROMs

The New Standards Primary Literacy Standards are unique and powerful for two reasons. First, they are clear and precise expectations, not fuzzy jargon. Second, student work accompanies standards that define the reading and writing skills. The standards are made tangible by reading performances and writing samples that exemplify the expectations and the results.

Moreover, the commentary on the student work explains the qualities of performances that meet the standards and answers the burning question, "How good is good enough?" The student work, collected from a diverse range of students in a wide variety of settings, shows the level of performance expected — and reachable — in these standards.

Reading and writing performances also are included on the CD-ROMs that accompany this book.

A Healthy Tension Between Theory and Practice

A major challenge in drafting standards is translating abstract theories of learning into concrete language for practice. In these standards, the language is specific enough to be useful, yet general enough to accommodate variability in K–3 students and literacy programs. At the same time, these standards invite active intellectual engagement from educators who use them in classroom practice.

A case in point: It is critical for educators to understand the distinction between invisible, cognitive processes inside students' minds and visible, behavioral indicators that these processes are occurring. For example, retelling a story is one way first graders may indicate that they comprehend what they have read or heard, but the comprehension itself may be invisible. The quality of the retelling contains clues about the accuracy, scope and depth of each child's comprehension — and it is up to the adult to pick up on these clues and assess their quality.

These standards spell out what students are expected to do, cognitively and behaviorally, rather than what curriculum and instruction should look like. There are, in fact, many effective ideas for organizing a strong literacy program. All of them are based on how children learn to read and write. To understand what the research says about these processes, turn to **Learning to Read**, page 17, and **Learning to Write**, page 29. These sections lay out the assumptions about reading and writing that are incorporated in the standards.

Design Features Make These Standards Easy to Use

Reading Standards

◆ Standard name

◆ A site map that shows where you are, where you've been and what comes next

◆ Video snapshot from the CD-ROM of student reading performances that meet the standard and demonstrate "how good is good enough"

◆ Insightful commentary that explains the student performances

---

The kindergarten standards have a special status due to the enormous variability that exists at this early level. Not only do students start kindergarten at different ages with diverse preschool literacy experiences, but also some kindergarten programs are full day and others only half a day. Educators should get as close to the kindergarten target as possible and do whatever is necessary over the summer and throughout first grade to put everyone on track to meet end-of-year standards in first grade.

Kindergarten Reading Standard 1: **Print-Sound Code**

During kindergarten, children should learn the basics of the print-sound code: how words break up into individual sounds and how words are constructed from individual sounds; the alphabet and how letters stand for sounds; and how a string of letters can stand for a string of sounds that make up a word.

Knowledge of Letters and Their Sounds

Children leaving kindergarten should know the letters of the alphabet and many of their corresponding sounds. The precise number of letters and sounds kindergartners should know is not important; what is essential is that children grasp the *idea* of how letters represent sounds. We expect children leaving kindergarten to:

◆ recognize and name most letters;

◆ recognize and say the common sounds of most letters and write a letter that goes with a spoken sound; and

◆ use their knowledge of sounds and letters to write

phonetically, representing consonant sounds with single letters in the correct sequence.

Phonemic Awareness

Children who readily develop phonemic awareness in kindergarten probably will learn to read easily. But lagging development of phonemic awareness is not an excuse for delaying work on the print-sound code; some children develop phonemic awareness by learning the sounds of letters and how to blend them.

Children who do not grasp the print-sound code until first grade will not necessarily have a hard time learning to read. With instruction in phonemic awareness and the print-sound code, these students can become readers in first grade.

Site map:

Kindergarten
Reading Standard 1:
Print-Sound Code
◆ Knowledge of Letters and Their Sounds
◆ Phonemic Awareness
◆ Reading Words

Kindergarten
Reading Standard 2:
Getting the Meaning
◆ Accuracy and Fluency
◆ Self-Monitoring and Self-Correcting Strategies
◆ Comprehension

Kindergarten
Reading Standard 3:
Reading Habits
◆ Reading a Lot
◆ Reading Behaviors
◆ Discussing Books
◆ Vocabulary

Rosanna

Reading Standard 1:
Print-Sound Code

Knowledge of Letters and
Their Sounds

Rosanna is asked to write a few simple, regularly spelled words with the consonant-vowel (CV) pattern, such as *go*, the consonant-vowel-consonant (CVC) pattern, such as *gas*, *dog* and *pin*, or the consonant-consonant-vowel-consonant (CCVC) pattern, such as *stop*. Despite some mistakes, Rosanna reveals through her writing that she clearly "gets" the idea that letters represent sounds.

She sounds out the word as she tries to match the sound with the letter that represents it. From her efforts, we know that she can identify some beginning sounds. She is not able to write ending sounds as consistently (although she can say them to herself in preparation for writing). She knows two sounds for the letter *o*. This is evident from her

correct spelling of the word *go* and her spelling of "DO" for the word *dog*.

Like many kindergarten children, Rosanna has the most difficulty hearing the middle sounds, including the second sound in a beginning blend and medial vowels. From watching Rosanna try to write the word *stop*, we know she hears the sound that *t* makes in the word because her first attempts show her writing the letters *st*. When the teacher repeats the word to see if she can identify more sounds, Rosanna erases the *t* from the blend *st* and substitutes a *p*, which represents the ending sound.

We expect children at the end of kindergarten to know the letters of the alphabet and some sounds and to get the idea that letters represent sounds.

The images and commentary in the reading section of this book refer to reading performances available on the CD-ROM.

Spelling Patterns
CV — consonant-vowel
CVC — consonant-vowel-consonant
CCVC — consonant-consonant-vowel-consonant

Writing Standards

◆ Standard name

◆ A site map that shows where you are, where you've been and what comes next

◆ Student work that meets the standard and demonstrates "how good is good enough"

◆ Informed commentary on the student writing

Second-Grade
Writing Standard 2: Writing Purposes and Resulting Genres

For second graders who are progressing according to standards, writing has become a meaningful activity with myriad purposes. More than ever, these children write to communicate with other people, to learn new things and to give evidence of their understanding. By the time they leave second grade, they have experimented with and produced many kinds of writing, including narrative account, response to literature, report and narrative procedure.

Sharing Events, Telling Stories: Narrative Writing
By the end of the year, second-grade writers should move beyond simply describing a sequence of events. The structures for extended pieces may be built around a cluster of memorable events (episodic memoirs), around problems and solutions, or around a central idea or a theme running through events. Second graders should be able to set the action of a narrative in a context that could include setting, relationships among characters, motives and moods — perhaps beginning with a classic story opening (for example, "Once there was a girl ... " or "It was a dark, dark night when ... "). Second graders should begin to use strategies for building pace and tension, such as giving more attention to some events than others, summarizing or skipping some events, and creating anticipation.

By the end of the year, we expect second-grade students to produce fictional and autobiographical narratives in which they:

◆ incorporate some literary or "writing" language that does not sound like speech (for example, "Slowly, slowly he turned," "For days and weeks and months, I've worked for this moment");

◆ create a believable world and introduce characters, rather than simply recount a chronology of events, using specific details about characters and settings and developing motives and moods;

◆ develop internal events as well as external ones (for example, the child may tell not only what happened to a character but also what the character wondered, remembered and hoped);

◆ write in first and third person; and

◆ use dialogue effectively.

**Second-Grade
Writing Standard 1:**
Habits and Processes

**Second-Grade
Writing Standard 2:**
Writing Purposes and Resulting Genres

  ◆ Sharing Events, Telling Stories: Narrative Writing

  ◆ Informing Others: Report or Informational Writing

  ◆ Getting Things Done: Functional and Procedural Writing

  ◆ Producing and Responding to Literature

**Second-Grade
Writing Standard 3:**
Language Use and Conventions

  ◆ Style and Syntax

  ◆ Vocabulary and Word Choice

  ◆ Spelling

  ◆ Punctuation, Capitalization and Other Conventions

"A New Teacher"

Writing Standard 2:
Writing Purposes and Resulting Genres

Narrative Writing

Bryan, the writer of this piece, produces a fairly mature story line, one with a strong message. The story is one of moral choice and perhaps was inspired by other stories built around such choices that are common in children's literature. Although the piece lacks some detail, it is typical of certain kinds of writing in which detail is not essential to the author's purpose — for example, fables. This sample meets the standard for narrative writing for second grade.

◆ Bryan develops a context for the story by introducing the central character and the one thing that is important to know about her initially: As a girl wanted to be a teacher and when she grew up she still wanted to be one. This characteristic is the piece of information on which the whole story hangs.

◆ Bryan layers our understanding about Judy through events in the story. She procrastinates ("She didn't study"), she worries ("'What will I do?'") and she resists the devil's suggestion (she believes in fairness even though her resistance may prevent her from achieving the one thing the writer has told us is important to her: becoming a teacher).

◆ Judy's emotions are not specified explicitly, but rather are suggested by internal dialogue ("'What will I do?'") and by descriptions of facial expressions ("as she smiled" [happiness]).

◆ The dialogue, though predictable, advances the story line. ▶ ▶

A New Teacher

Once there was a girl named Judy. She wanted to be a teacher*. She grew and she still wanted to be a techer*. "O.K.," said Mrs. Carter. "But you have to take a test." "O.K.," said Judy. Later it was all most* time for the test. She didn't study so she said, "What will I do?" It was night and Judy dremed* about the test. She was asleep and a little

*teacher
*teacher
*almost
*dreamed

*Translation of phonetically spelled words

About the Student Work

The reading performances and writing samples in this book come almost entirely from public school classrooms, many of them urban — and not from "gifted and talented" programs. The performances and student work were gathered from schools recognized for their good reading and writing programs. Even so, reading and writing samples come not from students who are superstars or unusually talented but from typical, normal children who work hard in good programs.

As a result, the levels of performance represent reasonable, attainable expectations where student effort and the opportunity to learn are in place.

Kindergarten

Kindergarten

Their belief that learning

is fun, easy, exciting —

that they already

almost know how —

sets kindergartners apart

from older students.

Emerging Readers and Writers

Virtually all kindergarten students enter their first real classrooms wide-eyed and eager to learn. They "take to" learning like fearless adventurers on an undiscovered trail, absorbing new information and mastering new processes with aplomb. Their belief that learning is fun, easy, exciting — that they already almost know how — sets kindergartners apart from older students.

Children enter kindergarten with widely different preparation for achieving literacy standards. Some come to school with a running start, already reading and writing at or near end-of-kindergarten standards. Other children have little knowledge of books, print, the alphabet or even the sounds that make up the words they know. However, differences in readiness are no excuse to lower expectations. Instead, these differences should lead schools to make extra efforts — to devote more time, give more attention and allocate more resources — to help kindergartners learn. Given good instruction, preferably in all-day programs, virtually every kindergartner can end the year prepared to succeed in first grade.

Children who have less exposure to language-building activities in their preschool years may need extra time, attention and resources to bring them up to speed. They may need strong literacy instruction during the summer after kindergarten and extra attention in first grade to meet first-grade standards.

The New Standards Primary Literacy Standards assume a full-day kindergarten with a rich literacy program. Children in half-day kindergarten programs probably will take longer to meet these standards.

Reading and Writing: What to Expect

During kindergarten, children learn how to handle books and navigate through them. They learn to hold books right side up, with the text facing towards them, and to turn the pages from front to back. "Reading," they discover, means figuring out the secrets of print — but in their minds, print still may be a confusion of pictures, random letters, numbers and squiggles. And, in fact, this is how kindergarten writing often appears at the beginning of the year. Kindergartners learn to follow the words of a book as their teacher reads it aloud; in doing so, they come to understand that the meaning of a story is linked to the text on the pages. Their vocabularies increase rapidly.

By the end of kindergarten, children should know the basics of the print-sound code. They should know that spoken words contain separate sounds, which correspond to the letters of the alphabet, and that letters combine to make

printed words. Kindergartners should be able to recognize or sound out some simple words on their own as they read easy books, such as *At the Zoo* from Houghton Mifflin's Little Reader series. They also begin to demonstrate their knowledge of the print-sound code in their writing.

Kindergartners usually approach writing with confidence and a spirit of adventure. Given writing implements and paper, nudges of encouragement, and large blocks of uninterrupted time, most kindergartners write eagerly. Determined to communicate and make meaning, they are resourceful and inventive in their use of drawings, words, letter strings, scribbles, graphic representations and letter approximations.

In kindergarten, children begin to learn the rhythms, pauses and rhymes of written language. By the end of kindergarten, students should be able to repeat, with fluent intonations and appropriate pauses, the words of familiar texts, using illustrations to support them. They should be able to follow the text as they read, pointing on occasion to the right words, turning pages at the appropriate time and practicing the performance of fluent reading. These characteristics of emergent reading are critical precursors of real reading that kindergartners should master.

Developing Literacy Habits

Kindergartners should be immersed in books and reading. At this stage of their schooling, they should read several books every day. This is a reasonable expectation for kindergartners; they read short books and, often, reread certain books many times. Students can read either independently or with assistance from peers, a teacher or another adult. In addition, kindergartners should hear good books read aloud to them every day. *For examples of the kinds of books kindergartners should read, see **Leveled Books to Read for Accuracy and Fluency**, page 58, and **What Books Should Kindergartners Read?**, page 65.*

Kindergartners also should write every day. To adults who may be averse to writing themselves, this may seem too rigorous for five- and six-year-old children. At this stage, however, writing is expressive, playful and fun.

Other activities support emerging readers and writers as well. Kindergartners can create classroom labels and signs, known as environmental print; write and send notes; and produce stories and poems. On their way to meeting reading and writing standards, kindergartners can incorporate writing into play activities by writing directions for a treasure hunt, for example, or a reminder to a parent to send lunch money. Dramatic play builds their sense of language as well.

Kindergartners also can play with language by producing and mimicking rhymes. Early on, their written efforts will mix pictures, letter strings and phonetic strings — and they will show little or no evidence of punctuation. Nor will kindergarten work be arranged carefully from left to right or top to bottom, with neat spaces between words or letter strings. This is fine. Kindergarten writers are trying out many new skills. Their work is important and meaningful in leading them toward literacy — even if adults cannot always read their phonetic spelling.

Drawing is a major, integral component of kindergarten writing. Kindergartners create detailed, even elaborate, drawings related to their writing topics. Many times, the drawings stand alone, telling stories without words. Other times, the drawings reflect how much students know about their topics, capturing more than they are able to write yet in words. Or drawings act as a placeholder that students use to hold ideas in their minds, a rehearsal to try out their thoughts or a plan to generate new ideas. Drawings commonly remain an integral part of student writing through first grade.

> The New Standards Primary Literacy Standards assume a full-day kindergarten with a rich literacy program. Children in half-day kindergarten programs probably will take longer to meet these standards.

The kindergarten standards have a special status due to the enormous variability that exists at this early level. Not only do students start kindergarten at different ages with diverse preschool literacy experiences, but also some kindergarten programs are full day and others only half a day. Educators should get as close to the kindergarten target as possible and do whatever is necessary over the summer and throughout first grade to put everyone on track to meet end-of-year standards in first grade.

Kindergarten
Reading Standard 1: **Print-Sound Code**

During kindergarten, children should learn the basics of the print-sound code: how words break up into individual sounds and how words are constructed from individual sounds; the alphabet and how letters stand for sounds; and how a string of letters can stand for a string of sounds that make up a word.

Knowledge of Letters and Their Sounds

Children leaving kindergarten should know the letters of the alphabet and many of their corresponding sounds. The precise number of letters and sounds kindergartners should know is not important; what is essential is that children grasp the *idea* of how letters represent sounds. We expect children leaving kindergarten to:

◆ recognize and name most letters;

◆ recognize and say the common sounds of most letters and write a letter that goes with a spoken sound; and

◆ use their knowledge of sounds and letters to write phonetically, representing consonant sounds with single letters in the correct sequence.

Phonemic Awareness

Children who readily develop phonemic awareness in kindergarten probably will learn to read easily. But lagging development of phonemic awareness is not an excuse for delaying work on the print-sound code; some children develop phonemic awareness by learning the sounds of letters and how to blend them.

Children who do not grasp the print-sound code until first grade will not necessarily have a hard time learning to read. With instruction in phonemic awareness and the print-sound code, these students can become readers in first grade.

**Kindergarten
Reading Standard 1:**
Print-Sound Code

- ◆ Knowledge of Letters and Their Sounds
- ◆ Phonemic Awareness
- ◆ Reading Words

**Kindergarten
Reading Standard 2:**
Getting the Meaning

- ◆ Accuracy and Fluency
- ◆ Self-Monitoring and Self-Correcting Strategies
- ◆ Comprehension

**Kindergarten
Reading Standard 3:**
Reading Habits

- ◆ Reading a Lot
- ◆ Reading Behaviors
- ◆ Discussing Books
- ◆ Vocabulary

Rosanna

Reading Standard 1:
Print-Sound Code

Knowledge of Letters and
Their Sounds

Rosanna is asked to write a few simple, regularly spelled words with the consonant-vowel (CV) pattern, such as *go,* the consonant-vowel-consonant (CVC) pattern, such as *gas, dog* and *pin,* or the consonant-consonant-vowel-consonant (CCVC) pattern, such as *stop.* Despite some mistakes, Rosanna reveals through her writing that she clearly "gets" the idea that letters represent sounds.

She sounds out the word as she tries to match the sound with the letter that represents it. From her efforts, we know that she can identify some beginning sounds. She is not able to write ending sounds as consistently (although she can say them to herself in preparation for writing). She knows two sounds for the letter *o.* This is evident from her correct spelling of the word *go* and her spelling of "DO" for the word *dog.*

Like many kindergarten children, Rosanna has the most difficulty hearing the middle sounds, including the second sound in a beginning blend and medial vowels. From watching Rosanna try to write the word *stop,* we know she hears the sound that *t* makes in the word because her first attempts show her writing the letters *st.* When the teacher repeats the word to see if she can identify more sounds, Rosanna erases the *t* from the blend *st* and substitutes a *p,* which represents the ending sound.

We expect children at the end of kindergarten to know the letters of the alphabet and some sounds and to get the idea that letters represent sounds.

The images and commentary in the reading section of this book refer to reading performances available on the CD-ROM.

Spelling Patterns

CV — consonant-vowel

CVC — consonant-vowel-
consonant

CCVC — consonant-
consonant-vowel-consonant

Phonemic Awareness
(Segmenting and Blending Sounds)

In kindergarten, children should be learning phonemic awareness, the ability to hear and say the separate sounds (phonemes) in words. Specifically, by the end of kindergarten, we expect children to:

◆ produce rhyming words and recognize pairs of rhyming words;

◆ isolate initial consonants in single-syllable words (for example, /t/ is the first sound in *top*);

◆ when a single-syllable word is pronounced (for example, *cat*), identify the onset (/c/) and rime* (-at) and begin to fully separate the sounds (/c/-/a/-/t/) by saying each sound aloud; and

◆ blend onsets (/c/) and rimes (-at) to form words (*cat*) and begin to blend separately spoken phonemes to make a meaningful one-syllable word (for example, when the teacher says a word slowly, stretching it out as "mmm — ahhh — mmm," children can say that the word being stretched out is *mom*).

Kindergarten Reading Standard 1: *Print-Sound Code*
◆ Knowledge of Letters and Their Sounds
◆ Phonemic Awareness
◆ Reading Words

Kindergarten Reading Standard 2: *Getting the Meaning*
◆ Accuracy and Fluency
◆ Self-Monitoring and Self-Correcting Strategies
◆ Comprehension

Kindergarten Reading Standard 3: *Reading Habits*
◆ Reading a Lot
◆ Reading Behaviors
◆ Discussing Books
◆ Vocabulary

* *Onset* and *rime* are linguistic terms. Onsets are speech sounds (/b/, /j/, /s/, /p/) before a vowel, and rimes are the vowel and what follows (-ack). If a word begins with a vowel, it only has a rime. Words are formed by combining onsets and rimes (*back, jack, sack, pack*).

Kimberly

Reading Standard 1:
Print-Sound Code

Phonemic Awareness
◆ Produce rhyming words

Kimberly is able to recognize and add a word to a series of rhymes. The teacher says a series of words and asks for a rhyme. Children can say a real word or a nonsense word. Kimberly successfully delivers all five rhyming words.

Rosanna

◆ Blend onsets and rimes

In this exercise, Rosanna is asked to listen to the puppet say a beginning sound (onset) and then the rest of the word (rime). She is asked to blend the onset and rime to make a word. She blends each onset and rime quickly and confidently.

Paul

◆ Blend onsets and rimes and begin to blend separately spoken phonemes

In this exercise, Paul is able to segment the initial sound from the rest of the word to make a new word. Interestingly, in an earlier exercise, he was not able to add a rhyming word to a series of rhymes and had trouble blending onsets and rimes. However, he is quite comfortable segmenting phonemes, often considered a more advanced skill. He successfully segments the initial phoneme from all five words. The teacher is careful not to tack a vowel onto the initial consonant sound, so Paul can hear the sound of the initial consonant clearly.

Eduardo

◆ Isolate consonants

In these two exercises, Eduardo is asked to identify the beginning sounds in one set of words and the ending sounds in another set of words. He successfully completes the tasks, often giving the letter name that represents the sound, which is more difficult to do. When the teacher asks him to say the sound of the letter he names, he answers correctly every time.

Lucas

◆ Blend phonemes

Lucas successfully blends three distinct phonemes to make a word. He does this well, even though the teacher is not as exact in her pronunciation as she could be. For instance, as the first phoneme in *gum*, he hears /*guh*/ instead of a sharp /*g*/. It is impossible to say how this affected him as he mentally worked through the exercise — he may have adjusted his efforts, or he may have been unaware. He still is able to blend the three phonemes accurately.

New Standards

Reading Words

By the end of kindergarten, children should have caught on to the alphabetic idea, i.e., how the writing system works with respect to sounds. We expect children leaving kindergarten to:

◆ use their knowledge of letter sounds to figure out a few simple, regularly spelled, single-syllable words (consonant-vowel-consonant);

◆ read simple texts containing familiar letter-sound correspondences and high-frequency words; and

◆ read some words on their own, including a small number (about 20) of simple, high-frequency words that are recognized by "sight" — that is, when children encounter the words in a story, they do not need to sound the words out.

About the 20-Word Sight Vocabulary

A 20-word sight vocabulary is a learning target, *not a teaching target.* The idea is not for children to memorize or "study" words from flash cards but to recognize words they encounter in their everyday lives. Students in print-rich classrooms, filled with word walls, labels and books, comfortably amass a 20-word sight vocabulary. Each student may know a different set of words.

Kindergarten Reading Standard 1:
Print-Sound Code

◆ Knowledge of Letters and Their Sounds

◆ Phonemic Awareness

◆ Reading Words

Kindergarten Reading Standard 2:
Getting the Meaning

◆ Accuracy and Fluency

◆ Self-Monitoring and Self-Correcting Strategies

◆ Comprehension

Kindergarten Reading Standard 3:
Reading Habits

◆ Reading a Lot

◆ Reading Behaviors

◆ Discussing Books

◆ Vocabulary

Lucas

Reading Standard 1:
Print-Sound Code

Reading Words
◆ Read simple texts containing familiar letter-sound correspondences and high-frequency words

In this performance, the teacher tells Lucas, "I have a book and I'm going to read some of it, but when I stop, I want you to read the word, OK?"

The text, *Jeff Helps With the Jet,* is designed to challenge the beginning reader with common sight vocabulary and regularly spelled two-, three- and four-letter words with the CV, CVC, CVCC and CCVC patterns. The illustrations are only partially helpful and not at all explicit.

◆ Read some words, including some "sight" words

Lucas demonstrates that he knows several "sight" words including *the* when he reads the first page. He also successfully decodes the word *up* on page 1. On page 2, Lucas reads *jet* with minimal help from the picture, which shows the front window of the plane with two persons sitting side-by-side.

◆ Use their knowledge of letter sounds

Lucas correctly reads the word *men,* even though only one man is pictured. Lucas struggles to read the word *fast* on page 4, which contains no picture clues. He mouths the sounds for the *f* and the *a.* Given more time, he may have been able to decode the last two sounds /st/ to read the word *fast.* He successfully tackles another CVCC pattern word when he false-starts and then decodes *land* in the sentence "The jet can land" on page 5.

Lucas' reading of *Jeff Helps With the Jet* demonstrates he has caught on to how the writing system works with respect to sounds. He uses his knowledge of letter sounds to figure out a few simple, single-syllable words with the CV, CVC, CVCC and CCVC patterns and recognizes some familiar high-frequency words.

Spelling Patterns

CV — consonant-vowel

CVC — consonant-vowel-consonant

CVCC — consonant-vowel-consonant-consonant

CCVC — consonant-consonant-vowel-consonant

Kindergarten
Reading Standard 2: Getting the Meaning

Accuracy and Fluency

Children at the end of kindergarten should understand that every word in a text says something specific. They can demonstrate this competence in the following ways:

◆ read Level B books that they have not seen before, but that have been previewed* for them, attending to each word in sequence and getting most of them correct; and

◆ read "emergently" — that is, "reread" a favorite story, re-creating the words of the text with fluent intonation and phrasing and showing through verbal statements or occasional pointing that they understand that the print on the page controls what is said.

Kindergarten
Reading Standard 1:
Print-Sound Code

◆ Knowledge of Letters and Their Sounds

◆ Phonemic Awareness

◆ Reading Words

Kindergarten
Reading Standard 2:
Getting the Meaning

◆ Accuracy and Fluency

◆ Self-Monitoring and Self-Correcting Strategies

◆ Comprehension

Kindergarten
Reading Standard 3:
Reading Habits

◆ Reading a Lot

◆ Reading Behaviors

◆ Discussing Books

◆ Vocabulary

*Previewing means telling the student the title of the book and what it is about, as well as introducing any difficult or unfamiliar vocabulary that is important to the story.

Leveled Books to Read for Accuracy and Fluency

Level B books are very easy for emerging readers to read. These books often focus on a single idea or simple story line that children can relate to their personal experience. The text and the pictures directly correspond. The language, while not exactly duplicating oral language, includes natural syntactic structures.

The format of Level B books is consistent, with text that is clearly separated from pictures appearing at the same place on every page. Most books have one to four lines of text (one or two sentences) for each page or illustration, with a full range of punctuation. The text is regular, clear and easy to see, with ample space between the words so that children can point and read. Several high-frequency words are repeated often throughout the text.

Shiori

Reading Standard 2:
Getting the Meaning

Accuracy

In this performance, Shiori attains 97 percent accuracy on her reading of *Animal Habitats*. She requests and receives help with only two words during this reading, *habitats* and *porcupine*. The teacher, after giving Shiori an opportunity to use decoding strategies to figure out the word, tells her in general terms what the book is about. This modest assistance is all the support Shiori needs to proceed. Because she did not know what a porcupine looked like, the picture was not helpful in making sense of the text.

The evidence shows that Shiori really is "reading" and not just telling the story from the pictures. For instance, on several pages, she correctly reads the text instead of substituting another, more conversational word for the word on the page. On page 8, she reads, "I am a whale. I live in the sea" (not water). And on page 4, "I am a deer. I live in the forest" (not woods).

A Kindergarten Running Record*

Book Title: _Animal Habitats_ (T)

Page 1:   I am a fish. I live in a lake.

Page 2:   I am a koala. I live in a gum tree.

Page 3:   I am a bat. I live in a cave.

Page 4:   I am a deer. I live in the forest.

Page 5:   I am a porcupine. I live in a log. (T)

Page 6:   I am a parrot. I live in a nest.

Page 7:   I am a wolf. I live in a den.

Page 8:   I am a whale. I live in the sea.

(Word count: 73)

T = Told the word

2 errors = 97% accuracy

*For more on running records, see page 21.

Fluency

Shiori reads the book with adequate intonation for a kindergarten student, pausing appropriately for periods at the end of each sentence. She also points to each word as she reads. Although an adult reader might put more fluctuation and drama into the reading to make it more interesting, Shiori's reading is considered fluent for the end of kindergarten.

Comprehension

Comprehension must be evaluated with more complex pieces of literature read aloud to students; however, kindergartners should be able to get the gist of texts they read independently. At first, Shiori recalls only that the book is about animals. However, after looking at the pictures again, she gives a succinct and accurate summary of the book: "It's about animals, where they live." This response is evidence that Shiori follows the meaning of what she is reading. Looking back at the pictures is the kindergarten version of "going back to the text" for assistance and is a strategy that should be encouraged.

(For more on Comprehension, see page 62.)

Self-Monitoring and Self-Correcting Strategies

When students are rereading a familiar book at the end of kindergarten, we expect them to self-monitor and self-correct when necessary to determine whether:

◆ they are looking at the correct page;

◆ the word they are saying is the one they are pointing to; and

◆ what they read makes sense.

When listening to stories read aloud, children should monitor whether the story is making sense to them. We expect children leaving kindergarten, for example, to:

◆ ask why a character would do that;

◆ say they don't understand something; or

◆ say the character "is scared because ... " or "did that because ... ."

Kindergarten Reading Standard 1:
Print-Sound Code

◆ Knowledge of Letters and Their Sounds

◆ Phonemic Awareness

◆ Reading Words

Kindergarten Reading Standard 2:
Getting the Meaning

◆ Accuracy and Fluency

◆ Self-Monitoring and Self-Correcting Strategies

◆ Comprehension

Kindergarten Reading Standard 3:
Reading Habits

◆ Reading a Lot

◆ Reading Behaviors

◆ Discussing Books

◆ Vocabulary

Thomas

Reading Standard 2:
Getting the Meaning

Accuracy and Fluency

Thomas reads the book *Going to School* accurately and fluently. Thomas has no trouble decoding the text, yet he continues to illustrate a good sense of how to monitor and correct his own reading.

Self-Monitoring and
Self-Correcting Strategies

◆ Determine whether they are looking at the correct page

◆ Determine whether the word they are saying is the one they are pointing to

◆ Determine whether what they read makes sense

On page 1, Thomas first reads, "We go to," but then catches himself, brings his finger back over the words again to check whether he is saying what he is pointing to and reads, "I go to … ." Thomas continues to scan the pictures to reinforce his understanding, even though he doesn't seem to need assistance with decoding. On the second-to-last page, Thomas realizes he has come to the end of the book but glances back again, flipping backward to make sure he has not skipped a page. This type of careful yet automatic self-monitoring is the mark of a successful reader.

Jacob

Jacob demonstrates several self-monitoring and self-correcting strategies during his reading of *At the Zoo,* a Level B book. Several times in this performance, Jacob shows that he knows he is saying the word he is pointing to. On the title page, he asks the teacher, "Did you notice that?" as he points to a sign.

The teacher asks, "What does it say, that sign?"

Jacob replies, "Monkeys!"

On page 1, after incorrectly reading the word "monkeys" for *monkey,* he corrects himself and rereads from the beginning of the sentence, "I like the monkey and the monkey likes me." On page 3, when Jacob comes to the word *giraffe,* he obviously checks the picture as if to see if what he has just said makes sense.

Comprehension

Then the teacher asks, "Can you tell me what happens in this book?"

Jacob demonstrates that he knows that the word he is saying is the one on the sign. Flipping through the pages of the book while sometimes pointing to and sometimes glancing at each sign, Jacob says, "It has signs, and it keeps on saying the same words every time, like … monkeys, bears, giraffes, tigers, alligators, elephants. And then you come to the end, and it has the exclamation mark here."

The teacher asks, "Why do you think it has an exclamation mark at the end?"

Jacob answers, "Because it's an exciting ending."

"Can you tell anything else that happens in the book?" the teacher asks.

Pointing to each word in turn, Jacob answers, "At first it keeps on saying, 'I like the giraffe, and the giraffe likes me.' But at the end it says, 'And the elephant loves me.'" Jacob's focus on each word as he pointed to it helped him notice that the pattern changed.

In this performance, Jacob uses several self-monitoring and self-correcting strategies, including looking at the right page when referring to the text and reading, pointing to words as he refers to them in the text and checking to see if what he says makes sense in relation to the picture.

(For more on Accuracy and Fluency, see page 58, and for more on Comprehension, see page 62.)

Comprehension

In addition to recognizing words, kindergartners should be able to get the gist of texts they read. When they read on their own with expected levels of accuracy and fluency (see page 58), we expect students at the end of kindergarten to be able to:

◆ give evidence that they are following the meaning of what they are reading (for example, retelling what they have read using their own words or colloquial phrasing).

Kindergarten children also should be able to concentrate on and make sense of texts they hear read to them. The following are visible indicators that comprehension is taking place.

By the end of the year, we expect kindergarten students to be able to:

◆ retell the story in their own words or re-enact it, getting the events in the correct sequence;

◆ respond to simple questions about the book's content (for example, "Can you tell me what this story was about?" "What was Maria trying to do?" "How did Sam feel?" "Why did Antoine hide under the bed?");

◆ create artwork or a written response that shows comprehension of the story that was read;

◆ use knowledge from their own experience to make sense of and talk about the text; and

◆ make predictions based on illustrations or portions of stories.

**Kindergarten
Reading Standard 1:**
Print-Sound Code

■ ◆ Knowledge of Letters and Their Sounds

■ ◆ Phonemic Awareness

■ ◆ Reading Words

**Kindergarten
Reading Standard 2:**
Getting the Meaning

■ ◆ Accuracy and Fluency

■ ◆ Self-Monitoring and Self-Correcting Strategies

■ ◆ Comprehension

**Kindergarten
Reading Standard 3:**
Reading Habits

■ ◆ Reading a Lot

■ ◆ Reading Behaviors

■ ◆ Discussing Books

■ ◆ Vocabulary

Cleopatra

Reading Standard 2:
Getting the Meaning

Comprehension
◆ Create artwork or a written response that shows comprehension of the story that was read
◆ Use knowledge from their own experience to make sense of and talk about the text
◆ Make predictions based on illustrations or portions of stories

Students listen to the teacher read the book *Here Comes the Train* by Charlotte Voake. The book emphasizes the sounds the trains make as they speed by.

Cleopatra then demonstrates her understanding of the story by creating a drawing of a train with a caption bubble with the letters "Shhhhh."

The teacher comments, "Look what you did over here!" as she points to the letters that Cleopatra included in her drawing. The teacher asks, "What does that sound say?"

Cleopatra answers, "It says, 'Shhh.'"
The teacher asks, "What's making that sound?"

Cleopatra answers, "The train."
With her drawing and caption, Cleopatra demonstrates she understood the story was about the sounds trains make. She also demonstrates that she knows how those sounds can be represented by letters.

Jennifer Purdy and Kindergarten Class

◆ Use knowledge from their own experience to make sense of and talk about the text

In the story *Here Comes the Train* by Charlotte Voake, a family rides bikes on a bridge and stops to watch and listen to the trains on the tracks below. Because the children in this classroom ride the subway in their daily lives, they are eager to discuss how the family in the story might get onto the train from the bridge.

Cleopatra asks, "How could they get on the train?"

Adam proposes an idea as a question: "They would take a ladder?"

Talya, a third child, challenges the logic of Adam's suggestion when she poses another question: "How could they take a ladder down because they have bikes? How could they bring their bikes down the ladder?"

During this interaction, these three children bring their own experience to bear on the task of comprehending text.

Bill Fulbrecht and Kindergarten Class

◆ Make predictions based on illustrations or portions of stories

The teacher introduces the children to the cover of the book *The Trip* by Ezra Jack Keats. The teacher asks, "Just from looking at the cover, what do you think this story is going to be about?"

Rhea predicts it might have something to do with a puppet show. Some other children merely point out things they notice about the cover illustrations.

Mercy seems to predict that this book will be similar to another Ezra Jack Keats book the class read together. She makes a connection to this new book when she says, "I think it looks like he was painting from the story ... the one with ... Peter." The teacher acknowledges her answer, commenting that the painting looks like it came from the book that Peter was in.

The teacher asks, "So I wonder who made that puppet?"

Alex predicts the story line when he points and says, "I think [the boy on the cover] made the puppet!"

During this class discussion, three children, Rhea, Mercy and Alex, use the comprehension strategy of making predictions to help themselves get meaning from illustrations.

Kindergarten
Reading Standard 3: **Reading Habits**

Kindergarten is the grade when the joys and habits of frequent reading should develop. Kindergartners should engage with books — either independently or with assistance — every day and hear a variety of interesting books read to them every day.

Reading a Lot
We expect kindergarten students to:

◆ choose reading as a way to enjoy free time and ask for books to be read aloud to them;

◆ listen to one or two books read aloud each day in school and discuss these books with teacher guidance;

◆ hear another one or two books read to them each day at home or in after-school care;

◆ "reread" or read along — alone or with a partner or adult — two to four familiar books each day; and

◆ engage with a range of genres: literature (stories, songs, poems, plays); functional texts (how-to books, signs, labels, messages); and informational texts (all-about books, attribute texts).

Reading Behaviors
We expect kindergarten students to:

◆ hold a book right side up and turn pages in the correct direction;

◆ be able to follow text with a finger, pointing to each word as it is read; and

◆ pay attention to what the words they read are saying.

Reading Behaviors
Being able to point to each word as they read indicates that children recognize individual words. This does not mean that children must always follow text with their fingers. In fact, pointing may sometimes interfere with proficient readers' fluency.

**Kindergarten
Reading Standard 1:**
Print-Sound Code

◆ Knowledge of Letters and Their Sounds

◆ Phonemic Awareness

◆ Reading Words

**Kindergarten
Reading Standard 2:**
Getting the Meaning

◆ Accuracy and Fluency

◆ Self-Monitoring and Self-Correcting Strategies

◆ Comprehension

**Kindergarten
Reading Standard 3:**
Reading Habits

◆ Reading a Lot

◆ Reading Behaviors

◆ Discussing Books

◆ Vocabulary

What Books Should Kindergartners Read?

Beyond leveled books, which are used for practice-reading, teaching, and testing for accuracy and fluency, kindergartners should read and reread a variety of books and other print material.

Many excellent fiction and non-fiction books do not appear on any leveled text lists. Classroom libraries should include a wide range of classic and modern books that will satisfy readers with various reading abilities and interests. Kindergartners need books at their own reading levels to practice new skills, books above their reading levels to stretch and challenge them, and books that teachers can read aloud to them. Most kindergartners will not be able to read the read-aloud books on their own, but they can understand and enjoy more advanced books — and they need to hear these books read aloud to absorb the rhythms and cadences of more sophisticated language.

There are many lists of recommended titles, including the Newbury and Caldecott Award winners, *The Read-Aloud Handbook* by Jim Trelease, *Books to Build on: A Grade-by-Grade Resource Guide for Parents and Teachers (Core Knowledge Series)* by E.D. Hirsch, and the *Elementary School Library Collection: A Guide to Books and Other Media.* The American Library Association also recommends titles.

Read-Aloud Books

Allard, Harry, *Miss Nelson Is Missing!*
Barrett, Judith, *Cloudy With a Chance of Meatballs*
Bemelmans, Ludwig, *Madeline* (series)
Blanco, Alberto, *Angel's Kite*
Carle, Eric, *The Very Hungry Caterpillar*
Cisneros, Sandra, *Hairs/Pelitos*
Cooney, Barbara, *Miss Rumphius*
Freeman, Don, *Corduroy*
Greenfield, Eloise, *Honey, I Love*

A Level B Text

Henkes, Kevin, *Chester's Way*
Hoban, Russell, *A Baby Sister for Frances*
Hurwitz, Johanna, *Rip-Roaring Russell*
Keats, Ezra Jack, *Regards to the Man in the Moon*
Keats, Ezra Jack, *The Snowy Day*
Keats, Ezra Jack, *The Trip*
Polacco, Patricia, *Babushka's Doll*
Polacco, Patricia, *Just Plain Fancy*
Steptoe, John, *Mufaro's Beautiful Daughters: An African Tale*
Voake, Charlotte, *Here Comes the Train*
Williams, Karen Lynn, *Galimoto*
Williams, Vera B., *A Chair for My Mother*
Wood, Audrey, *The Napping House*
Yolen, Jane, *Owl Moon*

Level B Texts

Houghton Mifflin Co., Little Reader, Peters, *At the Zoo*
Rigby, PM Starters One, *The Way I Go to School*
Rigby, PM Starters Two, Giles, *Ball Games*
Rigby, PM Starters Two, Randell, *Cat and Mouse*
Sundance Publishing, Little Red Readers, Sloan, *Animal Habitats*
Wright Group, Sunshine Community Books, *Going to School*
Wright Group, Sunshine Set C, *I Love My Family*

I am a deer.
I live in the forest.

4

I am a porcupine.
I live in a log.

5

Discussing Books

We expect children to discuss books every day. Such discussions allow children to use and extend their vocabularies, to explore the ideas presented in books, to develop and use comprehension strategies, and to show that they can engage in "accountable talk" — conversations in which children build ideas together as a group, argue respectfully and logically with one another, and attend carefully to the language of texts.

In kindergarten discussions, we expect children to:

◆ give reactions to the book, with backup reasons;

◆ listen carefully to each other;

◆ relate their contributions to what others have said;

◆ ask each other to clarify things they say; and

◆ use newly learned vocabulary.

Vocabulary

Most children enter kindergarten with vocabularies that are more than ample for what they read. But because the vocabulary of the books they will read in the first, second and third grades expands dramatically, children's vocabularies also must grow — even in kindergarten. Children should learn not only new words but also new meanings and uses for familiar words.

We expect kindergarten students to:

◆ notice words that they don't know when they are read to and talked with and guess what the words mean from how they are used;

◆ talk about words and word meanings as they are encountered in books and conversation;

◆ show an interest in collecting words and playing with ones they like; and

◆ learn new words every day from talk and books read aloud.

Public School 321 Kindergarten Class

Abby

Reading Standard 3:
Reading Habits

Discussing Books

◆ Give reactions to the book, with backup reasons

◆ Listen carefully to each other

◆ Relate their contributions to what others have said

While participating in a class discussion, Katie demonstrates she can back up her interpretation of a book she has heard read aloud. After reading the book *The Trip* by Ezra Jack Keats, the teacher asks the children, "Why did Louie make up that whole story? Why did he imagine what he imagined?"

Katie offers her opinion: "Because he wanted to see his friends again."

The teacher asks Katie to provide a reason for this opinion when he asks, "Why do you say that?"

She replies, "Because at the beginning it said, 'He knew no one!'" By paraphrasing the words from the text, Katie demonstrates she attends carefully to the language of the text and comprehends it.

During a class discussion, Abby demonstrates she can listen carefully and relate her contributions to what others have just said. Before reading the book *The Trip* by Ezra Jack Keats, the teacher asks the children, "What can you tell just from looking at the cover?"

Danny says, "That was the same puppet that [came] from the other book we read with the puppet show."

"What book was that?" the teacher asks. "Do you remember the name of that book? We could go back and check if there was a puppet in that show."

Demonstrating that she is listening to the conversation, Abby adds, "Umm, next time at morning meeting, I think, umm, I could find it. I mean, umm, maybe at story time, I think I could find it … . Yeah, with the puppet show where he peeked over and saw them." Abby's comment builds on and directly relates to the comments she heard Danny and the teacher make.

Kindergarten
Writing Standard 1: **Habits and Processes**

As early as kindergarten, children should write every day, choosing and developing their topics. Their beginning "texts" may include material that is spoken, drawn and acted out along with their attempts to print letters and words. With partners, they respond to one another's work and help each other — most often by encouraging "add that" — to extend the story and make it more interesting to a reader. Young writers don't always make the suggested additions in writing because the physical act of forming letters and the concentration required to sound out and spell words tire them out. What appears on the page usually only hints at the rich composing kindergarten children do mentally.

Frequently, kindergartners' writing and pictures are displayed on the classroom wall. On occasion, selected pieces are revised, edited and polished for audiences outside the classroom. They may be read aloud in a celebration or mailed to a parent or grandparent. These public displays commemorate young writers' evolving literacy.

We expect kindergarten students to:

- write daily;

- generate content and topics for writing;

- write without resistance when given the time, place and materials;

- use whatever means are at hand to communicate and make meaning: drawings, letter strings, scribbles, letter approximations and other graphic representations, as well as gestures, intonations and role-played voices; and

- make an effort to reread their own writing and listen to that of others, showing attentiveness to meaning by, for example, asking for more information or laughing.

"ABCD … "

Writing Standard 1:
Habits and Processes

These samples are drawn from the portfolio of Melissa, a kindergarten student who wrote on a daily basis. The full collection of Melissa's work shows she produced writing on a wide array of topics, including what she did on weekends, what she wanted for Christmas, who her friends were, what she liked about school and various attempts at fiction. Melissa's collection provides clear evidence that she wrote with enthusiasm — several of her pieces are more than two pages long. Some of her revised pieces are illustrated and presented with a titled cover sheet. The collection represents a performance that meets the standard for kindergarten.

The first sample, "ABCD … ," was generated in mid-September, about a week into the school year, after the teacher had distributed "writing journals" to the class and directed the students to write about anything they wanted her to read. The teacher's plan was to respond to these journals on a daily basis. Melissa's entry shows that she wanted her teacher to know that she knew some of the alphabet. As a writing sample this, of course, is limited, but it does demonstrate that Melissa has one of the basic tools of literacy.

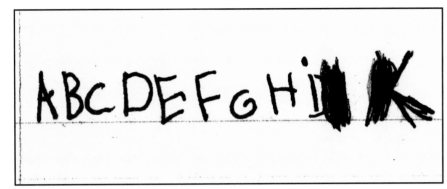

*I   like   jelly   beans

*Translation of phonetically spelled words

The second sample, "I LC GELLY BEN," is a simple piece of expressive writing dated Nov. 5. It illustrates that Melissa understands to write from left to right across the page (we could probably infer the left-to-right ordering from the alphabet sample, but we could not be certain). Melissa's sample also shows that she is attempting letter-sound correspondence (she has represented *like* with the beginning and ending sounds, though the ending sound is represented by the letter *c* rather than by the actual ending consonant). Melissa relies heavily on beginning and ending consonant sounds to represent whole words. She still is not creating word boundaries, and whether her writing could be read by another person, even someone who is knowledgeable about phonetic spelling, is doubtful.

(For more of Melissa's collection, see page 236.)

Kindergarten
Writing Standard 2: Writing Purposes and Resulting Genres

Most kindergartners are willing and eager to produce writing for its own sake; they think it is fun to express feelings and thoughts, and they like to make "stuff." But they have other reasons for wanting to write: to understand and make themselves understood and to participate in the grown-up world of written words and communication. Typically, they are determined and inventive in their often hybrid productions of writing. Kindergarten writing is practically a genre unto itself until children learn to control word boundaries and understand the more mature aspects of writing.

Young children write for a variety of purposes. But they write especially to share an event or tell a story, to convey information to others, to get something done, or to produce or respond to literature. The writing of kindergarten children is related closely to their talk. In fact, the writing of young children often contains many of the characteristics of oral language — it resembles written-down speech in which meaning relies on immediate context and on the reader's familiarity with the writer and the writer's opinions, feelings and ideas. Rather than waiting for children's writing to catch up with their thinking, it is acceptable for young children to express orally what later will become written text.

Sharing Events, Telling Stories: Narrative Writing

Because using language to share experiences and tell stories is such a basic part of being human, the narrative genre often emerges first as kindergarten children begin to produce writing. The stories initially are rather abbreviated glimpses into the life of the writer. They get longer as students develop the perseverance to write more and an awareness of the need to provide the audience with sufficient detail and context. Throughout kindergarten, however, these narratives are done both orally and in writing.

By the end of the year, we expect kindergarten students to produce narratives that:

♦ contain a "story" that may be only a single event or several events loosely linked, which the author may react to, comment on, evaluate, sum up or tie together;

♦ tell events as they move through time (control for chronological ordering);

♦ may include gestures, drawings and/or intonations that support meaning; and

♦ may incorporate storybook language (for example, "and they lived happily ever after").

"I WiT To MY Gamo s Has"

Writing Standard 2:

Writing Purposes and Resulting Genres

Narrative Writing

Jill's writing is typical of the bed-to-bed narratives frequently written by students through second grade. These narratives are distinguished by the writer's attempt to capture a series of events, but they are flawed in that they have no center or distinguishing event. They begin with an initiating event, which is followed by a list of subsequent events. The writer does not attempt to compress time, exclude extraneous events, or discriminate between what is or is not important.

Nevertheless, this piece meets the standard for narrative writing in kindergarten.

- This piece tells a story — a series of six events initiated by a trip to "MY Gamo s Has."

- The events are sequenced appropriately ("I PLad ByBLSu And uBLu PoPT in my iuy And [as a result] i wi in sid And i WocT My iuy").

- The story includes a drawing that illustrates what the writer is doing.

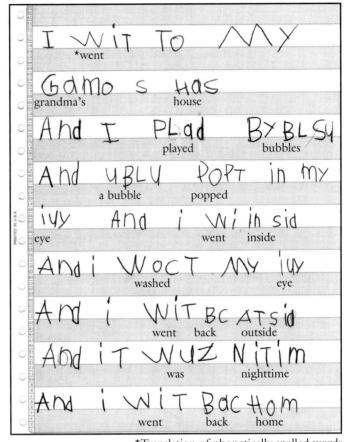

*Translation of phonetically spelled words

Writing Standard 3:

Language Use and Conventions

This piece meets the Language Use and Conventions Standard for kindergarten.

Style and Syntax

This story demonstrates the syntax of oral language typical of a kindergartner when recounting "what happened" in story form.

Vocabulary and Word Choice

This work shows Jill uses words that logically might be used in talk *(bubbles* and *popped)* but represents them phonetically ("ByBLSu" and "PoPT").

Spelling

This work provides evidence that the student creates text that a knowledgeable adult can decipher — words are represented phonetically with some consistency, especially in regard to initial consonants; there are also some high-frequency words included ("I," "to," "my," "and"). The writing also demonstrates an understanding of spaces between words and controls for left-to-right and top-to-bottom presentation.

(For more on Language Use and Conventions, see page 88.)

"I wit fihn"

Writing Standard 2:
Writing Purposes and Resulting Genres

Narrative Writing

Melissa's piece of narrative writing is a good example of a kindergartner narrating a sequence of events in chronological order. It represents narrative writing that meets the standard for kindergarten.

◆ Melissa produces a story with several events ("I wit fihn," "we clild hil," "we oalso coct 2 fih" and "on our wa bac we wrr fiidn roolepoles").

◆ She also includes reactions to these events ("it wizs andvihr!" and "it wizs finn!").

◆ She recounts events that move logically through time.

Writing Standard 3:
Language Use and Conventions

This piece meets the Language Use and Conventions Standard for kindergarten.

Style and Syntax

This work provides evidence that Melissa uses the syntax of oral language typically heard in children's recountings of "what I did."

Vocabulary and Word Choice

This work provides evidence that Melissa uses words drawn from oral vocabulary (*adventure* and *roly-poly*) but represents them phonetically ("andvihr" and "roolepoles").

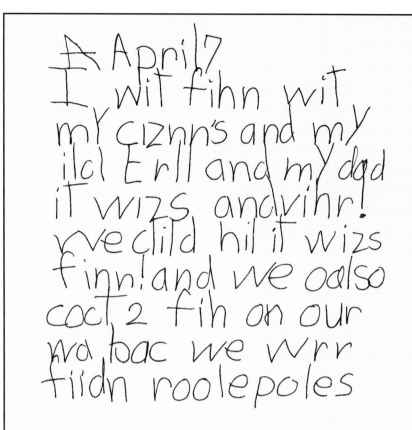

April 7
*I went fishing with
my cousins and my
Uncle Earl and my dad.
It was an adventure!
We climbed hill. It was
fun! And we also
caught 2 fish. On our
way back we were
finding roly-polys.

*Translation of phonetically spelled words

Spelling

This work provides evidence that Melissa creates text that is readable by adults familiar with phonetic spelling — in fact, this text is readable by even those who are inexperienced with phonetic spelling. She represents words with both initial and final consonants, and she represents many vowel sounds as well. Seven high-frequency words are spelled correctly. In addition, Melissa controls for left-to-right and top-to-bottom presentation and leaves space between words.

(For more on Language Use and Conventions, see page 88.)

New Standards

Research Perspectives

" Once children learn to write letters, they should be encouraged to write them, to use them to begin writing words or parts of words, and to use words to begin writing sentences. Instruction should be designed with the understanding that the use of invented spelling is not in conflict with teaching correct spelling. Beginning writing with invented spelling can be helpful for developing understanding of the identity and segmentation of speech sounds and sound-spelling relationships. Conventionally correct spelling should be developed through focused instruction and practice. Primary-grade children should be expected to spell previously studied words and spelling patterns correctly in their final writing products. Writing should take place regularly and frequently to encourage children to become more comfortable and familiar with it. "

From National Research Council, *Preventing Reading Difficulties in Young Children* (Washington, D.C.: National Academy Press, 1998), pp. 323–4.

Informing Others: Report or Informational Writing

Kindergarten writers on target to meet standards usually are full of their own new knowledge, and they delight in reporting it to others. They make lists that tell "all about" a particular topic (for example, "all about my brother," "about whales," "about me") and with prompting can reread these texts, leaving out information that is not about the topic.

They may mimic the informational reporting style of books they have encountered in the classroom.

By the end of the year, we expect kindergarten students to:

- gather, collect and share information about a topic;

- maintain a focus — stay on topic; and

- exclude extraneous information when prompted.

Kindergarten Writing Standard 1:
Habits and Processes

Kindergarten Writing Standard 2:
Writing Purposes and Resulting Genres

- Sharing Events, Telling Stories: Narrative Writing
- Informing Others: Report or Informational Writing
- Getting Things Done: Functional Writing
- Producing and Responding to Literature

Kindergarten Writing Standard 3:
Language Use and Conventions

- Style and Syntax
- Vocabulary and Word Choice
- Spelling
- Punctuation, Capitalization and Other Conventions

"bad somrs"

Writing Standard 2:
Writing Purposes and Resulting Genres

Report or Informational Writing

Lauren's writing is a good example of a kindergartner reporting information on a particular topic. She begins by naming the topic ("bad somrs") and by giving examples of these types of storms. Then she offers one characteristic of each of the examples given. This sample represents report writing that meets the standard for kindergarten.

- This piece relates information about two kinds of storms — those characterized primarily by thunder (and lightning) and those characterized by wind funnels (tornadoes). (See drawing.)

- The writing maintains a focus — each kind of storm is characterized as "bad," which is followed by an explanation ("tonados can cut up thns thnrsomrs can sakt thns"). In addition, the author includes no extraneous information.

- The writing also is accompanied by an illustration of the report topic — storm clouds and tornadoes. Reading this piece properly requires giving attention to the illustration, which shows both lightning and wind funnels.

Writing Standard 3:
Language Use and Conventions

This piece meets the Language Use and Conventions Standard for kindergarten.

Style and Syntax

Admittedly, the short length of the piece precludes Lauren's demonstrating syntactic range. However, the sentences that comprise the sample are complete syntactic units made up of subject-verb constructions. The first sentence draws its subject from the title of the piece ("bad somrs") and, hence, reads a bit awkwardly. It is not, however, incorrect.

Vocabulary and Word Choice

The vocabulary is appropriate for the topic. Lauren's word choice in this piece represents language that children would use orally or would hear spoken by peers.

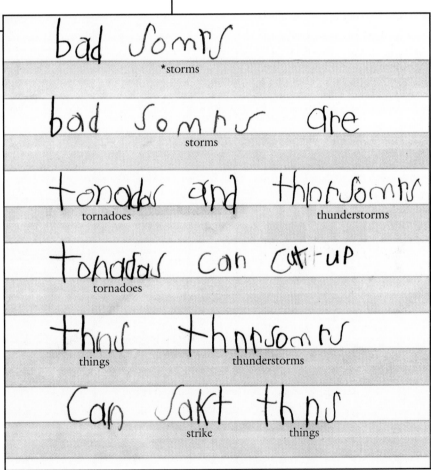

bad Somrs
*storms

bad Somrs are
storms

tonadar and thnrsomrs
tornadoes   thunderstorms

tonadar can cut-up
tornadoes

thns thnrsomrs
things   thunderstorms

can Sakt thns
strike   things

*Translation of phonetically spelled words

Spelling

This writing represents a kindergartner's understanding of phonetic spelling, as Lauren hears the sounds ("somrs" for *storms*). Misspellings are consistent throughout the piece. It also demonstrates knowledge of spacing and directionality.

(For more on Language Use and Conventions, see page 88.)

The Fort Worth Nature Center
by
Joe

"The Fort Worth Nature Center"

Writing Standard 2:
Writing Purposes and Resulting Genres

Report or Informational Writing

This report was produced after Joe's class took a trip to a nature center. He arranges information under four labels: "Buflo raNge," "Brdwok," "Mrsh" and "the tral." He illustrates and refines the report. That is, it is not a first draft. It is remarkable for its length — most kindergarten writing will not be this long. It is long because the trip galvanized the class; it was a remarkable experience and so inspired very good writing. Moreover, Joe worked over a period of several days to make the report a finished piece. This report clearly meets the standard for kindergarten informational writing.

♦ The piece is a thorough report about what happened and what Joe saw at a nature center. It is filled with information drawn from firsthand observation.

♦ The piece is organized into four sections, each of which focuses on happenings or objects associated with a particular location, such as the buffalo range.

♦ The text contains no digressions — all the information is pertinent.

Buflo raNge
*Buffalo

I saw a big buffalo.

I saw a big buflo

We Sol ded grass. We saw dead grass.

There were some baby deer.

There was some buffalo calves.

It smelled.

thar Wen Zom BABY dEr

THAt Was Zom Bafalo savs.

it smld.

BrdwoK   MNsh
Boardwalk   Marsh
            Marsh

thr Was MEnns There was minnows.

it had ANmis trAKs It had animal tracks.

They showed a dead skunk.

they shod a ded Skuk.

*Translation of phonetically spelled words

There were plants.

They showed us a dead fox.

There was some scum.

The Trail

The hike never ended.

Emil got hurt.

I heard a robin.

There were fossils.

My back started to hurt.

We got lost.

Writing Standard 3:
Language Use and Conventions

This piece meets the Language Use and Conventions Standard for kindergarten.

Style and Syntax

The style and syntax of this piece are fairly typical of oral language patterns used to detail information. Though the sentences are fairly short, the sentence stems are not all alike, as they might be with a writer as young as Joe ("I saw a buffalo," "I saw grass," "I saw a baby deer," etc.).

Vocabulary and Word Choice

Joe carefully uses words to explain what the class saw as well as what happened at the nature center. "Scum" and "FosuLs" are, of course, words that are appropriate for the experience and perhaps not part of Joe's everyday vocabulary. But the phrase "The hck navr indid" clearly echoes oral language.

Spelling

This text is readable by adults who are familiar with phonetic spelling. It is made up of words for the most part represented by appropriate initial and final consonants. Additionally, a number of high-frequency words are spelled correctly ("big," "was," "got"), as well as a number of words related to the nature center that may have been part of a word wall ("grAss" and "Scum").

(For more on Language Use and Conventions, see page 88.)

Getting Things Done: Functional Writing

Kindergartners should write for functional purposes both within the classroom and outside of school. Youngsters on their way to meeting standards find innumerable reasons for writing to get things done. A child who has erected a block castle might post a warning to classmates not to wreck it. A student whose birthday is coming up might create invitations to a party. A group of kids might make a list of feeding instructions for the class hamster or labels for special places in the room.

Kindergartners create imaginary phone messages. They compile menus. They write to tell people how to turn on the computer.

By the end of the year, we expect kindergarten students to be able to use writing to:

◆ tell someone what to do (for example, give directions, send messages); and

◆ name or label objects and places.

"WATER-sun-DErt SED-"

Writing Standard 2:
Writing Purposes and Resulting Genres

Functional Writing

This is a very early attempt at describing a procedure — it tells someone what to do: how to grow a flower. However, succinct as it is, it is nevertheless a correct and coherent statement. Like many early attempts at functional writing, Alex's sample actually is cast as a recounting — that is, he tells how to do something by recounting the experience as if done — hence, the "WE" that starts the piece off. This writing sample is a good example of a kindergartner using writing to explain how to do something for functional purposes. It represents functional writing that meets the standard for kindergarten.

◆ Alex begins with a list of ingredients ("WATER-sun-DErt SED-"), all necessary items for plant growth. Next, he simply states the directive ("PAt + SED-UNDR-DGrD [to] GrO- [the] FLWr").

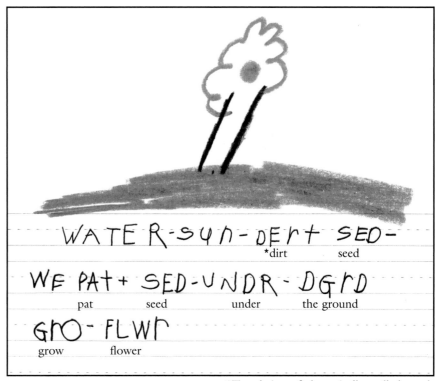

*Translation of phonetically spelled words

Writing Standard 3:
Language Use and Conventions

This piece does not meet the Language Use and Conventions Standard for kindergarten because it is marginal in terms of the syntax and vocabulary parts of the standard.

Alex clearly is abbreviating the language of oral speech, and the reader has to supply at least one additional word ("[to] grow flower[s]"). The piece does have some notable features, however.

This work provides evidence that Alex uses words from oral language and represents these words phonetically ("SED"). This work provides evidence that he independently creates text with words that an adult who is knowledgeable about spelling development and

the content of that particular child's piece of writing can decipher.

Alex frequently represents words with initial consonant sounds ("D" for *the*) and correctly spells two words ("WATER" and "sun"), though it is likely he copied them from a word wall or other source as the rest of the words indicate only control of consonant sounds ("FLWr"). The writing shows evidence of spacing between words, though Alex does use dashes and one plus sign to mark the spaces. He controls for directionality — left to right, top to bottom.

(For more on Language Use and Conventions, see page 88.)

"Haw to MaKa Jacltr"

Writing Standard 2:
**Writing Purposes and
Resulting Genres**

Functional Writing

This piece of writing is a good
example of a kindergartner using
writing to get things done by giving
directions. Lindsey provides the reader
a clear sense of the basic steps in making a jack-o'-lantern. This sample represents functional writing that meets
the standard for kindergarten. (To see
this same topic treated adequately by
students at other grades, see page 279.)

◆ Lindsey begins by identifying
and naming the materials one
will need to carve the pumpkin
("1. Got a nif And son").

◆ She sequences the steps from
beginning to end, segmenting the
steps by using numbers (1–6), so
the reader can easily follow the
directions.

Writing Standard 3:
Language Use and Conventions

This piece meets the Language
Use and Conventions Standard
for kindergarten.

Style and Syntax

Lindsey uses simple, short, almost
choppy sentences. It is, however, easy to
read this text and follow the directions,
and relatively short sentences are often
the norm in functional writing.

Vocabulary and Word Choice

Lindsey makes deliberate choices to
explain how to get this job done
("Coot The top of," "Dig owt ol of The
PulP" and "Put CaNDol Aer Flowhlot
into the Jak lotr") and to convey accurately the actions of the steps.

Spelling

This piece of writing is an excellent
example of a kindergartner showing
control of her knowledge of letter-
sound correlation. She represents
words by including beginning, ending
and some internal consonant sounds
along with internal vowels, although
the vowels are not always the correct
ones. There are also the beginnings
of spacing between words, along
with left-to-right and top-to-bottom
directionality.

Many sight words also are
included in the writing and are spelled
accurately ("And," "The," "You,"
"Put," "to" and "into").

(For more on Language Use and
Conventions, see page 88.)

Lindsey

Haw to maka lanltrs

1. Got a nip And Son

2. Coot The top of The Jank. lant

3. You Dig aut ol of The PulP in To a Bol.

5. You Cot aut The eiys And nos And maut

4. Cot aut The Fae

6 Put Can Dol Aer Flau h lot into bak the lotr

*How to Make a Jack-O'-Lantern

1. Get a knife and spoon.

2. Cut the top off the jack-o'-lantern.

3. You dig out all of the pulp into a bowl.

4. Cut out the face.

5. You cut out the eyes and nose and mouth.

6. Put candle or flashlight into the jack-o'-lantern.

*Translation of phonetically spelled words

Producing and Responding to Literature

Children on target for meeting kindergarten standards re-enact, retell, borrow and burrow into all forms of literature, including stories, songs, poems and plays. They do this both formally — in structured activities with whole-class support and teacher guidance — and informally — in improvised small groups, pairs and clusters, and individually — throughout the day. They are both reacting to the literary works they encounter and inventing their own. Initially, children's engagement with literature is mostly oral. Over the course of the year, children also will respond to literature in writing. As they initiate and participate in these activities, kindergartners should demonstrate their grasp of the rhythms and styles of the literary language they hear in the classroom. It is important to emphasize that children's proficiency at producing literature is dependent upon how deeply they are immersed in literary reading activities.

By the end of the year, we expect kindergarten students to produce literature and responses to literature in which they:

◆ re-enact and retell stories (borrow and burrow into stories, poems, plays and songs);

◆ create their own stories, poems, plays and songs; and

◆ use literary forms and language (for example, if they produce a poem, students should write with some poetic language, perhaps even using poetic devices such as imagery and repetition).

"ZoM"

Writing Standard 2:
Writing Purposes and Resulting Genres

Producing Literature

This poem is a very sophisticated effort for a kindergarten child. It creates two very powerful images: a plane traveling out over water (zooming) then turning back, and Evan's mind simultaneously doing a loop. These parallel images — each introduced by "As" — are organizationally very effective. There is also a careful employment of line breaks to support the meaning. This sample meets the kindergarten standard for producing literature.

◆ The sample creates vivid images, which are supported through the use of line breaks.

◆ The parallel structure of the images is supported by parallel syntactic patterns ("as Mi arPaN" and "as Mi MiD").

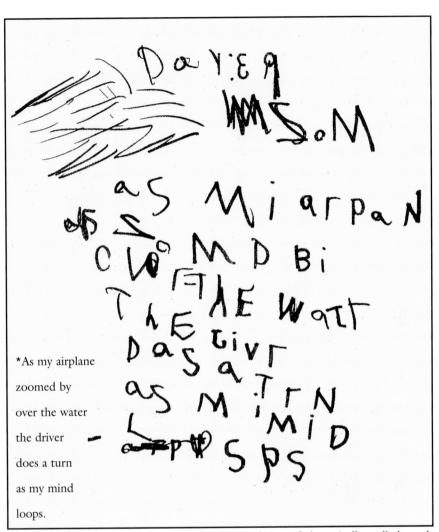

*As my airplane

zoomed by

over the water

the driver

does a turn

as my mind

loops.

*Translation of phonetically spelled words

Writing Standard 3:
Language Use and Conventions

This piece does not meet the Language Use and Conventions Standard for kindergarten because there are some problems with spelling and spacing. It does, however, have notable features.

The piece is a good example to illustrate control of form emerging much earlier than control of conventions. To someone not familiar with reading phonetic spelling, this sample is almost unintelligible. Two sight words ("as" and "ThE") are spelled correctly, but Evan more often represents words with initial and final consonants, occasionally embedding vowels that say their own name.

The poem shows that Evan understands that text moves left to right across a page and top to bottom down the page, but he does not control evenly for space between words.

Read simply as a sentence, not as a poem, the text reveals Evan's ability to craft a very sophisticated sentence.

(For more on Language Use and Conventions, see page 88.)

"WoNS. O. PoDuoM TiM"

Writing Standard 2:
**Writing Purposes and
Resulting Genres**

Producing Literature

This writing effectively demonstrates a kindergartner producing literature by creating a fictional story and threading his knowledge of literary language throughout the piece. Jason is able to sequence appropriately eight events that move from "WoNS. O. PoDuoM TiM" to "that Was the END oF the QWeN AND the keNG." The events read like an adventure video, but Jason clearly understands the format for such a genre. It represents work that meets the standard for producing literature in kindergarten.

- The writing creates a story, in this case one that draws from a combination of heroic tales and modern TV and movie venues.

- Jason uses literary language to introduce the piece ("WoNS. O. PoDuoM TiM").

Writing Standard 3:
Language Use and Conventions

This piece meets the Language Use and Conventions Standard for kindergarten.

Style and Syntax

This work provides evidence that Jason uses the syntax typically associated with literature ("WoNS. O. PoDuoM TiM" and "Ther LeviD"), as well as the syntax more typical of oral language ("AND ONe TiM they WeNt," "AND

theN the keNG" and "AND that Was the END oF the QWeN AND the keNG").

Vocabulary and Word Choice

This work provides evidence that Jason uses words in the text that are common to his spoken language (*bad guys,* which is represented phonetically, and "BLasteD"), as well as specialized words related to the content (*castle,* which is represented phonetically).

*Once upon a time there lived
a king and a queen and one time they
went in their ship and they went to the bad
guy's castle and they got the queen and then
the king rescued the queen and then
they ran to the ship and then the alarm
came on and then the bad guys
blasted the king and the queen
and that was the end of the queen and
the king.

*Translation of phonetically spelled words

Spelling

This work provides evidence that Jason creates text with words that an adult who is familiar with phonetic spelling can read. He also leaves space between words, though the spacing is somewhat uneven, and controls for left-to-right and top-to-bottom directionality. Jason represents most words with initial and ending consonants and correctly represents tenses in verbs ("WeNt," "LeviD," "RaN" and "BLasteD").

"HaVe You seen mY CAt"

Writing Standard 2:
Writing Purposes and Resulting Genres

Responding to Literature

Lauren's example is typical of a kindergartner retelling the essence of a picture book, in this case *Have You Seen My Cat* by Eric Carle. Her writing represents a response to literature that meets the standard for kindergarten.

◆ Lauren's piece offers a simple retelling of a familiar story.

◆ She makes an evaluative statement about the story being retold.

Writing Standard 3:
Language Use and Conventions

This piece meets the Language Use and Conventions Standard for kindergarten.

Style and Syntax

Lauren's syntax is somewhat problematic — tense shifts occur — and the writing is quite brief. If a reader inserts punctuation, the text actually reads as a single compound-complex sentence.

Vocabulary and Word Choice

The text is created with words that an adult who is familiar with phonetic spelling can read. Lauren controls for directionality and leaves space between words — actually she uses dashes to separate words, a strategy that is a precursor to spacing.

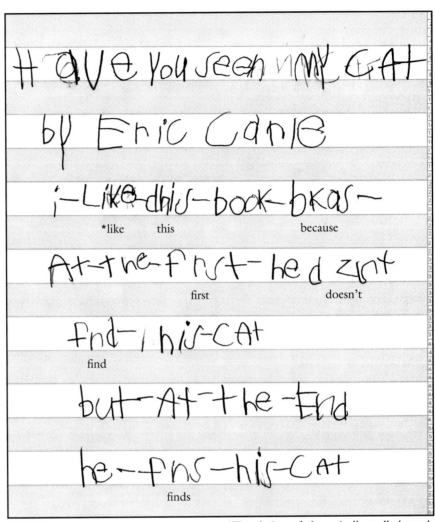

*like   this   because
first   doesn't
find
finds

*Translation of phonetically spelled words

Spelling

Words are represented with initial consonant sounds, and some high-frequency words are spelled correctly ("i," "LiKe," "At" and "the").

(For more on Language Use and Conventions, see page 88.)

"FraNkliN Is MeSSY"

Writing Standard 2:
Writing Purposes and Resulting Genres

Responding to Literature

This response to literature does three things. It recounts three events from the picture book *Franklin Is Messy* by Paulette Bourgeois, it illustrates each of these events, and it shows Max making a connection between the messy nature of the character in the book and the time when he was messy himself. The response is relatively brief and is, at best, a partial retelling. For kindergarten, however, this writing meets the standard for a response to literature.

◆ This piece of writing provides the reader with a brief retelling of a children's book.

◆ The piece actually is divided into two parts. One part is a retelling of three instances of Franklin's messiness ("He PuT A APPLe IN THe DOR," "He DiD NOT PiK THiNGS UP" and "He LeFT eRVAYTHiNG OUT"). These instances are accompanied by drawings. The second part is Max's making a connection to the character in the book ("I WAS MeSSY WeN MY ToY ROOM WAS VRAY MeSSY").

Writing Standard 3:
Language Use and Conventions

This piece meets the Language Use and Conventions Standard for kindergarten.

*Translation of phonetically spelled words

Style and Syntax

The work is laid out in such a way — sentences attached for the most part to pictures — that it is difficult to evaluate as "text." Yet each picture illustrates its corresponding sentence. The final sentence in the piece ("I WAS MeSSY WeN MY ToY ROOM WAS VRAY MeSSY") is not illustrated. (It is possible to assume this sentence was Max's way to connect to the story.) Each sentence begins with a capital letter and ends with a period.

Vocabulary and Word Choice

The words used in this text are words typical of kindergarten oral language.

Spelling

Most words are spelled correctly — but this may be the result of the words' being on a word wall or Max's having the book literally in hand and using the text to guide spelling. (Even the name of the author of the book is spelled correctly.) The vocabulary obviously correlates to the vocabulary of the book.

(For more on Language Use and Conventions, see page 88.)

Authors' Perspectives

"The special thing about the picture book is that it's a combination of both words and pictures, and the two of them work together to tell the story. I write with the illustration and with the words as well, and try to make the two of them dance together to tell the story. So they're both equally important to me when I'm putting one of my books together."

— Steven Kellogg

From Pamela Lloyd,
"How and Where Writers Write," *How Writers Write*
(Heinemann Educational Books, Inc., 1987), p. 3.

Kindergarten Writing Standard 3:
Language Use and Conventions

Kindergartners who are on target for meeting standards write freely in whatever manner they can, showing little or no concern for spelling, punctuation, capitalization and other conventions that will become important later. As a result, most of their writing is readable only by the author. And even then, although kindergarten children may be able to read their writing immediately after they have written it, they frequently cannot decipher the same piece several days later. By then meaning becomes elusive, particularly when the writer has relied (as is appropriate for a kindergarten student) on one or two letters to represent an entire word (for example, "LF" = *laugh*, "R" = *are*).

Style and Syntax

Kindergarten is early for young writers to notice conventional elements of style; however, the writings of kindergarten children do have a strong voice, even if it is consistently one of naïveté and wonder. The kindergarten writer's voice usually conveys a sense that the author is central to the message. As children grow, their voices will change; their writing will become easier to read aloud and will sound more like natural or story language.

Using one's own language
By the end of the year, we expect kindergarten students to produce writing that:

◆ uses the syntax of oral language and so is easy to read aloud.

Taking on language of authors
By the end of the year, we expect kindergarten students to produce writing (stories, songs, poems, rhymes) that:

◆ approximates some of the phrasing and rhythms of literary language.

Vocabulary and Word Choice

Just as kindergarten writers get their sense of syntax from the language they hear spoken, so do they rely on oral language for the vocabulary that captures their ideas.

Using one's own language
Kindergartners should be able to make choices about which of the words they know will convey accurately their intended meaning, not just use the first word that comes to mind. For example, they will write about a fire ant, not a bug.

By the end of the year, we expect kindergarten students to:

◆ use words in their writing that they use in their conversation, usually represented phonetically (see Spelling below).

Taking on language of authors

As kindergarten children are read to, their vocabularies increase, and new words begin to appear in their writing.

By the end of the year, we expect kindergarten students to:

◆ use in their writing some words they like from the books read to them; and

◆ make choices about which words to use on the basis of whether they accurately convey the child's meaning.

Spelling

Children in kindergarten write using initial sounds to represent words. At times, they use some end sounds correctly as well, most often in consonant-vowel-consonant words. The stories and other texts that kindergarten children compose over the course of the year as part of the writing curriculum should include consonants, but vowels may be missing.

Kindergartners should know how to write words in ways that show they are representing the individual sounds of the words systematically. For some children, written words are well spaced but may include only consonants. Other children may include vowels in their spelling but run the words together without spaces.

By the end of the year, we expect kindergarten students to show evidence of their ability to:

◆ independently create text with words that an adult (who is knowledgeable about spelling development and about the content of that child's piece of writing) can decipher;

◆ reread their own text, with a match between what they say and the words they have written on paper;

◆ pause voluntarily in the midst of writing to reread what they have written (tracking);

◆ leave space between words;

◆ control for directionality (left to right, top to bottom); and

◆ represent words frequently with the initial consonant sound.

Punctuation, Capitalization and Other Conventions

At this stage we do not expect the child to show any regularity in — or even awareness of — punctuation and conventions. Most kindergartners are so preoccupied with the new letter-sound puzzle that they literally don't see or react to such marks as capital letters and commas. When they do become aware of punctuation, kindergarten writers frequently use a period as a marker to separate words or designate the end of each line or page. Eventually, they will use the conventional placement of a period at the end of the sentence.

Students' Perspectives

At the begening of the year I was not a) ritr but I am a ritre now

First Grade

First Grade

When students understand that, together, the sounds of language and the sense of stories can help them become word problem-solvers, the puzzle of reading and writing begins to come together.

Exuberant Readers and Writers

Most first graders come to school filled with expectations about the classroom experiences in store for them. Kindergarten opened their eyes to school culture and classroom routines. By first grade, students settle in and know the rules — though these energetic young children aren't always attentive to them. Still, first graders realize that their teachers and parents expect them to learn. And they bring a can-do gusto to their schoolwork.

At the same time, first graders have expectations of their own. They expect to learn — and they expect help when they need it. First graders also expect to play and have fun. They don't expect to sit still for long.

Like kindergartners, first graders often come to school with dramatically different literacy experiences from their early childhood. Children who come from families, child care and kindergarten programs that provide strong literacy experiences likely will find reading and writing easier than will children less experienced in literacy. Hearing books read aloud, engaging in conversations, playing rhyming games and acting out make-believe dramas — experiences like these influence the levels of reading and writing proficiency that students bring to first grade. Rich literacy experiences also may improve the rate at which students acquire new literacy skills.

Beginning in first grade, literacy skills are important not only for students' academic success, but also for their social and emotional well-being. In kindergarten and at the beginning of first grade, students believe they are all pretty much the same. By the end of first grade, they know who is the "best" reader or the "best" artist in the class. This sensitivity to their own strengths — and weaknesses — gets stronger year by year.

Reading and Writing: What to Expect

First graders who come to school having had an array of experiences with speaking, listening, reading and language play generally are well prepared to meet the first-grade literacy standards. Other first graders must do a lot of catching up to understand the concepts that many of their classmates learned in kindergarten. They have to learn that sounds correspond to letters, that letters make words and that words make text. If students who are behind show rapid growth toward meeting kindergarten standards, and continue to make progress on the first-grade standards, their likelihood of eventually developing competent literacy skills is strong. While their end-of-year performances may not meet the standards, they should fall within a safe range.

In first grade, most students master the print-sound code. Over the course of the year, they will understand that print is made up of

words, words are made up of letters and letters correspond to sounds. When students understand that, together, the sounds of language and the sense of stories can help them become word problem-solvers, the puzzle of reading and writing begins to come together.

By the end of first grade, most children can read books with more elaborate story structures, episodes and themes than lower-level books. Simon & Schuster's *Hattie and the Fox* is an example of a text that most first graders can read by the end of the year. When they read aloud, their accuracy and fluency should indicate that they recognize most words, take some cues from punctuation and understand what they are reading. Students whose literacy skills are below the first-grade standards, however, may be able to read only simpler books. Even so, the expectations for accuracy and fluency remain firm.

For texts read independently, students should be able to demonstrate their comprehension by retelling or summarizing a story, sharing some new bit of information they discovered, or answering questions about the story.

When their teacher reads aloud from a more complex text, most first graders can, by the end of the year, extend the story, predict what will happen next, discuss the characters' motives, question the author's meaning or word choice, and describe the causes and effects of specific events. When they talk about books, first graders can, and often do, tie the reasons for their comments directly to the text.

In writing, too, first graders' proficiency varies. Their reading and writing skills, in fact, often are linked. The leap from kindergarten to first-grade writing is pronounced; by the end of first grade, students who are working at standard levels truly can communicate in writing. Details they would have added orally in kindergarten they now add routinely in their first-draft writing. Their oral responses to writing become more sophisticated as well. First graders reread their writing to monitor for meaning. They begin to use feedback from other children and adults to improve their writing — by adding more text or making minor revisions or edits. First graders can extend meaning by inserting text in the middle of their writing rather than merely adding on to the end of it — a big leap in writing development.

First graders use language deliberately, crafting their writing to achieve particular purposes and moods. Frequently, they play with print to make their meaning clear, punctuating excessively with exclamation points or writing with all capital letters, for example. Their style, a holdover from kindergarten, lends an exuberance to their writing, as in "I LOVE PENGUINS!!!" Like kindergartners, first graders write very much the way they talk — and they like to talk and write about what *I* like, how *I* feel, what *I* know. Even as they mimic their speech in their writing, they also mimic the language of books they read and hear.

First graders who begin the year with minimal understanding of letter-sound correspondence will produce writing that cannot necessarily be read yet. Over the course of the year, as they put the print-sound code together, their writing proficiency will grow by fits and starts as well. With good instructional support, they will catch up — although their focus on the print-sound code may distract them temporarily from paying attention to issues of craft or genre. Children who are working somewhat behind the first-grade expectations are not necessarily at risk in literacy development. As long as they are making regular progress in writing, their literacy skills should continue to develop. The best indicator of whether a child is in danger of falling behind irreparably is the rate of growth, rather than a particular inventory of skills. However, any child who is still writing in letter strings or relying primarily on pictures and single-word labels at the middle of first grade needs immediate, intensive intervention to catch up.

Developing Literacy Habits

First graders should continue to read a lot, immersing themselves in a range of texts that capture their interest, give them pleasure and reinforce their sense of themselves as readers.

By reading and discussing their favorite books again and again, first graders "study" the way language works, find more meanings and probe deeper into the stories they read. First graders should continue to read picture and story books. They should read widely from narrative, functional and informational genres.

By the end of the year, most first graders will read independently and with assistance from a classmate or teacher. Nevertheless, first graders also should listen to books and other texts read aloud to them every day. Listening to more sophisticated books develops language, knowledge and enjoyment of literature. *For examples of the kinds of books first graders should read, see* **Leveled Books to Read for Accuracy and Fluency,** *page 99, and* **What Books Should First Graders Read?,** *page 109.*

First graders on target to meet the reading and writing standards should engage in activities common to literate people. They should read their own writings and those of their classmates, re-enact plays, sing songs, and recite poems. They should read and understand the "environmental print" in the classroom, such as a sign warning them away from a wet painting on an easel. And they should read and follow simple instructions for feeding the resident tadpoles or booting up the classroom computer, for example.

Every day, first graders should have time to write. From stories, reports and poems to riddles, signs and letters, the writing students do should encompass many genres and purposes. First-grade writers should create stories that unfold sequentially, from "first" to "next" to "then." They should focus on a topic and set up rudimentary categories, such as "all about dogs" or "my new sister" — strategic thinking that eventually will lead to grouping ideas into paragraphs.

Most first graders still incorporate drawing into their writing. For some, the pictures expand the writing. Still others use drawing as a supportive scaffold. During first grade, drawing should assume less importance in students' writing.

First-Grade
Reading Standard 1: **Print-Sound Code**

First grade is the time when knowledge of the print-sound code should take root, as the phonemic awareness that children developed in kindergarten deepens and expands. By the end of first grade, students should be well on the way to mastering phonemic awareness. No longer working on sounds or letters separately, they now are able to put these elements of the code together to read meaningful, connected texts. The set of high-frequency words they recognize also has expanded since kindergarten.

Phonemic Awareness

By the end of the year, first-grade students' phonemic awareness should be consolidated fully. They should be able to demonstrate, without difficulty, all of the skills and knowledge expected at the end of kindergarten. The ability to segment and blend each of the sounds in words — which they began to develop in kindergarten — should now be developed fully. We expect students at the end of first grade to be able to:

◆ separate the sounds by saying each sound aloud (for example, /c/-/a/-/t/); and

◆ blend separately spoken phonemes to make a meaningful word.

Reading Words

By the end of the year, we expect first-grade students to:

◆ know the regular letter-sound correspondences and use them to recognize or figure out regularly spelled one- and two-syllable words (see Appendix, page 292);

◆ use onsets and rimes to create new words that include blends and digraphs;* and

◆ recognize about 150 high-frequency words as they encounter the words in reading.

**First-Grade
Reading Standard 1:**
Print-Sound Code

  ◆ Phonemic Awareness

  ◆ Reading Words

**First-Grade
Reading Standard 2:**
Getting the Meaning

  ◆ Accuracy

  ◆ Fluency

  ◆ Self-Monitoring and
    Self-Correcting Strategies

  ◆ Comprehension

**First-Grade
Reading Standard 3:**
Reading Habits

  ◆ Independent and
    Assisted Reading

  ◆ Being Read To

  ◆ Discussing Books

  ◆ Vocabulary

---

*In consonant blends, each consonant keeps its regular sound (*br, cr*). A digraph is a combination of two letters that, together, make one sound, which is different from either of the letter sounds alone. Consonant digraphs include letter combinations such as *ch, ph, sh, th* and *wh.* Vowel digraphs include combinations such as *ea* in *eat, ay* in *day, oi* in *oil* and *oa* in *coat.*

Print-Sound Code

Some children may continue to struggle with the print-sound code. Often their difficulties with translating letters to sounds stem from problems segmenting and blending sounds orally (*cat* into /c/-/a/-/t/ and vice versa), i.e., phonemic awareness. Phonemic awareness difficulties take the form of belabored word attack strategies as well as immature spelling (for example, "PRK" for *park* or "JRAGN" for *dragon*) at the end of first grade.

Christopher

Beatriz

Juan

Reading Standard 1:
Print-Sound Code

Phonemic Awareness

- Separate the sounds by saying each sound aloud

In this task, the teacher first asks Christopher to identify "the last sound in the word."

Christopher clarifies her instructions, asking, "You mean the ending sounds?" He then identifies all seven of the ending sounds. Christopher does this accurately and with great clarity, mentally segmenting and then speaking each phoneme distinctly.

- Separate the sounds by saying each sound aloud (identifying the middle sound in a word)

The teacher asks Beatriz to identify the middle sound in a series of regularly spelled three- and four-letter words. In all cases, she says the sounds clearly and is able to speak the correct phoneme. Beatriz handles this task with confidence; in this exercise, she easily identifies the short and long vowel sounds in the middle of the words.

- Separate the sounds by saying each sound aloud (replacing the beginning and ending sounds to form new words)

During a series of exercises, Juan demonstrates a fully developed phonemic awareness. He is able to hear and then replace the beginning and ending sounds to form new words. He stumbles on the third try when the teacher switches from replacing the beginning sound to replacing the ending sound, but on a second attempt, he switches gears and is successful. ▶▶

The images and commentary in the reading section of this book refer to reading performances available on the CD-ROM.

Yasmen

Christopher

Reading Standard 1:
Print-Sound Code

Phonemic Awareness
◆ Blend separately spoken phonemes
to make a meaningful word
(blending three separate phonemes
to make a word)

Yasmen meets the standard by being
able to hear distinct phonemes and
then blend them to make a word.
Though she is restless and not always
looking directly at the teacher when
she speaks, Yasmen is listening well and
successfully blends all eight words.

Reading Words
◆ Know the regular letter-sound
correspondences

In this dictation task, Christopher
shows that his phonemic awareness
is fully developed. His knowledge of
letter-sound correspondences has
deepened so that now he not only is
able to translate letters to sounds by
reading words in decodable text, but
he also can translate sounds to letters
to write regularly spelled three- and
four-letter words. The teacher says five
words (one containing an initial
blend), and Christopher spells all five
correctly. On this task, he works
silently, no longer needing to sound
out the separate phonemes as many
kindergartners do.

Read-Aloud Books

Bourgeois, Paulette, *Franklin in the Dark*

Cannon, Janell, *Stellaluna*

Cleary, Beverly, *Ramona the Pest*

Dahl, Roald, *The Minpins*

Dakos, Kalli, *If You're Not Here, Please Raise Your Hand: Poems About School*

Dorros, Arthur, *Abuela*

Fox, Mem, *Hattie and the Fox*

Gardiner, John Reynolds, *Stone Fox*

Henkes, Kevin, *Chrysanthemum*

Hess, Debra, *Wilson Sat Alone*

Hoffman, Mary, *Amazing Grace*

Kraus, Robert, *Leo the Late Bloomer*

Lindgren, Astrid, *Pippi Longstocking*

Martin, Bill, Jr. *Knots on a Counting Rope*

Mitchell, Margaree King, *Uncle Jed's Barbershop*

Munsch, Robert N., *Thomas' Snowsuit*

Polacco, Patricia, *The Keeping Quilt*

Polacco, Patricia, *Rechenka's Eggs*

Schwartz, Alvin, *And the Green Grass Grew All Around: Folk Poetry from Everyone*

Sendak, Maurice, *Chicken Soup With Rice*

Various authors, *The American Girls Collection* (series)

Viorst, Judith, *Alexander and the Terrible, Horrible, No Good, Very Bad Day*

Viorst, Judith, *Alexander, Who's Not (Do you hear me? I mean it!) Going to Move*

Viorst, Judith, *The Good-Bye Book*

Waber, Bernard, *Ira Sleeps Over*

Warner, Gertrude Chandler, *The Boxcar Children* (series)

White, E.B., *Charlotte's Web*

Yee, Paul, *Roses Sing on New Snow: A Delicious Tale*

Yolen, Jane, *Miz Berlin Walks*

Zolotow, Charlotte, *William's Doll*

Level I Texts

D.C. Heath & Co., Little Readers, Bloksberg, *The Hole in Harry's Pocket*

Houghton Mifflin, Little Readers, deWinter, *Worms for Breakfast*

Houghton Mifflin, Little Readers, Fear, *Ginger*

A Level I Text

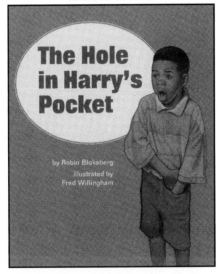

Rigby, Literacy 2000, *Jack and the Beanstalk*

Scholastic, Zimmerman, *Henny Penny*

Simon & Schuster, Alladin Paperbacks, Rockwell, *Apples and Pumpkins*

William Morrow & Co., Mulberry Books, Hutchins, *Tidy Titch*

Wright Group, Sunshine, Level 1, Luhrs, *Camouflage*

Wright Group, Sunshine Science Series, Cutting, *Ants*

Wright Group, Sunshine, Set 1, Cowley, *Quack, Quack, Quack*

Leveled Books to Read for Accuracy and Fluency

Level I books include a variety of texts with more complex story structures, more elaborate episodes and more sophisticated themes than lower-level texts. These books are more rich in meaning, giving students opportunities to explore different points of view, discuss new ideas and compare the books to others read independently or aloud in class. The characters are memorable.

Level I books also feature more pages, with more sentences per page and more specialized, unusual and challenging vocabulary in the sentences. Many words will be familiar to first-grade readers, however, so only unfamiliar words will test their problem-solving skills.

The illustrations provide minimal to moderate support to students as they try to interpret and extend the text.

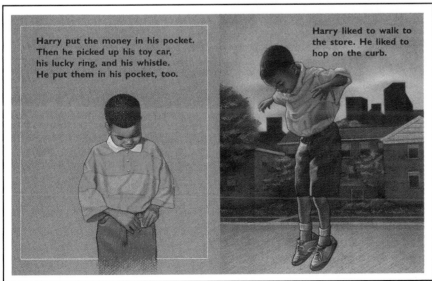

The Hole in Harry's Pocket by Robin Bloksberg, illustrated by Fred Willingham, from *Guided Reading, Collection 1* in *Houghton Mifflin Reading: Invitations to Literacy* by Pikulski, et al. Copyright © 1995 by Houghton Mifflin Company. Reprinted by permission of Houghton Mifflin Company. All rights reserved.

First-Grade
Reading Standard 2: **Getting the Meaning**

Accuracy

By the end of the year, we expect first-grade students to be able to:

◆ read Level I books that they have not seen before, but that have been previewed* for them, with 90 percent or better accuracy of word recognition (self-correction allowed).

Fluency

When they read aloud, we expect first graders to sound like they know what they are reading. Fluent readers may pause occasionally to work out difficult passages.**

By the end of the year, we expect first-grade students to be able to:

◆ independently read aloud from Level I books that have been previewed for them, using intonation, pauses and emphasis that signal the structure of the sentence and the meaning of the text; and

◆ use the cues of punctuation — including commas, periods, question marks and quotation marks — to guide them in getting meaning and fluently reading aloud.

**First-Grade
Reading Standard 1:**
Print-Sound Code

◆ Phonemic Awareness

◆ Reading Words

**First-Grade
Reading Standard 2:**
Getting the Meaning

◆ Accuracy

◆ Fluency

◆ Self-Monitoring and Self-Correcting Strategies

◆ Comprehension

**First-Grade
Reading Standard 3:**
Reading Habits

◆ Independent and Assisted Reading

◆ Being Read To

◆ Discussing Books

◆ Vocabulary

---

* Previewing means telling the student the title of the book and what it is about, as well as introducing any difficult or unfamiliar vocabulary that is important to the story.

** Such pauses, provided they are preceded and followed by fluent reading, are more likely to indicate use of self-monitoring strategies than lack of fluency.

Reading Standard 2:
Getting the Meaning

Accuracy

Christopher reads *The Hole in Harry's Pocket* with 98 percent accuracy and, therefore, meets the standard for accuracy. He mispronounces the name *Harry* as "Hah-ree" throughout the story, but it is counted as a single mistake. On page 3, he reads "into his pocket" rather than "in his pocket." And on page 12, he is unable to decipher the word *hurray*, even with help from his teacher. On two or three occasions, he stumbles a bit or transposes words, but he self-corrects on each occasion, and it does not affect his ability to read fluently.

Fluency

Christopher reads fluently, clearly demonstrating he understands the book's content. However, he could pause more appropriately at commas when they appear just before a quotation mark. Although he usually drops his voice to note the ends of sentences, the drop could be more emphatic. With a bit of coaching, he probably could improve this skill quickly. It is important that he refine his ability to notice punctuation clues so that he can maintain a level of comprehension when reading more difficult texts.

Christopher

Self-Monitoring and Self-Correcting Strategies

Christopher uses self-monitoring strategies successfully. For instance, on page 2, he first reads "didn't lose it" and then corrects to "don't lose it." On two occasions, he mispronounces the word *curb* as "crub" but then self-corrects. On page 14, he first reads "I did sure" but then corrects to "I sure did." These self-corrections show that he is listening well and scrutinizing his own performance.

(For more on Self-Monitoring and Self-Correcting Strategies, see page 102.)

Comprehension

Christopher shows that he gets the gist of the story when he says Harry is "shocked because he forgot all about [getting the milk]." He also lists from memory several of the things Harry carried in his pocket (the ring, the money and the whistle) and the amount of money given to him by his mother (a dollar). Evidence of comprehension also is found in the simple fact that he obviously enjoyed the book when he smiles and giggles over the outcome.

(For more on Comprehension, see page 104.)

A First-Grade Running Record*

> SC = Self-correction
> R = Repeated the word

the Pocket Hah-ree SC

Book Title: *The Hole in Harry's Pocket*

Hah-ree ^

Page 1: Harry looked in the refrigerator. "Mom!" he called. "There's no milk."

Page 2: "You'll have to go to the store and get some," said his mother.

didn't R SC

"Here's the money. Put it in your pocket so you don't lose it."

Hah-ree

Page 3: Harry put the money in his pocket. Then he picked up his toy car, his

to ^ SC

lucky ring, and his whistle. He put them in his pocket, too.

Hah-ree

Page 4: Harry liked to walk to the store. He liked to hop on the curb.

SC *looked the* R

Page 5: He liked to look in all the windows and count cracks in the sidewalk.

Hah-ree ^

Page 6: Harry got the milk. But when he looked for his money, it was gone!

What could he do?

Hah-ree

Page 7: Harry put the milk back. He started to walk back home.

Then he saw something on the sidewalk. It was a red toy car.

Hah-ree

Page 8: "Hmmm," Harry thought. "That looks like my toy car — the one I

had in my pocket." He picked it up.

Hah-ree SC

Page 9: Then Harry saw something near the curb. It was a shiny silver ring.

look *Hah-ree* R *That*

Page 10: "That looks like my lucky ring," Harry thought. "The one I had in ^

my pocket." He picked it up.

Hah-ree SC R

Page 11: Next, Harry saw a toy whistle. "That looks like my whistle," he

R

thought. "The one I had in my pocket." He picked it up, too.

Hah-ree *Hah-ree, hurry*

Page 12: Then Harry saw some money. Hurray! It was just what his mom

gave him!

Hah-ree

Page 13: Harry picked up the money. "I guess I have a hole in my pocket," he

thought. He held the money tightly and ran the rest of the way home.

Page 14: "Did you have a nice trip to the store?" asked his mother.

SC *did sure Hah-ree*

"I sure did!" Harry said.

Page 15: "Good," said his mom.

5 errors = 98% accuracy

"So where's the milk?"

(Word count: 279)

2 insertions
Hah-ree 1 mispronunciation
Hurray 2 misreads

*For more on running records, see page 21.

New Standards

Self-Monitoring and Self-Correcting Strategies

Whenever children read, they should use a variety of self-monitoring and word-recognition strategies to help them figure out words they do not recognize immediately. By the end of first grade, we expect children to monitor their own reading for accuracy and sense and to use successfully strategies to solve reading problems. To see these strategies — which normally are deployed privately and silently inside children's minds — it may be necessary to ask children to read aloud from books that are a bit of a stretch for them in terms of difficulty.

First-grade readers should stretch beyond books that are easy for them. When they read books like those that are more difficult, we expect to see more overt self-monitoring behaviors, less accuracy and fluency, and slower or less-precise comprehension.

By the end of the year, we expect first-grade students to:

◆ notice whether the words sound right, given their spelling;

◆ notice whether the words make sense in context;

◆ notice when sentences don't make sense;

◆ solve reading problems and self-correct, through strategies that include using syntax and word-meaning clues, comparing pronounced sounds to printed letters, gathering context clues from surrounding sentences or pictures, and deriving new words by analogy to known words and word parts (for example, using *tree* and *my* to get *try*); and

◆ check their solution to a difficult word against their knowledge of print-sound correspondences and the meaning of the text.

Chelsea

Gerardo

Jasmin

Reading Standard 2:
Getting the Meaning

Self-Monitoring and
Self-Correcting Strategies

Chelsea demonstrates strategies for solving reading problems by comparing pronounced sounds to printed letters when she encounters the word *curb* while reading a book. She tries reading it as "creb," "crub," "cirb" and "crib." When none of these words makes sense in the context, she looks to the teacher for help. When told that the word is *curb,* she demonstrates how much she knows about the print-sound code. She says, "There are all kinds of sounds for the *u* ... I would expect an *ir* or an *er* there, because we have a chart in our classroom that has the *er* sound, and we have *ur,* but I didn't expect it to be *ur.*" Although she was unsuccessful in decoding *curb* in this instance, she clearly has the strategy of trying the various sounds for the letters in a word and checking to see if her attempt makes sense in the sentence she is reading.

Gerardo has difficulty reading the book *The Hole in Harry's Pocket,* but he does show an excellent attempt to monitor his own efforts and self-correct. On page 3, he reads the first sentence correctly: "Harry put the money in his pocket." But then he seems to lose sight of the words on the next line, saying "pocket" for *picked* and becoming confused. However, he soon starts over, even verbalizing to himself, "No," and shaking his head. He begins again, rereading, "Then he picked up his toy car, his lucky ring, and his whistle." At first he placed "and" before "his lucky ring," but here again, he is aware that the word does not actually appear in the text. He says, "No," again and then rereads the phrase correctly.

Jasmin shows he is adept at self-monitoring while reading the book *Ants.* For instance, on the very first page, after he reads, "Is this a jaw?" he subvocalizes, "Yes, it is," as he checks the text against the illustrations. Next he comes across the word *hooks,* and he tries it first with a long /o/ sound and then a short /o/. When that does not work, he asks if the *h* might be silent. Finally, he connects the illustration of the ant's bent legs to the word and sees that it might be *hooks.*

Comprehension

By the end of first grade, we expect children to demonstrate their comprehension of books that they read independently or with a partner, as well as books that adults read to them. We also expect them to read and understand simple written instructions and functional messages.

When they independently read texts they have not seen before, we expect students at the end of first grade to be able to:

◆ retell the story;

◆ tell what the book is about (summarize it);

◆ describe in their own words what new information they gained from the text; and

◆ answer comprehension questions similar to those for kindergartners.

The texts that adults read to first graders usually have more complex conceptual and grammatical features than the texts the children read independently, permitting greater depth in the kinds of comprehension children can display.

For texts that are read to them, we expect children at the end of first grade also to be able to:

◆ extend the story;

◆ make predictions about what might happen next and say why;

◆ talk about the motives of characters; and

◆ describe the causes and effects of specific events.

Alyssa

Reading Standard 2:
Getting the Meaning

Comprehension
◆ Make predictions about what might happen next and say why

This class is engaged in an author study about Judith Viorst. The teacher has read aloud several books by this author, and the class has discussed them. While reading *The Good-Bye Book* aloud to the class, the teacher stops and asks the class to compare it to other books they have read. Thinking about how the book might end, Alyssa makes a connection to two other books by Judith Viorst. She says, "Maybe at the end, he, it's going to be happy, happier just like in *Alexander, Who's Not (Do you hear me? I mean it!) Going to Move* and in *Alexander and the Terrible, Horrible, No Good, Very Bad Day* ... because at the end, it's always getting happier."

Although she does not specifically refer to parts from the other books that remind her of this one, Alyssa claims that the books are similar because the endings in all of these books are happier than their beginnings. This comment demonstrates that she is using her knowledge about two other books by this author to make a prediction about how this one will end.

First-Grade
Reading Standard 3: **Reading Habits**

It is important that first graders continue to read a lot. Through first and second grades, expectations for independent and assisted reading are elaborated separately from those for being read to. Books read to students are chosen for their interest and literary value; they usually have greater complexity than a student can handle reading independently or with assistance.

**First-Grade
Reading Standard 1:**
Print-Sound Code
  ◆ Phonemic Awareness
  ◆ Reading Words

**First-Grade
Reading Standard 2:**
Getting the Meaning
  ◆ Accuracy
  ◆ Fluency
  ◆ Self-Monitoring and
    Self-Correcting Strategies
  ◆ Comprehension

**First-Grade
Reading Standard 3:**
Reading Habits
  ◆ Independent and
    Assisted Reading
  ◆ Being Read To
  ◆ Discussing Books
  ◆ Vocabulary

Independent and Assisted Reading

We expect first-grade students to:

◆ read four or more books every day independently or with assistance;

◆ discuss at least one of these books with another student or a group;

◆ read some favorite books many times, gaining deeper comprehension;

◆ read their own writing and sometimes the writing of their classmates; and

◆ read functional messages they encounter in the classroom (for example, labels, signs, instructions).

Being Read To

We expect first-grade students to:

◆ hear two to four books or other texts (for example, poems, letters, instructions, newspaper or magazine articles, dramatic scripts, songs, brochures) read aloud every day; and

◆ listen to and discuss every day at least one book or chapter that is longer and more difficult than what they can read independently or with assistance.

Discussing Books

Daily discussion of books continues to be essential in first grade. Children now can deal with more complex and longer texts and relate books to each other. In classroom and small-group discussions of their reading and of books read to them, we expect students finishing first grade to be able to:

◆ demonstrate the skills we look for in the comprehension component of Reading Standard 2: Getting the Meaning;

◆ compare two books by the same author;

◆ talk about several books on the same theme;

◆ refer explicitly to parts of the text when presenting or defending a claim;

◆ politely disagree when appropriate;

◆ ask others questions that seek elaboration and justification; and

◆ attempt to explain why their interpretation of a book is valid.

Hannah and Matt

Ashanti

Reading Standard 3:
Reading Habits

Discussing Books

In this class discussion, the children are thinking about the father character in several books. In *William's Doll,* the father brings the boy a basketball and, on a different occasion, an electric train to distract him from wanting a doll. Matt says, "Um, his father is just making it worse — he's pushing it. Every time he brings him something, he thinks about [the doll] more, so he wants it more."

The teacher comments that the father in *William's Doll* reminds her of the father in *Leo the Late Bloomer.* She asks, "Do you guys remember what the father there does?"

Jose responds, "He sneaks, and he always watches him without letting him know."

The teacher, agreeing with Jose, reads the section from *Leo the Late Bloomer* that makes his point that the father is not being helpful.

Hannah challenges this interpretation when she tells the teacher, "I have two things to say. One is that I disagree with, with, you a little bit. When Leo's father, um, it's just like the father in

that book, because [Leo's] father's trying to be nice and trying to wait for the blooming to come, and [William's] father just doesn't want his son to have a doll. But maybe he's kinda being nice, um, in *William's Doll,* because he's maybe thinks that, maybe, if he gets the doll, that everyone will notice and they'll tease him, and he doesn't want his son to, like, be really teased."

The teacher asks Matt, "What do you think, Matt? What do you want to say back to Hannah about that?"

Matt replies, "I disagree with her. That was pretty mean because he will still want it."

Hannah and Matt demonstrate success in discussing books. Their comments show their attempts to explain why their interpretations of the book are valid. In doing so, they refer to specific parts of the texts. They listen to each other carefully and identify when their opinions differ. They politely point out how what they think is different from what someone else has said, and they give reasons for their opinions.

In the book *William's Doll,* the grandmother wants to get William the doll he desires so much. After hearing several pages read aloud, Ashanti offers her interpretation of the grandmother's motivation and connects it to her own life. She says, "Maybe his grandmother, um, knows that it doesn't matter if a boy has a girl thing and if a girl has a boy thing. It is sort of like my life, because my brother plays with my dolls." With this comment Ashanti justifies her interpretation by citing an example from personal experience.   ▶▶

Allegria

Reading Standard 3:
Reading Habits

Discussing Books

The children in this class discuss several books they have decided should go together in the "Trying Center" because the main characters in these books all try to do something. The teacher asks, "Who can start us off by doing some comparing?"

Allegria says, "I think *William's Doll* is a little different from *Leo the Late Bloomer* and *Today Is a Terrible Day** and *Wilson Sat Alone* and *Franklin in the Dark*. Because, um, all these are ones, um, are people are naturally growing up and they're trying to do it but they can't, but in *William's Doll*, he's trying to get a doll."

The teacher attempts to paraphrase Allegria's meaning and checks for understanding. Allegria shakes her head no, disagrees with the teacher's paraphrase of her comment and tries again. "Like, um, in *Wilson Sat Alone* and *Today is a Terrible Day* and *Franklin in the Dark* and *Leo the Late Bloomer*, they are growing up, growing up and trying to do stuff … naturally, but in, umm, *William Wants a Doll,*** he just wants a doll, he's not like growing up or anything."

In this book discussion, Allegria is able to identify an element that four of the books have in common that the fifth book does not share. She politely disagrees with the teacher and restates her point.

*The actual name of the book is *Alexander and the Terrible, Horrible, No Good, Very Bad Day.*

**The actual name of the book is *William's Doll.*

Vocabulary

Like kindergartners, first graders know more words than they can read or write. They still acquire most of their new vocabulary by listening to spoken language and hearing books read aloud, though reading and discussing books enhances the quality and breadth of their word knowledge. Children easily absorb into their vocabulary new words that come up and recur in conversation and reading.

We expect first-grade students to:

◆ make sense of new words from how the words are used, refining their sense of the words as they encounter them again;

◆ notice and show interest in understanding unfamiliar words in texts that are read to them;

◆ talk about the meaning of some new words encountered in independent and assisted reading;

◆ know how to talk about what words mean in terms of functions (for example, "A shoe is a thing you wear on your foot") and features (for example, "Shoes have laces"); and

◆ learn new words every day from talk and books read aloud.

**First-Grade
Reading Standard 1:**
Print-Sound Code

◆ Phonemic Awareness

◆ Reading Words

**First-Grade
Reading Standard 2:**
Getting the Meaning

◆ Accuracy

◆ Fluency

◆ Self-Monitoring and Self-Correcting Strategies

◆ Comprehension

**First-Grade
Reading Standard 3:**
Reading Habits

◆ Independent and Assisted Reading

◆ Being Read To

◆ Discussing Books

◆ Vocabulary

What Books Should First Graders Read?

Beyond leveled books, which are used for practice-reading, teaching, and testing for accuracy and fluency, first graders should read and reread a variety of books and other print material.

Many excellent fiction and nonfiction books do not appear on any leveled text lists. Classroom libraries should include a wide range of classic and modern books that will satisfy readers with various reading abilities and interests. First graders need books at their own reading levels to practice new skills and books above their reading levels to stretch and challenge them. When they read books that are difficult for them, they will exhibit more overt self-monitoring behaviors, less accuracy and fluency, and slower or less-precise comprehension.

First-grade classrooms also should include books that teachers can read aloud to the students. Most first graders will not be able to read the read-aloud books on their own, but they can understand and enjoy more advanced books — and they need to hear them to absorb the rhythms and cadences of more sophisticated language.

There are many lists of recommended titles, including the Newbury and Caldecott Award winners, *The Read-Aloud Handbook* by Jim Trelease, *Books to Build on: A Grade-by-Grade Resource Guide for Parents and Teachers (Core Knowledge Series)* by E.D. Hirsch, and the *Elementary School Library Collection: A Guide to Books and Other Media*. The American Library Association also recommends titles.

First-Grade
Writing Standard 1: **Habits and Processes**

In good programs, first graders write every day, both independently and with a partner or partners. When given blocks of time for writing, students take responsibility for choosing a topic (unless otherwise directed) and developing text around it. Quite often students work for more than a single day on creating a piece of writing. Taking selected pieces of their work through the processes of planning, drafting, getting response, revising and editing is very much the norm for first-grade writers. Students meeting standards have a growing awareness of what constitutes good writing and can work together to generate criteria for judging the quality of their written work. They can generate ideas for their writing, confer with other students and the teacher about what they have written, and make suggested changes in a piece, sometimes consulting word lists and classmates for more correct spellings. Working in response groups or partnerships with classmates, they are able to ask for and give each other feedback. They work toward producing the best writing they can, paying closer attention to spelling correctly and using periods than they did as kindergartners.

Throughout the year, students should revise, edit and polish selected pieces of writing for audiences beyond the classroom. Polished pieces are placed on display, read aloud, presented to someone the child cares about or acknowledged in some public way. Such displays are important ways of recognizing young writers' accomplishments.

We expect first-grade students to:

◆ write daily;

◆ generate topics and content for writing;

◆ reread their work often with the expectation that others will be able to read it;

◆ solicit and provide responses to writing;

◆ revise, edit and proofread as appropriate;

◆ apply a sense of what constitutes good writing (that is, apply some commonly agreed-upon criteria to their own work); and

◆ polish at least 10 pieces throughout the year.

First-Grade
Writing Standard 1:
Habits and Processes

**First-Grade
Writing Standard 2:**
*Writing Purposes and
Resulting Genres*

◆ Sharing Events, Telling Stories: Narrative Writing

◆ Informing Others: Report or Informational Writing

◆ Getting Things Done: Functional Writing

◆ Producing and Responding to Literature

**First-Grade
Writing Standard 3:**
*Language Use and
Conventions*

◆ Style and Syntax

◆ Vocabulary and Word Choice

◆ Spelling

◆ Punctuation, Capitalization and Other Conventions

"I Lik My Clas"

Writing Standard 1:
Habits and Processes

Amie's sample comes from her writing folder, which contains all the pieces she produced during first grade, including those pieces that were refined (edited and revised) over several drafts. The collection of pieces in the folder provides evidence that she meets the Writing Habits and Processes Standard. Amie wrote every day. She generated topics that interested her. She also responded to topics provided by her teacher. Amie's folder holds pieces on which she wrote herself notes about where and how to make revisions. It is reasonable to assume such notes came from the suggestions of response partners. Her final drafts are carefully refined pieces.

Amie wrote the first sample, "I Lik My Clas," on the first day of school. She spells four of the seven words phonetically, and she spells the other three words correctly, controlling for word boundaries and demonstrating left-to-right and top-to-bottom movement. Her message can be read — although "Agspeshale" may give readers some problems. A picture accompanies the text, though it is doubtful whether the picture ties to the text.

(For more of Amie's collection, see page 245.)

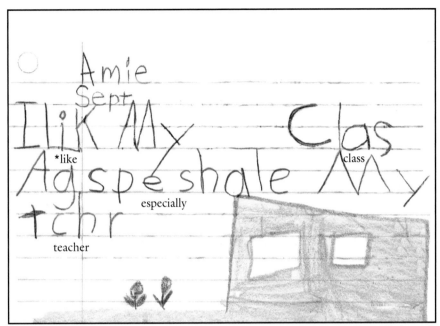

*Translation of phonetically spelled words

First-Grade
Writing Standard 2: **Writing Purposes and Resulting Genres**

Much of what children did orally when they were in kindergarten — sharing events and telling stories, producing and responding to literature, issuing instructions to get things done, and informing others — they do more extensively in writing by the end of first grade. But both the written and the continuing oral work are done with more elaboration and confidence

than was evidenced in kindergarten. As writers, many begin to show an intention to really connect with a reader by, for example, producing text that strives to be interesting or surprising.

Sharing Events, Telling Stories: Narrative Writing

First graders draw primarily on their own experience and knowledge as the source of material for their writings. They also borrow from and build on the stories read to them, as well as create their own fiction. Their narratives become longer and more detailed, clear and sequential.

By the end of the year, we expect first-grade students to produce narrative accounts — both fictional and auto-biographical — in which they:

◆ evidence a plan in their writing, including making decisions about where in a sequence of events they should enter;

◆ develop a narrative or retelling containing two or more appropriately sequenced events that readers can reconstruct easily, which the author then often reacts to, comments on, evaluates, sums up or ties together;

◆ frequently incorporate drawings, diagrams or other suitable graphics with written text, as well as gestures, intonation and role-played voices with oral renditions;

◆ demonstrate a growing awareness of author's craft by employing some writing strategies, such as using dialogue, transitions or time cue words; giving concrete details; and providing some sense of closure (for example, "The End," "And I will never forget that day," "I was glad to have my dog back. I will never forget to love him again");

◆ imitate narrative elements and derive stories from books they have read or had read to them; and

◆ in some cases, begin to recount not just events but also reactions, signaled by phrases like "I wondered," "I noticed," "I thought" or "I said to myself."

"On Saturday"

Writing Standard 2:
Writing Purposes and Resulting Genres

Narrative Writing

Amie's writing sample is a good example of a first grader narrating one focused event with more elaboration supporting the initial event. The narrative is told in simple story form, drawing from Amie's own personal experience. As a piece of writing, the text is typical of "bed-to-bed" narratives — a list of events flowing from "frust" through to the end, with no discrimination. However, she controls the focus of the story; that is, the events are all relative to a particular situation: looking at lights. It represents narrative writing that successfully meets the first-grade standard.

◆ Amie plans the writing by establishing an initiating event ("On Saturday I went to look at the lights").

◆ The piece develops a series of events that flow from the initiating event ("my mom and dad told me thet we wur going," "I got on my cot," "we wet to look at the lights," "we sol ol uv the pepul … had bels, and ajuls, and cande cangs," "And I sol suntclos to," etc.).

◆ She demonstrates an awareness of craft by signaling the chronology of events through transition words ("frust" and "Then"), providing some concrete detail ("a culurfol cande cang") and establishing a sense of closure ("The End"). ▶▶

Amie

On Saturday

On Saturday I went to look at the lights. And frust [*first]
my mom and dad told me thet [that] we wur [were] going. Then
I got on my cot [coat]. Then we wet [went] to look at
the lights. On the the Strets [streets] we sol [saw] ol [all] uv [of] the
pepul [people] thet [that] wur [were] on that stret [street]. had bels [bells], and ajuls [angels], and
cande cangs [candy canes]. And I sol [saw] lights most uv [of] the time. And I

*Translation of phonetically spelled words

sol Sunt clos to. And he
(saw) (Santa) (Claus) (too.)
gav me a culurfol comde
(gave) (colorful) (candy)
cang, Then we sol mor
(cane.) (saw) (more)
uv lights. Then I went
(of)
home, And wocht some tvi
(watched)
Then I went to get
my doll, Then I went
to slep, Then I had a
(sleep)
drem, Then I woc up!
(dream) (woke)
The End

Writing Standard 3:

Language Use and Conventions

This piece meets the Language Use and Conventions Standard for first grade.

Style and Syntax

The style of this piece clearly reflects Amie's efforts to "take on" the language of authors. Almost two-thirds of the sentences begin with a transitional word — most frequently, "Then." In fact, these transitional words provide most of the organizational framework for the writing. For the most part, Amie uses simple sentences, but there are two complex sentences as well.

Vocabulary and Word Choice

This work provides evidence that Amie uses words common to her speaking vocabulary — she has not modified her word choice by using shorter words to control for spelling. For example, Amie uses "culurfol" to describe the candy canes, a very precise word choice.

Spelling

This work provides evidence that Amie controls the spelling of many high-frequency words ("On," "went," "the," "look," "at," etc.). Amie produces text that can be read easily by others. Even words that are misspelled can be read because they are represented phonetically.

Punctuation, Capitalization and Other Conventions

This work provides evidence that Amie consistently controls for the use of capital letters at the beginning of sentences and periods at the end.

(For more on Language Use and Conventions, see page 136.)

"Once up on a hill"

Writing Standard 2:
Writing Purposes and Resulting Genres

Narrative Writing

Shauna's fictional narrative incorporates many of the elements that comprise the genre. This is a first-draft piece and is incomplete because Shauna ran out of time and space (though one can infer a coherence to an ending because of how she structures the last sentence — "the turtle was the savedy garde so when the baby chickens fell in the water … "). Time was also a factor in her lack of punctuation — Shauna explained that she was in a hurry to get the story out and that she would "fix up" punctuation later. This sample meets the standard for narrative writing for first grade.

◆ The piece clearly has been planned — the hero is a chicken who is really a turtle and so is capable of swimming and saving his friends. Shauna enters the sequence very early on — notice how she explains how a turtle is part of this story about chickens (solving the problem of the hen who couldn't lay an egg).

◆ This narrative actually is made up of two series of events, one series about the hen who couldn't lay an egg and a second series about the heroic act of the turtle who saves the lives of the chickens who mocked him.

Shauna

Once up on a hill a farmer lived and there wos a chichen pen. All the chickens had babys [chicken babies] except for one white chicken. and the farmer called her Peracalla [Priscilla] and she tried to lay an egg but it was no joys. she even could't [couldn't use] lay a single egg. so she put a note by her nest and ran away and whlie [while] she was runing [running] she triped [tripped] over someting [something]. She looked at it. It was an egg she took it to the chicken pen fast and qickly [quickly] and when she got there she mad [made] the egg warm and the cicken [chicken] sarted [started] to nit [knit] some overalls and a short [shirt]. and when the egg hached [hatched] the baby chicken was a turtle and the mom chicken thaunt [thought] it was a palayn [plain] baby chicken so she just dressed him and sent him outside with the other baby chicken they where [were] playing sager [soccer] the baby turtle said could I play a chicken said wat [what]

*Translation of phonetically spelled words

◆ The piece incorporates several writing strategies: dialogue, including the use of "HELP!" in all capital letters to indicate desperation, and literary language ("Once up on a hill a farmer lived").

◆ Shauna uses concrete details ("she took it to the chicken pen fast and qickly").

◆ The writing evidences a plot/subplot structure — the plot built around the turtle's heroism and the subplot built around how the turtle becomes a part of a chicken colony in the first place.   ▶▶

◆ This sample builds on and weaves together several common story lines from children's books. In particular, the introductory sentences mimic the syntax common to children's books, though all the syntax is fairly sophisticated.

Writing Standard 3:
Language Use and Conventions

This piece meets the Language Use and Conventions Standard for first grade.

Style and Syntax

Shauna employs an array of syntactic patterns. The piece is made up of simple, compound and complex sentences — although not all are properly punctuated. There are prepositional phrases, various kinds of clauses, and both noun and verb modifiers. "Once up on a hill" is a variation on "once upon a time." There is also an unusual placement of adverbs ("took it to the chicken pen fast and qickly").

Vocabulary and Word Choice

Shauna uses words from her everyday vocabulary and words she is not wholly familiar with ("nit some overalls and a short").

Spelling

The spelling in this piece is relatively consistent. Certainly, she evidences much control for a first-draft effort. The words can be read by another person, and the misspelled words correspond to phonetic attempts to record sound. Notice particularly Shauna's attempts to spell *middle*

("midol" and "mitle") in which each attempt represents a different, though logical, pronunciation of this word.

Punctuation, Capitalization and Other Conventions

Shauna exhibits knowledge of capitalization and end punctuation at the beginning of this story. Her control is inconsistent after that.

(For more on Language Use and Conventions, see page 136.)

are you I'm a chicken he laft [laughed] and said a chicken then the baby turtle cried and walk away then he saw them get on a boat that was made out of a box he wanted to get on the boat but he was to late [too] they had gone out in the midol [middle] of the pond but suddunly [suddenly] one side of the boat brok [broke] the baby chickens fell in to the water the baby chickens cried HELP! the baby turtle ran to the pond swam in the mitle [middle] of the pond and put them on his back and carried them to shor [shore] when the baby chickens woke up they playd [played] piret [pirate] and the turtle was the savedy garde [safety guard] so when the baby chickens fell in the water the turtle

Authors' Perspectives

"I'm a compulsive writer. I get up in the morning and I have all these things inside me that want to come out. Sometimes I'm struck by a story that will never be told unless I tell it. And once I start telling it, I want to tell it in the very best way I can. It's never perfect when I write it down the first time, or the second time, or the fifth time. But it always gets better as I go over it and over it."

— Jane Yolen

From Pamela Lloyd, "Why Writers Write," *How Writers Write* (Heinemann Educational Books, Inc., 1987), p. 143.

Informing Others: Report or Informational Writing

Like kindergartners, most first graders love to tell people "all about" various subjects. Students on target to meet first-grade standards produce inventories of things they like or things they know, as well as informational reports — from simple lists to more elaborately detailed descriptions — that enumerate what they have learned about a topic. These first graders have a growing sense of the reader or listener and the need to communicate clearly, along with an emerging sense of control of information, which they exhibit by sorting facts and ideas into major categories. Their work seems to say, "I'm trying to teach you, and I have a lot of good stuff to tell." They may use headings like the ones they have seen in "all-about" or chapter books: *Kinds of Dogs, Choosing a Dog, Caring for a Dog.* They may include pictures, diagrams, maps or other graphics to add detail. And they generally make some effort to wrap things up or close with a flourish.

By the end of the year, we expect first-grade students to produce reports in which they:

◆ gather information pertinent to a topic, sort it into major categories — possibly using headings or chapters — and report it to others;

◆ independently recognize and exclude or delete extraneous information according to appropriate standards governing what "fits"; and

◆ demonstrate a growing desire and ability to communicate with readers by using details to develop their points; sometimes including pictures, diagrams, maps and other graphics that enhance the reader's understanding of the text; and paying attention to signing off.

"Plankton"

Writing Standard 2:
Writing Purposes and Resulting Genres

Report or Informational Writing

Maggie's sample is a typical report that organizes information into chapters. This piece of writing clearly owes its organization to chapter books with which she is familiar. It represents informational writing that meets the standard for first grade.

◆ The sample uses the title as an introduction to the topic and defines plankton, which is a common introductory strategy for a report in first grade.

◆ Maggie seems to have written it over time because an apparent ending ("thats all I have for naw") is followed by a promise ("mabe on the nekst caprtr youll will find owt mrr") and then delivery of more information in subsequent chapters.

◆ The sample includes many concrete details and an impressive number of facts. While a reader sees some repetitions and irrelevancies, the report contains 21 facts ("plankton is a littll plant," "gros undr wotr," "high a-nuf so it can git some sun," etc.). ▶▶

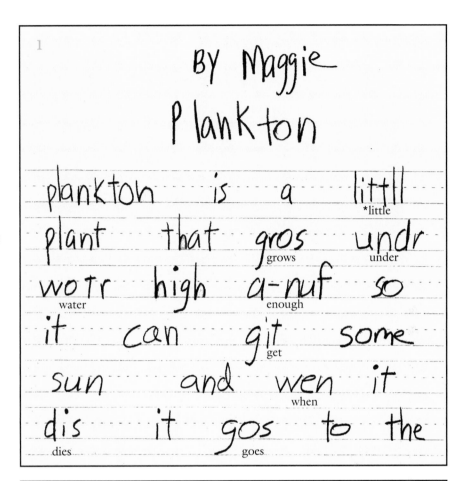

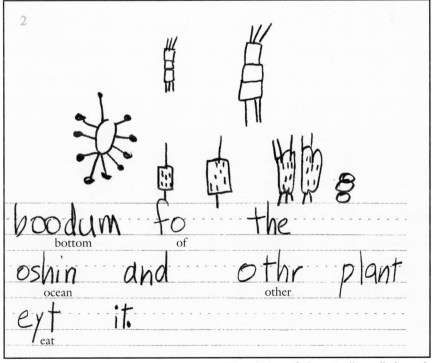

*Translation of phonetically spelled words

New Standards

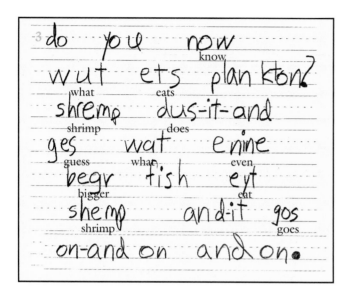

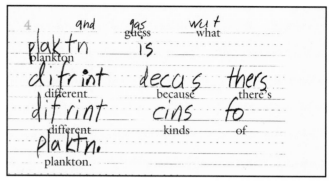

Writing Standard 3:

Language Use and Conventions

This piece does not meet the Language Use and Conventions Standard for first grade because of overall lack of attention to conventions. Admittedly, this piece is a first draft, which was written over several days, so correctness was not necessarily an issue. Maggie sometimes uses dashes to mark spaces, and she does not seem to make a consistent attempt to use capital letters to begin sentences or periods to end them. The piece does have some notable features, however.

Maggie mostly uses directly stated sentences, which are characteristic of reports of information. She likewise uses present-tense verbs that are appropriate for this kind of report and includes rhetorical questions as a way of introducing information ("do you now wut ets plankton?").

Maggie mixes everyday oral language (repetition of "and" and "gas/ges wat") with rhetorical questions — language that shows the influence of reading informational books. In addition, she employs a number of specialized terms related to the topic ("plant," "fish," "kelp," "snalls," etc.). She correctly spells both a number of high-frequency words and a number of the specialized words. Additionally, she shows awareness of letter-sound correspondence for initial and ending consonants and spells correctly some words with short vowels ("sun," "it," "to" and "do"). Maggie shows a discernible logic in spelling other words ("a-nuf," "wen," "boodum," etc.).

Maggie uses periods at the end of declarative sentences and question marks for some interrogative sentences. While Maggie uses few capitals, she knows to capitalize the personal pronoun *I*.

(For more on Language Use and Conventions, see page 136.)

6

kelp levs (lives) in
now (New) sea land (Zealand) and
sath (South) afca (Africa)
Kelp—livs (lives) in cold wotr (water).

Kelp froest-are-fand (forests are found)
oft (off) the west and
noth (North) and acros (across)
amarca (America) and ther (the)
suthun (southern) cost (coast)
to-in- (of) oshst-raly (Australia)

7

I like
Kelp
kelp chajes (changes) weth (with)
the sesin (season). But
in the wentr (winter)
~~ses~~ ~~gevn~~ navs (waves)
it dis (dies)
~~fo~~ ~~the plant~~

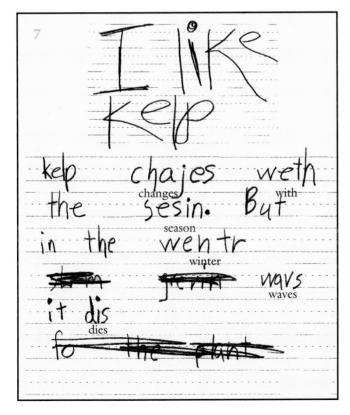

8

sea otrs (otters) hep Kelp.
they (there) are menie (many)
anmils (animals) that grow
in the kelp frest (forest)
that are stag (strange)
loking (looking).

9

the kelp hepes (helps)
may (many) anmils (animals)
sea slags (slugs)
are snalls (snails) weth (with)
awt (out) eney (any) shell
and thay (they) are
defrent (different) sisis (species) jest (just)
like kelp

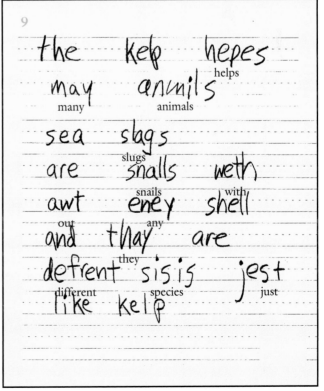

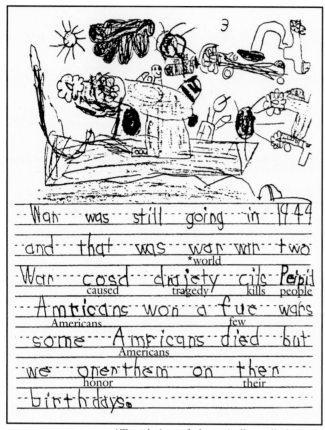

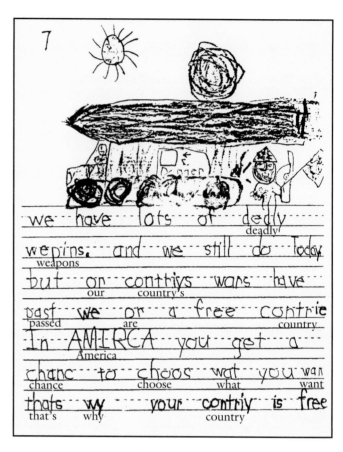

*Translation of phonetically spelled words

"Wars"

Writing Standard 2:
Writing Purposes and Resulting Genres

Report or Informational Writing

This sample is part of a 10-page report entitled "War in the History of America." The whole text is richly illustrated and distinguished both by Chuck's knowledge of the topic and by his vocabulary. The three pages reproduced here are representative of the report as a whole. Although the piece is marred by an overall lack of organization, control of 10 pages of text far exceeds reasonable expectations for first-grade writing. Basically, this sample is a very mature example of an "all-about" text.

This piece reflects a broad knowledge of the topic (Chuck's father was in the military), but even this knowledge reflects a naive understanding ("war war two" for *World War II*). Essentially, the piece is remarkable for its breadth; each of the many topics is elaborated on by no more than a single fact. It represents writing that meets the standard for informational writing in first grade.

◆ The piece is organized pictorially rather than by categories. Chuck provides very detailed drawings of fighter planes during an attack, huge missiles and a modern bomber landing. Under each picture is text about what the picture illustrates.

◆ The information clearly fits in with the overall topic.

◆ The information is drawn from Chuck's background knowledge and is presented to the reader with sufficient detail to be coherent. For example, on page 7, Chuck moves from the picture of a missile to telling the reader that America has deadly weapons. He then states that ours is a free country and goes on to say that we have freedom of choice and that is what constitutes being a free country.

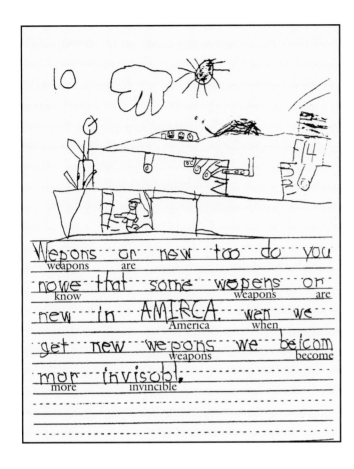

Writing Standard 3:
Language Use and Conventions

This piece meets the Language Use and Conventions Standard for first grade.

Style and Syntax

Chuck's syntax is relatively sophisticated. There are a variety of sentence patterns used, and though the piece is lengthy, there is no sense that he relies on chaining (generating text by using the end topic of one sentence to begin a new sentence), which is sometimes the case with writing of this length produced by very young authors. Chuck uses a rhetorical question ("do you nowe that some wepens or new in AMIRCA") and takes on syntactic patterns that are quite adult ("War cosd drajety cils Peipil" or "contriys wars have past we or a free contrie").

Vocabulary and Word Choice

The vocabulary of this writing is impressive. "Oner," "dedly wepins" and "invisobl" are all words not commonly associated with first-grade writing, but they are words that work naturally, given the topic. It is safe to assume that these words have been part of family conversations and subsequently are incorporated into associations with the topic. It is often the case that when students like Chuck address a topic they know a great deal about, their vocabulary will be quite technical and sophisticated to convey precise meaning.

Spelling

The spelling in this piece is uneven. Chuck uses an impressive number of high-frequency words, which are spelled correctly. And he attempts many words that are too advanced to be spelled correctly. Even so, a reader who is familiar with phonetic spelling is able to understand these difficult words because they are represented phonetically. This is a polished piece of writing; Chuck may have solicited some help with spelling.

Punctuation, Capitalization and Other Conventions

The punctuation and capitalization in this piece are not consistent. Nevertheless, Chuck demonstrates an awareness of beginning capitalization and punctuation.

(For more on Language Use and Conventions, see page 136.)

Getting Things Done: Functional Writing

First-grade students write for many of the same functional purposes that they did as kindergartners. They create signs, announcements, invitations, letters, lists and labels that support the myriad activities going on in their lively classrooms and sometimes outside school. They also may compose instructions that explain, albeit in minimal detail, how to make or do something. Their early functional writing is the foundation for narrative procedures that students will be expected to write in later grades.

By the end of the year, we expect first-grade students to produce functional writings that:

◆ give instructions;

◆ describe, in appropriate sequence and with a few details, the steps one must take to make or do a particular thing; and

◆ claim, mark or identify objects and places.

**First-Grade
Writing Standard 1:**
Habits and Processes

**First-Grade
Writing Standard 2:**
*Writing Purposes and
Resulting Genres*

◆ Sharing Events, Telling
Stories: Narrative Writing

◆ Informing Others: Report
or Informational Writing

◆ Getting Things Done:
Functional Writing

◆ Producing and
Responding to Literature

**First-Grade
Writing Standard 3:**
*Language Use and
Conventions*

◆ Style and Syntax

◆ Vocabulary and
Word Choice

◆ Spelling

◆ Punctuation, Capitalization
and Other Conventions

*Translation of phonetically spelled words

"On Haw to Make a Jackanolaner"

Writing Standard 2:
Writing Purposes and Resulting Genres

Functional Writing

Mary's sample is a rich example of a child's literacy development. It has been polished — that is, Mary worked on it to correct gross misspellings and a sequencing problem (see the editing arrow at the bottom right). It represents functional writing that meets the standard for first grade. (To see this same topic treated adequately by students at other grades, see page 279.)

◆ This piece of writing provides the reader a general sense of the steps involved in making (carving) a jack-o'-lantern.

◆ The piece begins by explaining to the reader where to get a pumpkin ("at the stor") and then sequences the steps from the beginning ("get The face That you want") to the end ("Put ... a candle in and at night Put it out sied").

◆ Although the detail is minimal ("get a Pumkin at the stor" and "get [carve] The face That you want"), the reader has a clear sense of the "what" of the process, though not exactly of the "how."

◆ Mary demonstrates a familiarity with the genre by labeling the work as a functional work ("a haw To Book") and by ascribing a reading level to it ("an I Can Read Book").

◆ Mary also creates a title page that is formatted and illustrated appropriately.

◆ She makes the text coherent through the use of transitional words ("first," "Then" and "Last").

Writing Standard 3:
Language Use and Conventions

This piece does not meet the Language Use and Conventions Standard for first grade because Mary shows no awareness of end punctuation. It does have some notable features, however.

Mary uses an informal beginning ("O.K.") at the start of this writing sample, clearly connecting it to the patterns of oral language. At the same time, she uses transition words that obviously mark the piece's association with written text. This piece has varied sentence openers rather than a repeated sentence stem to scaffold ideas: The syntax is primarily a subject-verb patterning of simple sentences introduced by a variety of appropriate transition words.

Mary uses words from her daily vocabulary ("mese") as well as words familiar to the genre of directions ("first," "Then" and "Last"). Her work contains a large proportion of correctly spelled, high-frequency words and can be read by others because most of the perceived sounds are phonetically represented. Familiar words and word endings are spelled correctly. There are actually only six misspellings.

(For more on Language Use and Conventions, see page 136.)

A

How To Tacke *take
A Test

How to tack
a test I will tell *take
you. First your
techer. will *teacher
pass out the
booklets. Next
you get your

2

pennsels redey *pencils *ready
for your test.
Then you open
your book when
your seayel is *seal
broken. Then
you read the
instruchches. *instructions
to your self. *yourself

*Translation of phonetically spelled words

"How To Tacke A Test"

Writing Standard 2:
**Writing Purposes and
Resulting Genres**

Functional Writing

This piece of functional writing grows naturally out of Amie's own experience. The tone is both informative and conversational ("How to tack a test I will tell you"). It obviously is written student-to-student. Although fairly general — there's no information about how to read the questions and problems or how to decide on a correct answer — the steps described could lead a reader through the process. The writing is enhanced by the use of transition words and the illustration to show how and where students are positioned when tested — four to a table, seated on separate sides. This is writing that meets the standard for first-grade functional writing.

◆ Amie provides instructions that, though general, explain how to take a test ("First your techer will pass out the booklets").

◆ She describes in appropriate sequence what a student should do during a standardized testing situation ("open your book when your seayel is broken ... read the instruchches to your self ... mark your anser ... strech").

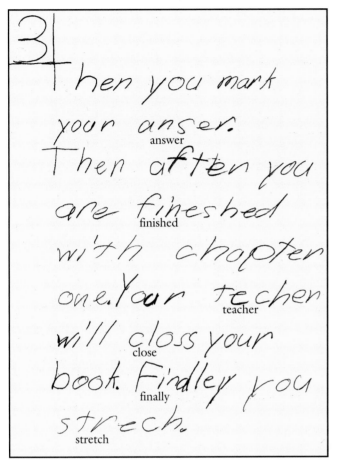

3) Then you mark your anser. *(answer)* Then after you are fineshed *(finished)* with chopter one. Your techen *(teacher)* will closs *(close)* your book. Findley *(finally)* you strech. *(stretch)*

4) Thats *(that's)* the way to tack *(take)* atest.

Writing Standard 3:
Language Use and Conventions

This piece meets the Language Use and Conventions Standard for first grade.

Style and Syntax

Amie uses both simple and complex sentences. Most of her sentences are relatively short and introduced by transitional words common to functional writing.

Vocabulary and Word Choice

This work provides evidence that Amie uses vocabulary appropriate for describing the procedure, even attempting words beyond the range expected for first graders ("instruchches"). She also employs the transitional words commonly used in procedures ("First," "Next," "Then" and "Findley").

Spelling

This work provides evidence that Amie controls for the spelling of a large percentage of high-frequency and familiar words ("How," "to," "test," "will," "tell," "you," "First," "pass" and "out"). She writes text easily read by others because misspelled words are represented phonetically ("techer").

Punctuation, Capitalization and Other Conventions

This work provides evidence that Amie uses punctuation correctly — she controls for the use of capitals to begin sentences and periods to end them.

(For more on Language Use and Conventions, see page 136.)

Producing and Responding to Literature

First graders who have opportunities to immerse themselves in all forms of literature do the same kinds of re-enacting, retelling, borrowing and burrowing that they did in kindergarten. They notice the wide variety of genres and work to write in all these forms, each to suit an appropriate purpose. To do this, first graders try to use in their own writing the writing techniques they have learned. Literary language may begin to appear in their writing, and they may approximate especially appealing generic forms,

such as the distinctive rhythmic scheme of a particular poem or a familiar and predictable story line. But where kindergartners' responses to literature consist mostly of recounting, first graders move into evaluating. They may mark favorite passages with Post-it Notes™ and talk about what they liked. They may draw comparisons to events and people in their own lives. During first and even second grades, these evaluative responses to literature usually take oral forms such as conversation, presentation or group discussion. Later, we will expect students to be able to produce written responses to literature, but to get ready for this, it is important that they begin learning the form of a response to literature. At this stage, as earlier, it is important that children be allowed to respond orally so that the physical act of writing does not get in the way of the response to literature.

Producing literature

By the end of the year, we expect first-grade students to be able to:

◆ write stories, memoirs, poems, songs and other literary forms;

◆ demonstrate not only an awareness of but also an ability to reproduce some of the literary language and styles they hear and read in the classroom (these may include alliteration, metaphor, simile, rhythm, complex syntax, descriptive detail, sound effects, dialogue, gestures, familiar story grammars or plot lines, and poetic line breaks and rhyme schemes); and

◆ imitate a text or write in a genre when they respond to it.

Responding to literature

By the end of the year, we expect first-grade students to be able to:

◆ re-enact and retell stories, songs, poems, plays and other literary works they encounter;

◆ produce simple evaluative expressions about the text (for example, "I like the story because," "I like the part where");

◆ make simple comparisons of the story to events or people in their own lives;

◆ compare two books by the same author;

◆ discuss several books on the same theme;

◆ make explicit reference to parts of the text when presenting or defending a claim; and

◆ present a plausible interpretation of a book.

"what is Blue?"

Writing Standard 2:
Writing Purposes and Resulting Genres

Producing Literature

Kyla's poem "what is Blue?" is a good example of how children's literature can inspire students to produce original pieces with similar formats on their own. This sample is reminiscent of various poems, songs and picture books, which all try to provide rich examples of a particular color. Kyla's poem explores what blue is. She names blue objects and then adds further description ("Blue are my eyes/BiG and wondrous," "Blue is the moon/BiG and round"). This poem meets the standard for producing literature in first grade.

◆ This piece uses literary language and style. The repetitive sentence openers work well as a means of organizing the rich imagery of the poem.

◆ The piece includes very precise descriptive detail ("a sea deeP sea").

◆ The writing uses poetic line breaks and imagery ("Blue is my memory trailing behind me/Locked in my mind forever more").

Writing Standard 3:
Language Use and Conventions

This piece meets the Language Use and Conventions Standard for first grade. It is a polished final draft and is virtually error-free.

Style and Syntax

Kyla employs literary language ("Locked in my mind forever more") and syntax obviously mimicking the structure and format of a familiar piece.

Vocabulary and Word Choice

She uses words common to first-grade writing as well as words that convey a sense of imagery ("sea deeP sea").

Spelling

There are no misspellings.

Punctuation, Capitalization and Other Conventions

The piece has been polished, so it is logical to assume that Kyla had help with spelling, punctuation and capitalization.

(For more on Language Use and Conventions, see page 136.)

The cow boy
and The *cowboy pingwin
penguin

BY Shawn

*Translation of phonetically spelled words

Once upon a time
in the dezert dy
desert   by
a hill of snow there
was a cow boy one
cowboy
day he wint up onto
went
the hill of snow.
Then he saw a cav
cave
he wint in it to
went
see wat was there,
what

"The cow boy and The pingwin"

Writing Standard 2:
Writing Purposes and Resulting Genres

Producing Literature

Shawn's work is a good example of a fictional narrative. He has pulled ideas from a variety of stories he has read to produce his own unique story, a strategy employed often by novice writers. This piece meets the standard for narrative writing in first grade.

◆ It has an appropriate story line containing a problem and a solution: The cowboy seeks gold, he goes on a quest and he finds gold.

◆ There is some use of literary language ("Once upon a time in the dezert dy a hill of snow there was ... " and "And thay livd haply ever after").

◆ The piece employs dialogue.

◆ The story follows a plot line: The cowboy takes on a quest, is successful, marries "the pridyist girl he nod" and lives happily ever after.

out in the uld west.

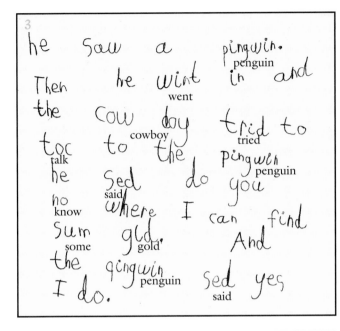

3

he saw a pingwin.
[penguin]
Then he wint in and
[went]
the cow boy trid to
[cowboy] [tried]
toc to the pingwen
[talk] [penguin]
he sed do you
[said]
no where I can find
[know]
sum gld. And
[some] [gold]
the qinguin sed yes
[penguin] [said]
I do.

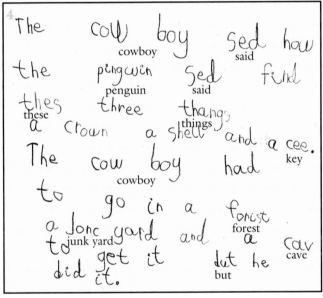

4
The cow boy sed how
[cowboy] [said]
the pingwin sed find
[penguin] [said]
thes three thangs
[these] [things]
a crown a shell and a cee.
[key]
The cow boy had
[cowboy]
to go in a forist
[forest]
a Jonc yard and a
[junk yard]
to get it cav
[cave]
did it. but he
[but]

5

Then he had to
find three cavs
[caves]
with the stone poctt
[pocket]
plas it took him
[place]
6 weeks
weecs then
it perd gld on him,
[poured] [gold]
And he mered the
married
pridgist girl he hod.
[prettiest] [knowed [knew]]
And thay livd
[they] [lived]
haply ever after.
[happily]

The end

Writing Standard 3:
Language Use and Conventions

This piece meets the Language Use and Conventions Standard for first grade.

Style and Syntax

Shawn moves between the syntax of oral language — particularly the dialogue — and the syntax of literary language ("One day he wint up onto the hill of snow"). His piece contains a variety of sentence openers and syntactic patterns.

Vocabulary and Word Choice

The vocabulary Shawn used in this piece is appropriate for first-grade expectations. There is language clearly influenced by books ("it perd gld on him") and language more representative of oral language.

Spelling

The text clearly can be read by people other than Shawn. Words he did not spell correctly can be deciphered because they are represented phonetically. He spelled some high-frequency words correctly.

Punctuation, Capitalization and Other Conventions

Both correct beginning capitalization and end punctuation are captured in this first-grade piece. It is only around quotations that Shawn runs into problems, but such problems are to be expected.

(For more on Language Use and Conventions, see page 136.)

"The Stre uvthe three Bers"

Writing Standard 2:
**Writing Purposes and
Resulting Genres**

Responding to Literature

Cristina generated this piece in
response to an assignment that asked
students to retell a story. The piece is
a remarkably complete retelling. It is a
good example of one of several kinds
of responses students may be asked to
do. This piece meets the standard for a
response to literature in first grade.

◆ The retelling is a complete and
faithful recounting of a familiar
story.

The Stre uvthe three Cristina
Bers. On spon atim the three
Bers witfour a wock in the forest.
Then Godinlos cameto the
three bers hasse. She Nocke
on the door. no wun wus ther
At the hasse. Then She tastid the
Popus porch. She sed it wus to hot
Then She tastid the momus porch it wusto
cod. then She tasid the babebers
Porch it wusqis rit. sow She dsirit
To tak a litle Sit. She sit on PoPuscher
It wus to hrd. Sow she Siton momus
Cher it wus to Soft. So w She Sit on the babe
Bers cher but it broka fart. Sow She wit
Up Stersto tak a nap She slepton Popus
Bed it wus to hard. So w sheslept on momus
Bed it wus to sofd. sow she wit to babebers
Bed it wusqis rit sowshe wit u slep.

*The Story of the Three Bears
Once upon a time the three
bears went for a walk in the forest.
Then Goldilocks came to the
three bears' house. She knocked
on the door. No one was there
at the house. Then she tasted the
papa's porridge. She said it was too hot.
Then she tasted the mama's porridge; it was
too cold. Then she tasted the baby bear's
porridge; it was just right. So she decided
to take a little sit. She sat on Papa's chair.
It was too hard. So she sat on Mama's
chair; it was too soft. So she sat on the baby
bear's chair, but it broke apart. So she went
upstairs to take a nap. She slept on Papa's
bed; it was too hard. So she slept on Mama's
bed; it was too soft. So she went to baby bear's
bed; it was just right, so she went to sleep.

*Translation of phonetically spelled words

Writing Standard 3:
Language Use and Conventions

This piece meets the Language Use and Conventions Standard for first grade.

Style and Syntax

The style and syntax of Cristina's writing sample are what one would expect in a faithful retelling. That is, she begins with literary language ("On Spon atim") and then switches to the almost singsong cadences created by the repetitions in the story ("She sit on popuscher It wus to hrd. Sow she Sit on momus cher it wus to soft"). Many of the sentences begin with transitions ("Then") or words to signal cause ("Sow").

Vocabulary and Word Choice

Her vocabulary and word choice are determined by the story. For example, Cristina mentions "Porch" (porridge), possibly not a common word in her day-to-day vocabulary. On the other hand, she mentions that Goldilocks "dsirit To tak a litte sit" (decided to take a little sit) and so employs language that is clearly not part of the story.

Spelling

The spelling is easy to read because Cristina represents almost each sound in a word phonetically. The misspellings are logical and do not inhibit the reading of the piece. She spells many high-frequency words correctly.

Then the three bears came to the house. The papa said, "Someone been sleeping in my bed," said the papa bear. "Someone been sleeping in my bed," said the mama bear. "Someone been sleeping in my bed, and there she is." Then up jump Goldilocks. She ran as fast as she could and never came back again.

Punctuation, Capitalization and Other Conventions

Cristina's control of capitalization and punctuation is quite consistent for a piece of this length. Some words are capitalized that should not be ("Porch" for *porridge* and "Bed" for *bed*).

(For more on Language Use and Conventions, see page 136.)

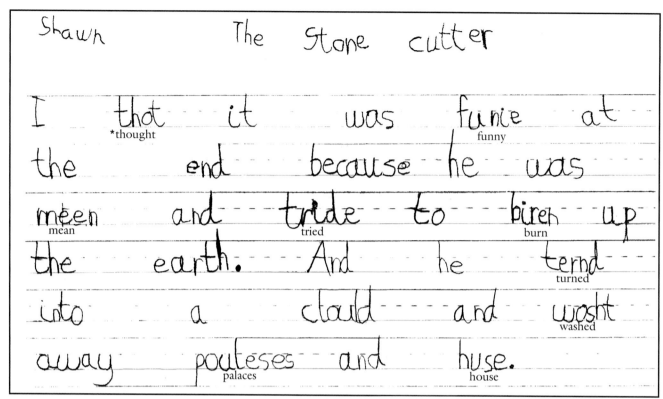

Shawn   The Stone cutter

I thot it was funie at
*thought   funny

the end because he was

meen and tride to biren up
mean   tried   burn

the earth. And he ternd
turned

into a claud and wosht
washed

away pouleses and huse.
palaces   house

*Translation of phonetically spelled words

"The Stone cutter"

Writing Standard 2:
Writing Purposes and Resulting Genres

Responding to Literature

Shawn's response to literature was produced when he was asked what he thought about the story *The Stone Cutter*. The writing, though brief, explains why the book appealed to Shawn. The writing meets the standard for a first-grade response to literature.

◆   Shawn begins with a judgment ("I thot it was funie at the end because … ").

◆   Shawn makes an explicit reference to a particular part of the text ("at the end") that is being commented upon and for which he defends his claim: It is funny because he "tride to biren up the earth. And [yet] he ternd into a clould and wosht away pouleses and huse."

Writing Standard 3:
Language Use and Conventions

This piece meets the Language Use and Conventions Standard for first grade.

Style and Syntax

The sentence structure of this very short piece is representative of the syntax of oral language. Shawn uses causal reasoning in the first sentence and links the ideas using an independent clause ("I thot") and a dependent clause ("because he was").

Vocabulary and Word Choice

The vocabulary is appropriate for a first grader. He uses words that adequately convey his thinking.

Spelling

The spelling is read easily by another person with the possible exception of the last word, "huse." He spelled the

14 high-frequency words correctly, and the other words are represented logically.

Punctuation, Capitalization and Other Conventions

The writing shows Shawn's control of capital letters at the beginning of sentences and periods at the end.

(For more on Language Use and Conventions, see page 136.)

Research Perspectives

"Written text places high demand on vocabulary knowledge. Even the words used in children's books are more rare than those used in adult conversations and prime-time television (Hayes and Ahrens, 1988). Learning new concepts and the words that encode them is essential for comprehension development. People's ability to infer or retain new words in general is strongly dependent on their background knowledge of other words and concepts. Even at the youngest ages, the ability to understand and remember the meanings of new words depends quite strongly on how well developed one's vocabulary already is (Robbins and Ehri, 1994)."

From National Research Council,
Preventing Reading Difficulties in Young Children
(Washington, D.C.: National Academy Press, 1998), p. 217.

First-Grade Writing Standard 3: Language Use and Conventions

As they did in kindergarten, first graders still write mostly in their own language, producing text that mirrors the sentence structure and vocabulary of their speech. Although they are beginning to develop a sense of writing for a reader, their writers' voices still are mostly egocentric. When first graders read books aloud and when they hear increasingly sophisticated spoken language from adults, they begin to appropriate new vocabulary and more complex elements of style and syntax for their own writing. That is, they can make more choices about which words to use, in which form and in what order. They also may produce text containing fragments of the language of other writers or speakers such as literary or "book-ish" language or turns of phrase heard in adults' speech.

Style and Syntax

In good programs, first graders are exposed throughout the year to increasingly sophisticated written and spoken language — and the elements of style embedded in both. By the end of the year, they are able to make more choices about which words to use and in what order. These first-grade writers produce text that mirrors the sentence structure and vocabulary of their oral language, sometimes enriched by literary language or the syntax of other genres they have been reading or hearing read.

Using one's own language
By the end of the year, we expect first-grade students to:

- vary sentence openers instead of relying on the same sentence stem (for example, "I like books," "I like dogs," "I like my mom"); and

- use a wide range of the syntactic patterns typical of spoken language.

Taking on language of authors
By the end of the year, we expect first-grade students to:

- embed literary language where appropriate; and

- sometimes mimic sentence structures from various genres they are reading.

Vocabulary and Word Choice

Using one's own language
By the end of the year, we expect first-grade students to:

- produce writing that uses the full range of words in their speaking vocabulary; and

- select a more precise word when prompted.

Taking on language of authors
By the end of the year, we expect first-grade students to:

- use newly learned words they like from their reading, the books they hear read, words on the classroom walls and talk.

First-Grade
Writing Standard 1:
Habits and Processes

First-Grade
Writing Standard 2:
Writing Purposes and Resulting Genres

- Sharing Events, Telling Stories: Narrative Writing
- Informing Others: Report or Informational Writing
- Getting Things Done: Functional Writing
- Producing and Responding to Literature

First-Grade
Writing Standard 3:
Language Use and Conventions

- Style and Syntax
- Vocabulary and Word Choice
- Spelling
- Punctuation, Capitalization and Other Conventions

Spelling

First-grade students still are experimenting with print and with the conventions that make print meaningful to a reader. By the end of the year, they should use appropriate letters to represent most of the sounds they hear in a word and so be able to produce writing that both they and others can read. This is not to say that the spelling is correct (conventional). Most first-grade writers use the segmenting and sounding-out strategies of phonetic spelling, but they also draw on a repertoire of other resources. For example, they may rely on meaningful parts of words that they know (*-tion, -ing, -ly*) and familiar word families with consistent (the *oo* in *book*) or inconsistent (*thay* for *they*) sound-spelling patterns.

By the end of the year, we expect first-grade students to:

◆ produce writing that contains a large proportion of correctly spelled, high-frequency words;

◆ write text that usually can be read by the child and others — regardless of the scarcity of correctly spelled words — because most of the perceived sounds in unfamiliar words are phonetically represented;

◆ draw on a range of resources for deciding how to spell unfamiliar words, including strategies like segmenting, sounding out, and matching to familiar words and word parts; and

◆ automatically spell some familiar words and word endings correctly.

Punctuation, Capitalization and Other Conventions

First-grade writers usually are aware of punctuation and are interested in trying to use it, albeit somewhat erratically. A collection of a first grader's writing over the year should show attempts to use exclamation points, quotations marks, ellipses and colons to add emphasis, create a mood, be clear or direct the reader's voice to use particular intonations. First-grade students also borrow conventions from their favorite authors. Though they often use them incorrectly, children at this age usually are beginning to show some control over periods, question marks, and the use of capital letters for names and sentence beginnings. Mostly, though, they like to play with using punctuation and conventions — like using all capital letters (for example, "HELP"), multiple underlinings (for example, "He was <u>very</u> sad"), serial exclamation points (for example, "We won!!!") and other graphic representations that emphasize elements of a text.

First graders should demonstrate an awareness of punctuation marks by attempting to use them to direct a reader, to provide emphasis and intonation, to create mood in a piece, to borrow the conventions used by published authors, or to be clear.

Although first-grade students will not have consistent control over punctuation, capitalization and other conventions, by the end of the year we expect them to:

◆ demonstrate interest and awareness by approximating the use of some punctuation, including exclamation points, quotation marks, periods, question marks, ellipses, colons, and capitalization of proper names and sentence beginnings; and

◆ use punctuation accurately and sometimes use conventions that are borrowed from a favorite author to add emphasis, suggest mood, be clear and direct readers to use particular intonations.

"I went to the park"

Writing Standard 3:
Language Use and Conventions

This piece describes Joey's trip to the park. The narrative meets the standard for Language Use and Conventions. The style and syntax part of the standard, however, is not met as fully as the other three criteria. The narrative does not meet the standard for Writing Purposes and Resulting Genres because it is such a simple recounting.

Style and Syntax

Joey relies almost entirely on simple sentences beginning with the subject and verb. (The exception comes at the end of the piece when the construction is object/subject/verb with an elliptical clause as the object.) Each sentence is lined up at the left margin except the final one. Although most of the language is straightforward, the piece does include one simile ("high as a bird"). Another interesting syntactic feature is Joey's use of a quotation tag at the end of the sentence ("'Time to go' she said") instead of a more natural structure ("She said, 'Time to go.'").

Vocabulary and Word Choice

Joey uses the language of everyday speech for this piece. Although he does not use literary vocabulary, his word choice is adequate to convey the series of events.

Spelling

The sample contains 36 words with only two misspellings ("road" for *rode* and "scaired" for *scared*). Although there are many high-frequency words in the sample, this level of correctness is remarkable for first grade.

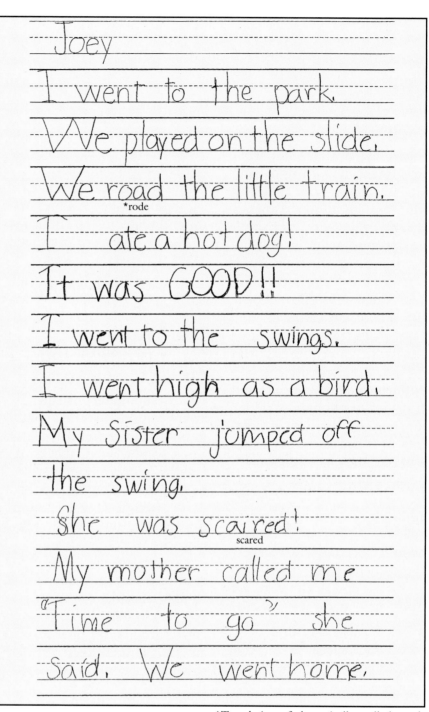

*Translation of phonetically spelled words

Punctuation, Capitalization and Other Conventions

This piece has no punctuation errors except for the omission of the comma after the quotation at the end of the piece. The first word of each sentence is capitalized, and question marks are used appropriately. The writer also uses capital letters and double exclamation marks to indicate emphasis and cue intonations in oral reading.

New Standards

Second Grade

Second Grade

Most second graders

eagerly attempt to write

in many genres,

from poems to reports to

memoirs, tailoring their

compositions for specific

audiences and purposes.

Budding Readers and Writers

Second grade is a critical year for budding readers and writers, a year when the transition from "learning to read" to "reading to learn" accelerates. Second graders, like kindergartners and first graders, come to school with an assortment of literacy experiences and skills. Their confidence as readers and writers varies widely as well.

Second graders who were reading fluently at the end of first grade — and who spent time reading throughout the summer vacation — are likely to pick up on reading and writing where they left off. Students who did not read over the summer, however, likely will have lost some fluency and will need extra help to catch up. Moreover, by second grade, students realize that they all should be good readers. Students who aren't reading well know it — and so do their classmates. Without instructional assistance to get them back on track, the academic problems of poor readers may mushroom into larger social and emotional difficulties as well.

Typically, most second graders are eager to please adults and classmates alike. They burst with pride when their teacher selects their best work for public display — and they eagerly share their work with family and friends.

Reading and Writing: What to Expect

Most second graders make significant leaps in reading and writing. Though their confidence and proficiency vary dramatically, most second graders should be readers. When they read independently, they can understand and enjoy books that are considerably longer and more complex in plot, vocabulary, syntax and structure than the books they read in first grade. Second graders begin to independently read chapter books, such as Penguin Group's mystery book *Cam Jansen and the Mystery of the Stolen Diamonds* in the Puffin Books series. They like to choose their own books — and with instruction, they usually select books they can read on their own.

Second graders also puzzle out difficult words, suspending the story's meaning in their minds as they do so. They use what they have learned about phonemes, chunks, rhyming words, onsets and rimes, contextual clues, and the sounds of sentences to figure out new words.

Second graders' writing skills should progress in tandem with reading improvements. As these standards show, the two are intertwined closely. Indeed, second graders often incorporate strategies from familiar books into

their own writing. For example, second graders commonly write poetry with refrains and alternating long and short lines, just as they have heard their teacher read aloud in class. And second graders imitate favorite authors or make use of intriguing writing strategies, such as dialogue, sound effects or detailed chronologies.

Most second graders eagerly attempt to write in many genres, from poems to reports to memoirs, tailoring their compositions for specific audiences and purposes. The variety of writing types they undertake helps them learn how the cadences of written language differ from those of speech.

Developing Literacy Habits

Second graders, like all primary schoolchildren, must continue to read a lot — a longer book or several chapters every day. They should read widely from both fiction and nonfiction sources, including poetry, picture books, adventure books and functional texts. Most of this reading should be done independently.

It is still essential, however, for teachers to read aloud to second graders every day. These readings should come from worthwhile texts, such as classic or modern literature, with the language, craft and excitement of good writing. Usually, read-aloud texts are beyond second graders' independent reading range. But hearing good books and stories read aloud is invaluable for students in developing their own reading and writing skills. They acquire new vocabulary because more advanced writing contains more unusual words than students are likely to encounter in everyday conversation or in the books they can read independently. And read-alouds help students develop syntactic awareness; again, written language contains more complex sentence structures than does most spoken language.

For examples of the kinds of books second graders should read, see **Leveled Books to Read for Accuracy and Fluency,** *page 146, and* **What Books Should Second Graders Read?,** *page 155.*

Second graders on target for meeting end-of-year standards recognize features of different reading and writing genres and, in classroom discussions, can compare works by different authors within a genre. Their inventory of "accountable talk" skills should grow throughout the year as well. That is, second graders increasingly are able to build ideas together as a group, argue respectfully and logically with one another, and attend carefully to the language of texts.

Having familiarized themselves with the nature of stories, reports, and informational and responsive writing in kindergarten and first grade, second graders firm up their understanding of the organizing structures of these and other genres. For example, discussing how writers organize factual books to provide infor-

> Second graders increasingly are able to build ideas together as a group, argue respectfully and logically with one another, and attend carefully to the language of texts.

mation gives second graders a sense of how to convey "all I know about" an important subject. Students may learn that the author of a book about dinosaurs organizes the text by classification and analysis. Second-grade factual writing may lack this sophisticated organization — and it may lack coherence and unity. Still, second graders can present facts backed by appropriate details within an obvious organizational framework.

Students who meet end-of-year standards for second grade understand and use important writing concepts and techniques. They can learn prewriting techniques that writers typically use, such as clustering and listing, drafting leads, and planning with a friend. They understand first drafts. They commonly start over on a piece of writing, make additions and take out extraneous information, reorganize to correct a sequence of events or "tell it right," and work to clarify their meaning with descriptive details. Second graders rely less on drawings to support their writing.

Proficient second-grade writers also produce much longer texts than they did in first grade. They can write a lot on a single topic, exploring the subject and trying different ways of writing about it — although most students can integrate large amounts of information into a cohesive piece of writing only with help. Second graders often seek out and use comments from their classmates, teachers and other adults to improve their writing. And they can give constructive feedback to their peers.

Second-Grade Reading Standard 1: Print-Sound Code

By the end of second grade, students should have a firm grasp of the print-sound code and be able to read the full range of English spelling patterns.

By the end of the year, we expect second-grade students to:

- read regularly spelled one- and two-syllable words automatically; and

- recognize or figure out most irregularly spelled words and such spelling patterns as diphthongs,* special vowel spellings and common word endings.

*A diphthong is a vowel sound that changes as it is spoken. In the word *boy,* for example, the *oy* sounds almost as if it were two sounds, /o/ and /e/. Other examples of diphthongs include the /ay/ sound in *day* or the /ow/ sound in *cow.*

Jasmin

Lucinda

Reading Standard 1:
Print-Sound Code

Jasmin appears to a have a solid grasp of the print-sound code as she reads an excerpt from *Young Jackie Robinson: Baseball Hero.* She sometimes repeats a word to refine her pronunciation or cadence, and she shows good attention to the text, even when reading a sign in the illustration. She has no trouble with common word endings *(-ry, -ly* or *-ing).* She easily reads vowel digraphs* found in such words as *treated* and *unfairly* and also deals with silent consonants such as those in *fighting.* This near mastery of the print-sound code means that she will be able to use her knowledge automatically to work through more difficult texts.

Lucinda also shows a firm grasp of the print-sound code as she reads an excerpt from *A Baby Sister for Frances.* In addition to easily reading one- and two-syllable words, she automatically reads words with digraphs *(ch, th* and *ng),* common word endings *(-ing* and *-zy)* and common endings where they appear in made-up words such as *rattley.* In addition, she reads the dialogue with good expression and voice.

*A digraph is a combination of two letters that, together, make one sound, which is different from either of the letter sounds alone. Consonant digraphs include letter combinations such as *ch, ph, sh, th* and *wh.* Vowel digraphs include combinations such as *ea* in *eat, ay* in *day, oi* in *oil* and *oa* in *coat.*

The images and commentary in the reading section of this book refer to reading performances available on the CD-ROM.

Second-Grade Reading Standard 2: **Getting the Meaning**

Accuracy

By the end of the year, we expect second-grade students to be able to:

◆ independently read aloud unfamiliar Level L books with 90 percent or better accuracy of word recognition (self-correction allowed).

Fluency

By the end of the year, we expect second-grade students to be able to:

◆ independently read aloud from unfamiliar Level L books that they have pre-viewed silently on their own, using intonation, pauses and emphasis that signal the meaning of the text; and

◆ use the cues of punctuation — including commas, periods, question marks and quotation marks — to guide them in getting meaning and fluently read-ing aloud.

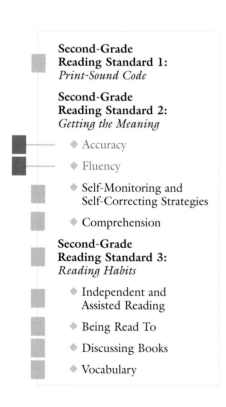

Second-Grade Reading Standard 1:
Print-Sound Code

Second-Grade Reading Standard 2:
Getting the Meaning

◆ Accuracy

◆ Fluency

◆ Self-Monitoring and Self-Correcting Strategies

◆ Comprehension

Second-Grade Reading Standard 3:
Reading Habits

◆ Independent and Assisted Reading

◆ Being Read To

◆ Discussing Books

◆ Vocabulary

Leveled Books to Read for Accuracy and Fluency

Level L books are markedly different from texts at lower levels. These books typically are longer chapter books with only a few illustrations that provide much less support for readers. The text size is smaller, and the word spacing is narrower.

Level L books feature more characters who are involved in more complex plots. The language struc-tures are more sophisticated, detailed and descriptive. The vocabulary is challenging.

In general, Level L books require higher-level conceptual thinking for students to understand the subtleties of plot and character development. Students must sustain their reading over several days to finish the book. Most of the reading is done silently and independently, but some parts of the book may be read aloud for emphasis or interest. Group discussion may support readers during and after they read Level L books.

Griffin

Reading Standard 2:
Getting the Meaning

Accuracy

Griffin reads *Cam Jansen and the Mystery of the Stolen Diamonds* with 98 percent accuracy. He mispronounces a few words or deletes a word occasionally but then self-corrects. For example, he says "assessment" but then corrects to "assignment." He occasionally will insert a word where it does not appear, such as "and then she closed her eyes" instead of "and then closed her eyes," but these few mistakes do not affect the meaning of the text.

Fluency

Griffin reads aloud fluently as far as clear and correct pronunciation of words is concerned. His verbal emphasis on words and phrases signals the meaning of the text. However, his intonation and pacing could be improved. He does not pause long enough within sections of dialogue to signal the end of the speaker's words. Sometimes he runs from one sentence right into another. Interestingly enough, Griffin tends to slow down when he approaches a difficult word. In this case, he phrases more emphatically as though he is stressing the words to assist his own comprehen-

▶▶

A Second-Grade Running Record*

SC = Self-correction
O = Omitted the word
R = Repeated the word

Book Title: *Cam Jansen and the Mystery of the Stolen Diamonds*

Page 3: It was the first morning of spring vacation. Cam Jansen and her friend Eric Shelton were sitting on a bench in the middle of a busy shopping mall. While Eric's mother was shopping, they were watching Eric's baby brother, Howie. And they were playing a memory game.

Eric's eyes were closed.

"What color jacket am I wearing?" Cam asked.

"Blue."

"Wrong. I'm not wearing a jacket."

Page 4: Eric opened his eyes. "It's no use," he said. "I'll never have a memory like yours."

"You have to keep practicing," Cam told him. "Now try me."

Cam looked straight ahead. She said, "Click," and then closed her eyes. Cam always said, "Click" when she wanted to remember something. She said it was the sound her mental camera made when it took a picture.

Eric looked for something he could be sure Cam hadn't noticed. Then he asked, "What does the sign in the card store window say?"

"That's easy, 'Mother's Day Sunday May 11. Remember your mother and she'll remember you.'"

"You win," Eric said.

Cam still had her eyes closed. "Come on, ask me something else."

Cam had what people called a photographic memory.

Her mind took a picture

*For more on running records, see page 21.

Page 5:   of whatever she saw. Once, she forgot her notebook in school.

O

She did her homework problems—ten math problems—all from the

assessment/SC

picture of the assignment she had stored in her brain.

When Cam was younger, people called her Jennifer. That's her real

name. But

Page 6:   when they found out about her amazing memory, they started

O

calling her "The Camera." Soon "The Camera" was shortened to

"Cam."

R

"All right," Eric said. "What color socks am I wearing?"

for

Cam thought a moment. "That's not really fair," she said. "I never

saw your socks."

But Cam didn't open her eyes. "You're wearing green pants, a green

your

belt, and green sneakers," she said. "I'll bet your socks are green,

too."

"You're too much, Cam."

"No, you're too neat."

"It's my turn now," Eric said.

Eric look carefully at all the stores and people in the shopping mall.

He closed his eyes. But he quickly opened them again. Howie was

crying.

R

"What do we do now?" Cam asked. "Should I look for your

mother?"

Page 7:   Eric shook his head. "Let's wait. Maybe Howie will go back to

sleep."

O/SC

"But what if he doesn't?" Cam asked.

"Then I have to find out whether he wants to be held, fed, or

---

sion. Since he does this naturally when necessary, it probably would take only the teacher's suggestion to encourage him to use better intonation to improve his verbal performance.

Self-Monitoring and Self-Correcting Strategies

Griffin exhibits strong self-monitoring and self-correcting strategies. His few mistakes do not interrupt the flow of his reading, even when he goes back to self-correct. On page 3, he leaves out a word crucial to the meaning of the sentence, reading at first "Wrong. I'm wearing a … " instead of "Wrong. I'm not wearing a jacket." But he notices his mistake, whispering, "Wait a minute," and then retraces three lines back to reread that section of dialogue accurately. On page 4, Griffin is scanning ahead as he reads, slowing down as he approaches two unfamiliar words, *sound* and *mental*. He manages "sound" but at first reads the second word as "metal." He repeats the word twice, finally inserting the *n*.

(For more on Self-Monitoring and Self-Correcting Strategies, see page 150.)

Comprehension

Griffin clearly comprehends and retains what he is reading. When asked to summarize what has happened thus far, he first reminds the teacher that he has read only the first chapter. He then goes on to set the scene: It is spring vacation, the characters are at the shopping mall playing a memory game. One of the characters, Eric, always loses. Even though the text does not make it explicit, Griffin predicts that one of the characters in the illustration is a jewel thief. He even combines information from another part of the book, referring to a second illustration on the book jacket. He explains his prediction because the man is "pushing everybody aside so the owner can't catch him." He notes that Cam studies the thief and says, "Click," which reconnects the action to the beginning of the chapter.

(For more on Comprehension, see page 152.)

changed. I have everything I need right here." Eric patted the insu-

lated bag strapped to the front of the carriage.

Eric and Cam watched to see what Howie would do. He

squirmed, turned his head from side to side, and then went back to

sleep.

"Let's play another memory game," Cam said.

"Let's not. I'm tired of losing." Eric rocked the carriage. "Rocking

relaxes a baby," he told Cam.

Cam was an only child so she didn't know much about babies. Eric

was the oldest of four children. Besides Howie, who wasn't even a

year old, Eric had twin sisters who were seven.

Page 8:   Eric rocked the carriage gently while he and Cam talked about the

fifth-grade science fair. It was being held right after spring vacation.

Eric was making a sundial, and Cam was making a box camera.

Suddenly a loud bell rang. It woke Howie and he started to cry.

Cam jumped up on the bench. "It's Parker's Jewelry Store!" she

yelled. "Their alarm just went off."

Eric pulled at Cam's sneakers. "Get down from there."

"No, wait. Maybe something is happening."

Something *was* happening. A tall, heavy man with a mustache

and wearing a dark suit ran out of the jewelry store toward the cen-

ter of the mall. He was in a real hurry. He pushed people aside—

including Eric. Cam looked straight at the man and said, *"Click."*

(Word count: 631)

12 errors = 98% accuracy

Self-Monitoring and Self-Correcting Strategies

At second grade, self-monitoring should be a well-established habit, and all the strategies developed earlier should be used regularly and almost automatically. In addition, second graders' strategies should be more focused than before on comprehension and meaning of extended sequences of text. Readers' fluency continues to drop when harder texts require them to monitor overtly for accuracy and sense and to use strategies for solving reading problems and self-correcting.

By the end of the year, we expect second-grade students to:

◆ know when they don't understand a paragraph and search for clarification clues within the text; and

◆ examine the relationship between earlier and later parts of a text and figure out how they make sense together.

Second-Grade Reading Standard 1:
Print-Sound Code

Second-Grade Reading Standard 2:
Getting the Meaning

◆ Accuracy

◆ Fluency

◆ Self-Monitoring and Self-Correcting Strategies

◆ Comprehension

Second-Grade Reading Standard 3:
Reading Habits

◆ Independent and Assisted Reading

◆ Being Read To

◆ Discussing Books

◆ Vocabulary

Self-Monitoring

When students become adept at using self-monitoring strategies, their self-monitoring behaviors become less visible. Asking children to talk about the strategies they are using is a way to make self-monitoring more overt. However, children who have been taught specific ways to solve reading problems sometimes learn to talk about the methods without being able to actually apply them. It is, therefore, important to notice whether what students say they are doing matches what they do.

Jade

Daniella

Jeffrey

Reading Standard 2:
Getting the Meaning

Self-Monitoring and
Self-Correcting Strategies

Jade demonstrates a successful reading of *A Baby Sister for Frances*. She makes her only mistakes when the speed of her reading gets the best of her. On those occasions, she looks too far ahead in the text and speaks so swiftly that she sometimes misreads an article, such as "the" for *a,* or shortens the preposition *into* to "in." Jade shows signs of being able to read with dramatic inflection; however, the effect often is lost because she reads too quickly. To her credit, Jade notices when she needs to slow down, and she automatically falls back on self-correcting strategies. On one occasion, she stops, catches her breath and uses a strategy she probably does not need very often: trailing her finger over the words, pointing to each one as she says it. Jade is a strong reader, but she should be encouraged to slow down and enunciate each word clearly.

Daniella is reading a passage from *The Giant Jam Sandwich,* a book that is a little too difficult for her. With the rhyming and alliteration, it might be easy for her to slip over her mistake, but she does not. She self-corrects "slap and slap" to "slap and slam." When asked why, she describes quite articulately her own mental processes — citing a self-check that prompts her to return to the text and study the word more carefully, letter by letter. When she does that, she is able to see that she pronounced the letter *m* incorrectly as /*p*/. This type of backtracking in the text is the mark of a careful reader.

While reading *How Ants Live,* Jeffrey's attempt to sound out a word he is not familiar with is an excellent example of a self-monitoring strategy. The word is *cities,* and at first, he tries it with the hard /*c*/ sound. Finally, just as the teacher is about to help him, he says the word correctly. When asked to describe his efforts, Jeffrey explains that when one sound for the letter *c* did not make sense, he tried another. Once he tried saying *cities* with a soft *c,* he could tell that he was right because the word made sense in the text.

Comprehension

By the end of second grade, we expect children to demonstrate their comprehension of a variety of narrative, literary, functional and informational texts that they read independently or with a partner, as well as texts that adults read to them.

For books that they read independently, including functional and informational texts, we expect children at the end of second grade to be able to do all of the things we expected of them in first grade, both orally and in writing. In addition, we expect them to:

◆ recognize and be able to talk about organizing structures;

◆ combine information from two different parts of the text;

◆ infer cause-and-effect relationships that are not stated explicitly;

◆ compare the observations of the author to their own observations when reading nonfiction texts; and

◆ discuss how, why and what-if questions about nonfiction texts.

The texts that adults read to second graders usually have more complex conceptual and syntactic features than the texts the children read independently, and this permits greater depth in the kinds of comprehension children can display. For texts that are read to them, we expect children at the end of second grade to be able to do all of the things they can do for independently read texts. In addition, we expect them to:

◆ discuss or write about the themes of a book — what the "messages" of the book might be;

◆ trace characters and plots across multiple episodes, perhaps ones that are read on several successive days; and

◆ relate later parts of a story to earlier parts, in terms of themes, cause and effect, etc.

Rachel

Daniel

Samir

Reading Standard 2:
Getting the Meaning

Comprehension

◆ Recognize and be able to talk about organizing structures

Rachel clearly understands how to recognize, talk about and use the organizing structures of a text to her advantage. She explains that the table of contents is a guide to what information is in the book and that, furthermore, in nonfiction books like this "you can choose which one you want to read, you don't have to, like, just choose one, like straight down," and she gestures down the column of contents. Rachel trails her finger across the page, explaining that after selecting the chapter title, you find the page number: "Right across it has the number of the page, where it is." The teacher asks Rachel if she can find other chapters that cover a similar topic. She immediately turns back to the table of contents and uses the title clues to identify two promising chapters.

◆ Compare the observations of the author to their own observations when reading nonfiction texts

Daniel reads a page of text and then correctly recounts all the different habitats where frogs and toads might be found. Based on his own knowledge of the animals, he expresses surprise at what he reads: "It surprised me that they could survive in desert environments." When the teacher suggests he read on to find out more, he uses illustration clues to ascertain that they are on the right track. He points to a picture and explains, "Well, here it looks like a frog in the desert, so maybe we could find out there." He reads one sentence quite dramatically to stress his surprise: "The frogs swell with water, which they use to survive until the next rainfall; this might be years away."

◆ Discuss how, why and what-if questions about nonfiction texts

Samir reads *Turtle Nest* quite comfortably and then discusses the information he has gained. He knows that the giant turtle comes out of the sea to "lay babies," commenting more broadly that she does this to "make the family keep going." Samir knows from the text that the turtle lays eggs in the sand where they stay warm, and even though the opposite is not stated explicitly, he is able to make the inference that "if she kept it cold at night, they might not hatch." Samir remembers that when the eggs are hot, they grow, and "when they grow, they go out and start their life." When asked to make a general summary of what he has learned, Samir correctly notes that the book tells "how giant turtles live, and how they make their family, and how their babies start their life."

Second-Grade
Reading Standard 3: **Reading Habits**

Children in second grade read more complex books that are considerably longer than books read in first grade and that often have chapters. Because of the length and complexity of these texts, second graders often do not reread whole books in a single day. They must continue to read a lot — a longer book or several chapters per day — not only for the purpose of learning to read, but also for the sheer enjoyment of reading. They also should be reading to learn throughout the school day in all areas of the curriculum. Most of their reading should be done indepen-

dently or with assistance from a peer partner. Nonetheless, every day, students should have read to them worthwhile literature beyond their own reading range. Such books should show the language and craft of good writing. This develops vocabulary, more complex syntax and conceptual structure, new ideas, and author's craft.

Books second-grade students read or have read to them should cross a range of genres. It is especially important that they read all the genres they are writing (see Writing Standard 2: Writing Purposes and Resulting Genres). Knowledge of genres is needed to be a good reader and writer. Each genre carries expectations shared by the writer and the reader. Each genre has its typical patterns of organizational structure. Once students understand the characteristics of a genre, reading and writing in the genre become much easier.

By second grade, students should recognize and be able to discuss literary qualities of the children's literature they read. They should identify and talk (or write) about similarities in different books by the same author; differences in similar books by different authors; genre features; and the effects of author's craft, including word choice, plot, beginnings, endings and character development.

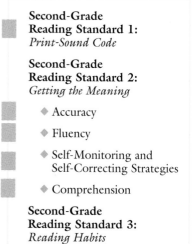

**Second-Grade
Reading Standard 1:**
Print-Sound Code

**Second-Grade
Reading Standard 2:**
Getting the Meaning

◆ Accuracy

◆ Fluency

◆ Self-Monitoring and Self-Correcting Strategies

◆ Comprehension

**Second-Grade
Reading Standard 3:**
Reading Habits

◆ Independent and Assisted Reading

◆ Being Read To

◆ Discussing Books

◆ Vocabulary

Independent and Assisted Reading

We expect second-grade students to:

◆ read one or two short books or long chapters every day and discuss what they read with another student or a group;

◆ read good children's literature every day;

◆ read multiple books by the same author and be able to discuss differences and similarities among these books;

◆ reread some favorite books or parts of longer books, gaining deeper comprehension and knowledge of author's craft;

◆ read narrative accounts, responses to literature (pieces written by other students, book blurbs and reviews), informational writing, reports, narrative procedures, recountings, memoirs, poetry, plays and other genres;

◆ read their own writing and the writing of their classmates, including pieces compiled in class books or placed on public display;

◆ read the functional and instructional messages they see in the classroom environment (for example, announcements, labels, instructions, menus and invitations) and some of those encountered outside school; and

◆ voluntarily read to each other, signaling their sense of themselves as readers.

Being Read To

In second grade, we expect all students, every day, to:

◆ have worthwhile literature read to them to model the language and craft of good writing; and

◆ listen to and discuss at least one text that is longer and more difficult than what they can read independently or with assistance.

Additionally, we expect students to:

◆ hear texts read aloud from a variety of genres; and

◆ use reading strategies explicitly modeled by adults in read-alouds and assisted reading.

What Books Should Second Graders Read?

Beyond leveled books, which are used for practice-reading, teaching, and testing for accuracy and fluency, second graders should read a variety of books and other print material.

Many excellent fiction and non-fiction books do not appear on any leveled text lists. Classroom libraries should include a wide range of classic and modern books that will satisfy readers with various reading abilities and interests. Second graders need books at their own reading levels to practice new skills and books above their reading levels to stretch and challenge them.

Second-grade classrooms also should include books that teachers can read aloud to the students. Most second graders will not be able to read the read-aloud books on their own, but they can under-stand and enjoy more advanced books — and they need to hear these books read aloud to learn new vocabulary and more sophisticated syntax.

There are many lists of recom-mended titles, including the Newbury and Caldecott Award winners, *The Read-Aloud Handbook* by Jim Trelease, *Books to Build on: A Grade-by-Grade Resource Guide for Parents and Teachers (Core Knowledge Series)* by E.D. Hirsch, and the *Elementary School Library Collection: A Guide to Books and Other Media.* The American Library Association also recommends titles.

Discussing Books

By second grade, children should discuss books daily in peer groups as well as in teacher-led groups. Their discussions are more extended and elaborate than earlier, and students are likely to challenge and argue with one another.

In classroom discussions of their reading, we expect students finishing second grade to be able to:

◆ demonstrate the skills we look for in the comprehension component of Reading Standard 2: Getting the Meaning;

◆ recognize genre features and compare works by different authors in the same genre;

◆ discuss recurring themes across works;

◆ paraphrase or summarize what another speaker has said and check whether the original speaker accepts the paraphrase;

◆ sometimes challenge another speaker on whether facts are accurate, including reference to the text;

◆ sometimes challenge another speaker on logic or inference;

◆ ask other speakers to provide supporting information or details; and

◆ politely correct someone who paraphrases or interprets their ideas incorrectly (for example, "That's not what I meant ... ").

**Second-Grade
Reading Standard 1:**
Print-Sound Code

**Second-Grade
Reading Standard 2:**
Getting the Meaning

◆ Accuracy

◆ Fluency

◆ Self-Monitoring and Self-Correcting Strategies

◆ Comprehension

**Second-Grade
Reading Standard 3:**
Reading Habits

◆ Independent and Assisted Reading

◆ Being Read To

◆ Discussing Books

◆ Vocabulary

Vocabulary

We expect second-grade students to:

◆ recognize when they don't know what a word means and use a variety of strategies for making sense of how it is used in the passage they are reading;

◆ talk about the meaning of some new words encountered in reading after they have finished reading and discussing a text;

◆ notice and show interest in understanding unfamiliar words in texts that are read to them;

◆ know how to talk about what nouns mean in terms of function (for example, "An apple is something you eat"), features (for example, "Some apples are red") and category (for example, "An apple is a kind of fruit"); and

◆ learn new words every day from their reading and talk.

**Susan Dillon's
Second-Grade Class**

Reading Standard 3:
Reading Habits

Discussing Books

After hearing one book by Chris Van Allsburg read aloud, the children in this class requested that the teacher read several more of his works to them. In this lesson, the teacher asks the children what they have come to expect in books by this author, and she charts their responses. As the segment begins, Alexa suggests, "Bizarre things happen. Like in, um, *The Wretched Stone*, um, they turn, they turn into apes and it's bizarre."

The teacher agrees, "That is bizarre. What does *bizarre* mean?"

Alexa responds, "Weird."

The teacher restates Alexa's point that weird and bizarre things happen in Van Allsburg's books, notes this on the chart, and says, "So, you think today's book might be a little bizarre. We'll see."

Next, referring to a comment made earlier in the class discussion, Eliza politely challenges the teacher and her classmates when she says, "When you said that we found Fritz [the dog] in every book, um, we didn't find him in *The Wretched Stone*."

Several classmates politely contradict her and say almost simultaneously, "Yes, we did. We found his tail."

The teacher acknowledges that it was very tricky to find the dog in this book and says, "Maybe later you can have Jeremy help you find him."

Continuing their discussion of recurring themes in Van Allsburg's work, another child says, "The book might be weird."

The teacher asks for support for this statement by asking, "Can you give me an example of something bizarre or weird that happened in one of the books that we read already?"

The student replies, "In *Jumanji* and *The Wretched Stone*. In *Jumanji*, when they, um, turn on the dice and when they turn on the, um, piece, then the thing written on them comes true."

Then the teacher asks, "What about the endings of a lot of these books?"

Branden responds, "They are not clear enough."

The teacher pushes for clarification of this idea by asking, "What do you mean they're not clear? You're confused? Or can you tell me more about what you mean?"

"Yeah, he doesn't say what happens," Branden says. "It doesn't say what happened at the end."

Daniel adds on to Branden's point: "They leave you with questions and thinking."

Alexa, Eliza, Branden and Daniel show expertise in discussing books. In this discussion, they each identified a recurring theme they have come to expect in the works of Chris Van

Allsburg and cited evidence from the texts for their opinions. In addition to expecting bizarre and weird things to occur, they noted that this author always leaves his readers thinking and asking questions. This performance also shows Eliza politely challenging the teacher and her classmates about the accuracy of a statement made during the discussion. The children politely contradict her and offer to prove their point at another time by referring to the illustrations.   ▶▶

Hannah Schneewind and Second-Grade Class

Reading Standard 3:
Reading Habits

Discussing Books
◆ Discuss recurring themes across works

In this video performance, the teacher recaps what the class has read thus far and then continues a discussion of the book *The Hundred Dresses*. In the last part of the reading, a lonely child leans dejectedly against a wall in the schoolyard. The students discuss how this familiar theme appears in other books they have read. Debra compares Wanda from *The Hundred Dresses* to Patricia Polacco from *Thank You, Mr. Falker*. She says, "I think [Wanda], umm, feels like, umm … Patricia Polacco felt in *Thank You, Mr. Falker*." When the teacher asks her to say more, Debra explains that Wanda appears to experience a feeling similar to that of Patricia who "felt dumb because everybody in her class could read and she couldn't."

Her classmate Jose says, "I agree with Debra, and I want to add on because I remember on the part when, umm, that big kid was bothering her in the playground … and she used to go in the bathroom like in that little place and, umm, um, I wonder if [the character in current reading] is going to try hiding somewhere."

Read-Aloud Books

Ancona, George, *The Piñata Maker/ El Piñatero*

Araujo, Frank P., *The Perfect Orange: A Tale from Ethiopia*

Asch, Frank, *Pearl's Promise*

Banks, Lynne Reid, *The Indian in the Cupboard*

Castañeda, Omar S., *Abuela's Weave*

Estes, Eleanor, *The Hundred Dresses*

Gray, Libba Moore, *My Mama Had a Dancing Heart*

Hong, Lily Toy, *Two of Everything*

Hopkins, Lee Bennett, *Side by Side: Poems to Read Together*

Kline, Suzy, *Song Lee in Room 2B*

Lord, Bette Bao, *In the Year of the Boar and Jackie Robinson*

MacLachlan, Patricia, *All the Places to Love*

McCloskey, Robert, *Homer Price*

Parish, Peggy, *Amelia Bedelia*

Polacco, Patricia, *Mrs. Katz and Tush*

Polacco, Patricia, *Thank You, Mr. Falker*

Ringgold, Faith, *Tar Beach*

Sachar, Louis, *Sideways Stories from Wayside School*

Smith, Robert Kimmel, *Chocolate Fever*

Soto, Gary, *Too Many Tamales*

Uchida, Yoshiko, *The Bracelet*

Van Allsburg, Chris, *Jumanji*

Van Allsburg, Chris, *The Wretched Stone*

White, E.B., *The Trumpet of the Swan*

Level L Texts

Bantam Doubleday Dell Books, Yearling Books, Giff, *The Powder Puff Puzzle*

Bantam Doubleday Dell Books, Yearling Books, Giff, *The Secret at the Polk Street School*

Crabtree Publishing Company, Crabapples, Kalman, *Wings, Wheels, & Sails*

HarperTrophy, Hoban, *A Baby Sister for Frances*

Penguin Group, Puffin Books, Adler, *Cam Jansen and the Mystery of the Monster Movie*

Penguin Group, Puffin Books, Adler, *Cam Jansen and the Mystery of the Stolen Diamonds*

Random House, Knopf Paperbacks, Cameron, *More Stories Julian Tells*

Random House, Knopf Paperback, Cameron, *The Stories Julian Tells*

Richard C. Owen Publishers, Books for Young Learners, Schaefer, *Turtle Nest*

Rigby, Literacy 2000, Murdoch and Ray, *It's a Frog's Life*

Scholastic, Cartwheel Books, Hutchings, *Picking Apples and Pumpkins*

Scholastic, Marzollo, *Happy Birthday Martin Luther King*

Troll Associates, Troll First-Start Biography, Farrell, *Young Jackie Robinson: Baseball Hero*

William Morrow & Co., Thayer, *The Puppy Who Wanted a Boy*

A Level L Text

Eric opened his eyes. "It's no use," he said. "I'll never have a memory like yours."

"You have to keep practicing," Cam told him. "Now try me."

Cam looked straight ahead. She said, *"Click,"* and then closed her eyes. Cam always said, *"Click,"* when she wanted to remember something. She said it was the sound her mental camera made when it took a picture.

Eric looked for something he could be sure Cam hadn't noticed. Then he asked, "What does the sign in the card store window say?"

"That's easy. 'Mother's Day Sunday May 11. Remember your mother and she'll remember you.'"

"You win," Eric said.

Cam still had her eyes closed. "Come on, ask me something else."

Cam had what people called a photographic memory. Her mind took a picture

4

of whatever she saw. Once, she forgot her notebook in school. She did her homework—ten math problems—all from the picture of the assignment she had stored in her brain.

When Cam was younger, people called her Jennifer. That's her real name. But

5

Second-Grade
Writing Standard 1: **Habits and Processes**

If second graders are to develop the expected levels of proficiency as writers, their daily writing habits must continue and expand. They need large blocks of time for writing so they can sustain their work longer, say more and provide more detail than they have in the past.

Working independently, second-grade children who are meeting standards make plans for their writing. They use specific criteria to decide what to write about — what is important to them, what they know something about, what will yield a good product, what will reach the audience. They make decisions about which pieces they will work on over several days and often revisit topics. They reread their writing, get help from their teachers or peers, and revise and adjust to make their writing understandable to their audience. They develop a sense of what counts as good writing by engaging in discussions about favorite books and favorite authors. They write for a growing variety of purposes and audiences and have an expanding range of sources from which they can learn more about the topics they choose. They understand there are choices about how to write about a topic, and they are able to select a genre, develop an angle or conjure a vision to frame their writing.

Second-grade students frequently keep notebooks in which they record favorite lines of poetry or prose, scenes from their day-to-day lives, ideas to develop into writing, phrases of conversation that are worth remembering, and other sources they can draw upon as writers. Students can use these notes as resource materials to develop their own texts.

We expect second-grade students to:

◆ write daily;

◆ generate their own topics and make decisions about which pieces to work on over several days or longer;

◆ extend pieces of writing by, for example, turning a narrative into a poem or a short description into a long report;

◆ regularly solicit and provide useful feedback;

◆ routinely reread, revise, edit and proofread their work;

◆ take on strategies and elements of author's craft that the class has discussed in their study of literary works;

◆ apply commonly agreed-upon criteria and their own judgment to assess the quality of their own work; and

◆ polish at least 10 pieces throughout the year.

Second-Grade
Writing Standard 1:
Habits and Processes

**Second-Grade
Writing Standard 2:**
*Writing Purposes and
Resulting Genres*

◆ Sharing Events, Telling Stories: Narrative Writing

◆ Informing Others: Report or Informational Writing

◆ Getting Things Done: Functional and Procedural Writing

◆ Producing and Responding to Literature

**Second-Grade
Writing Standard 3:**
*Language Use and
Conventions*

◆ Style and Syntax

◆ Vocabulary and Word Choice

◆ Spelling

◆ Punctuation, Capitalization and Other Conventions

"i Like"

Writing Standard 1:
Habits and Processes

Nora's writing sample is drawn from a collection of her second-grade work. A review of the collection reveals that Nora wrote daily, that she took responsibility for generating topics, that she willingly went back into a piece to make revisions (these often came out of response groups), and that she refined and edited (sometimes illustrating) her work. The complete collection provides evidence of Nora's meeting the second-grade standard for Writing Habits and Processes.

The first piece, done in September, is a basic list of what Nora likes and loves. The writing is justified to the left margin and is made up entirely of one-clause units. Of the six ideas expressed, five of them are made up of only three words — two in which the subject and predicate are the same. This pattern is fairly typical of first-grade writing and is familiar to readers of easy books. Most of the words are spelled correctly. The last idea breaks the pattern. The clause begins with a qualifying phrase ("And mostasl"), and the verb changes from "Like" to "Love." This modification in the wording of the last idea is very common in books written for emergent readers, and it is, therefore, possible to infer that Nora modeled her writing on these early books.

(For more of Nora's collection, see page 251.)

*Translation of phonetically spelled words

Second-Grade
Writing Standard 2: Writing Purposes and Resulting Genres

For second graders who are progressing according to standards, writing has become a meaningful activity with myriad purposes. More than ever, these children write to communicate with other people, to learn new things and to give evidence of their understanding. By the time they leave second grade, they have experimented with and produced many kinds of writing, including narrative account, response to literature, report and narrative procedure.

Sharing Events, Telling Stories: Narrative Writing

By the end of the year, second-grade writers should move beyond simply describing a sequence of events. The structures for extended pieces may be built around a cluster of memorable events (episodic memoirs), around problems and solutions, or around a central idea or a theme running through events. Second graders should be able to set the action of a narrative in a context that could include setting, relationships among characters, motives and moods — perhaps beginning with a classic story opening (for example, "Once there was a girl ... " or "It was a dark, dark night when ... "). Second graders should begin to use strategies for building pace and tension, such as giving more attention to some events than others, summarizing or skipping some events, and creating anticipation.

By the end of the year, we expect second-grade students to produce fictional and auto-biographical narratives in which they:

◆ incorporate some literary or "writing" language that does not sound like speech (for example, "Slowly, slowly he turned," "For days and weeks and months, I've worked for this moment");

◆ create a believable world and introduce characters, rather than simply recount a chronology of events, using specific details about characters and settings and developing motives and moods;

◆ develop internal events as well as external ones (for example, the child may tell not only what happened to a character but also what the character wondered, remembered and hoped);

◆ write in first and third person; and

◆ use a variety of writing strategies such as dialogue, transitional phrases, time cue words, etc.

"A New Teacher"

Writing Standard 2:
Writing Purposes and Resulting Genres

Narrative Writing

Bryan, the writer of this piece, produces a fairly mature story line, one with a strong message. The story is one of moral choice and perhaps was inspired by other stories built around such choices that are common in children's literature. Although the piece lacks some detail, it is typical of certain kinds of writing in which detail is not essential to the author's purpose — for example, fables. This sample meets the standard for narrative writing for second grade.

◆ Bryan develops a context for the story by introducing the central character and the one thing that is important to know about her initially: As a girl she wanted to be a teacher and when she grew up she still wanted to be one. This characteristic is the piece of information on which the whole story hangs.

◆ Bryan layers our understanding about Judy through events in the story. She procrastinates ("She didn't study"), she worries ("What will I do?"") and she resists the devil's suggestion (she believes in fairness even though her resistance may prevent her from achieving the one thing the writer has told us is important to her: becoming a teacher).

◆ Judy's emotions are not specified explicitly, but rather they are suggested by internal dialogue ("'What will I do?'") and by descriptions of facial expressions ("as she smiled" [happiness]).

◆ The dialogue, though predictable, advances the story line. ▶▶

A New Teacher

Once there was a girl named Judy. She wanted to be a techer. She grew and she still wanted to be a techer.

*teacher

"O.K.," said Mrs. Carter.

"But you have to take a test."

"O.K.," said Judy. Later it was all most time for the test. She didn't study so she said,

*almost

"What will I do?"

It was night and Judy dremed about the test.

*dreamed

She was asleep and a little

*Translation of phonetically spelled words

Writing Standard 3:
Language Use and Conventions

This piece does not meet the Language Use and Conventions Standard for second grade.

The number of spelling errors is not acceptable in an edited piece. The syntax, too, is less than what we would expect of second-grade writers. Most of the sentences are quite short, so when read aloud, the writing seems choppy. The vocabulary and word choice are adequate to tell the story, but that is all. The punctuation, however, is particularly good for second grade.

(For more on Language Use and Conventions, see page 182.)

angel came. The angel said, "You can't chete. [cheat] It's not fair." Then came the devil. He said, "Chete!" [cheat] Judy said, "NO!" This was the real test and Judy past it. [passed] The next day Mrs. Carter said, "Tomorrow you will be a techer." [teacher] "O.K.," said Judy as she smiled.
She became Mrs. Martin, the best new techer of the hole world! [whole]
Author: Bryan

"My favorite rainy day"

Writing Standard 2:
**Writing Purposes and
Resulting Genres**

Narrative Writing

Shannon's writing sample is a fine example of a young writer's internalization of narrative writing. She clearly controls a number of the elements of narrative writing. She recounts a chronology of events, introduces characters who act realistically, uses details effectively to describe a setting, and conveys to the reader both motives and moods of the characters. This piece represents narrative writing that meets the standard for second grade.

◆ Shannon not only recounts a chronology of events ("One morning I woke up"), but she also switches to an antecedent action ("My dad said he woke up around midnight") and then returns to the time of action that is maintained by revealing the time of events ("At about 10:00").

◆ Shannon introduces characters who act realistically: The father goes to the store for flashlights; Cassie eats "one whole hotdog!"; the mother makes a fire and takes the children for a walk; Ted uses his headphones to tell the news to Shannon and her family.

◆ The setting is described using effective details ("woke up around midnight," "it was pouring," "two red flashlights," "sat in the recliner and did math by the light of the fire," "tree had fallen down

My favorite rainy day
One morning I woke up
and it was raining and the
power was out. My dad said
he woke up around midnight
and the clock was off the
went out to the living room
and relized the electricity
*realized
was out and that it was pouring
outside. We had know light at
no

*Translation of phonetically spelled words

because of all the wind" and "cheered and danced").

◆ Shannon clearly conveys motives and moods by indicating the parents' roles (the father wakes at midnight, and the mother makes a fire) and implying the sister's enjoyment of unusual circumstances (she eats more than usual).

◆ Shannon consistently uses the first person.

◆ She effectively shows indirect dialogue and attempts to use direct dialogue, though it is unpunctuated ("What an exciting day I said").

◆ She documents the chronology by naming clock times and using transition words.

◆ Shannon anticipates the reader's questions by including statements clearly explaining specific details ("The reizen why his head phones still worked was because it ran on bateries"). ▶▶

New Standards

Writing Standard 3:
Language Use and Conventions

This piece meets the Language Use and Conventions Standard for second grade.

Style and Syntax

While Shannon uses sentence patterns typical of spoken language including the use of "and" to string clauses together, she also incorporates literary language ("One morning I woke" and "The rest of the day we read, wrote and did things that didn't use eletricity").

Vocabulary and Word Choice

She uses words from her speaking vocabulary ("I was done with it" and "The reizen why") while using language specific to the story ("electricity," "flashlights" and "recliner").

Spelling

The piece contains a high proportion of correctly spelled high- and low-frequency words. She uses a discernible logic to guide the spelling of unfamiliar words such as "relized," "bateries" and "noiticed."

Punctuation, Capitalization and Other Conventions

Shannon uses capital letters at the beginning of most sentences, places periods at the ends and uses an exclamation mark for emphasis. She also demonstrates correct punctuation of clock times and contractions.

(For more on Language Use and Conventions, see page 182.)

> all because we had know [no]
> flashlights and the sun hadn't
> came up yet. Then my mom
> made a fire and my dad
> went to the store and bought
> two red flashlights. At about
> 10:00 I read my chapter book
> by 11:00 I was done with it.
> Between 11:00 and 11:30 I sat
> in the recliner and did math
> by the light of the fire. At 12:00
> we had hotdogs we cooked
> them in the fire place and
> Shannon

Cassie ate one whole hotdog!
She usally only eat one half.
usually
Nicole wasn't born yet. The
rest of the day we read, wrote
and did things that didn't use
eletricity soon it stoped raining
electricity _stopped_
but the eletricity was not
electricity
back yet. So my mom took us
out for a walk and we saw
Ted our neighborHe had a
pair of head phones.The reizen
headphones _reason_
why his head phones still worked
headphones _batteries_
was because it ran on bateries
Shannon

He told us what was on the
news and weather.When we
went down the sidewalk
we noitced that a tree had
noticed
fallen down.because of all
the wind.Later that evening
around 6:00 the power came
back.We all cheered and danced
around.We were so happy the
power was back.Right away I
terned on the T.V.What an exciting
turned
day I said.

Informing Others: Report or Informational Writing

Second graders write reports on a variety of subjects that are familiar from their day-to-day lives or because they have studied them in school. Their reports, then, are drawn both from their personal knowledge (for example, "My brother…") and from research (for example, "Planets") and are frequently accompanied by diagrams, charts or illustrations. Organization is maintained most often by the use of headers, a strategy borrowed from chapter books. Second graders develop their reports through a recital of facts accompanied by detail. There is generally a concluding sentence or section.

By the end of the year, we expect second-grade students to produce reports that:

◆ have an obvious organizational structure (often patterned after chapter book headings);

◆ communicate big ideas, insights or theories that have been elaborated on or illustrated through facts, details, quotations, statistics and information;

◆ usually have a concluding sentence or section; and

◆ use diagrams, charts or illustrations as appropriate to the text.

"Bottlenose Dolphins"

Writing Standard 2:
**Writing Purposes and
Resulting Genres**

Report or Informational Writing

Amanda's sample effectively combines factual material gained from outside sources and information and opinions gained from personal experience. It displays her clear understanding of the report genre. It meets the standard for report writing for second grade.

◆ The piece demonstrates appropriate organizational structure by presenting similar information together, so the reader can easily understand the information.

◆ Amanda uses both pictures and a chart appropriate to the text.

◆ She uses facts with very specific details to develop the topic ("Its habitat is salt water," "found in coastal waters," "eat up to four pounds of fish a day," etc.).

◆ The ending is a personal experience with dolphins, which she uses to round out and humanize the report.   ▶▶

Amanda

Bottlenose dolphins

Its habitat is salt water. Dolphins are found in coastal waters around the world. Dolphins eat up to four pounds of fish a day. They eat inshore fish like capelin, anchovy, salmon, and shrimp. Dolphins can eat 6 feet under water and can stay down for 15 minutes.

Dolphins can live up to 50 years. Its coat is smooth and like rubber. A dolphin is a mammal.

When dolphins sleep, the female sleeps on top of the water and the male sleeps on the bottom. When the male needs air, it goes up to the top the water to get it and then it goes back down.

Some people let balloons go and they go into the ocean. Dolphins think it is food and eat it and can die. Other pollution like gas and soda cans can hurt dolphins. When a dolphin is sick it cries to get help from other dolphins who try to help it to the top so it can breathe. We can help dolphins by not polluting the ocean.

When I was in Hawaii, I swam with the dolphins. I fed them squid. The grossest part was when I had to feed them because there were dead squid and we had to hold them. I think what was neat about swimming with the dolphins was when we got to race with the them. Guess who won? The dolphins did. What was cool about it was when three dolphins at a time came out of the water and jumped up. Dolphins like to play in the ocean.

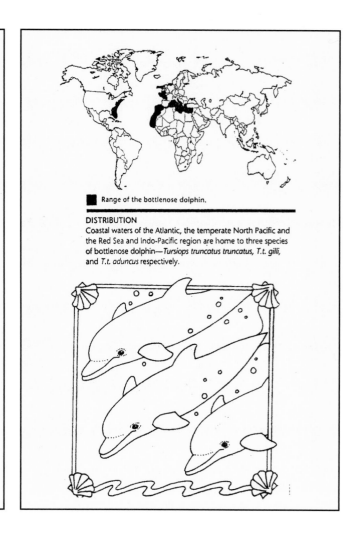

■ Range of the bottlenose dolphin.

DISTRIBUTION
Coastal waters of the Atlantic, the temperate North Pacific and the Red Sea and Indo-Pacific region are home to three species of bottlenose dolphin—*Tursiops truncatus truncatus, T.t. gilli,* and *T.t. aduncus* respectively.

Writing Standard 3:
Language Use and Conventions

This piece meets the Language Use and Conventions Standard for second grade.

Style and Syntax

Amanda relies on title, title page and book format to introduce the topic. She seems to organize the information section (paragraphs 1–4) somewhat arbitrarily but gears the personal section (final paragraph) toward conveying information important to her. In both the factual and the personal sections, she uses complex sentence structures.

Vocabulary and Word Choice

Amanda uses language specific to the topic ("Bottlenose dolphins," "habitat," "coastal waters," "mammal" and "pollution"). Amanda has widened her writing vocabulary by using these words, which she found while gathering information from outside sources.

Spelling

Since this report is the result of an obvious process that includes revision, the final copy contains correctly spelled words.

Punctuation, Capitalization and Other Conventions

This sample shows Amanda's ability to consistently use periods at the ends of declarative sentences and to employ commas to denote items in a series and after introductory clauses. She correctly capitalizes both at the beginning of sentences and in place names.

(For more on Language Use and Conventions, see page 182.)

"Our class room Doves"

Writing Standard 2:
Writing Purposes and Resulting Genres

Report or Informational Writing

This piece of work is an informational report that has been formatted as a brochure. The purpose is to inform classroom visitors about two doves that are class pets. Because it is about two specific doves and their care, there is no generic information about doves as a type of bird. The tone is friendly and straightforward, and the writer has anticipated questions a visitor might ask. The writing meets the standard for second-grade reports.

- The writing is well organized. It is laid out as a trifold and then broken out into three major headings ("OUR CLASSROOM DOVES," "CARING FOR THE DOVES" and "BABY DOVES").

- The writer mixes observation ("They make strange noises") with fact ("It takes the eggs 14 days to hatch"). There is also much detail in this report: the names of the two doves, how much food they are given and why that precise amount, who cleans the doves' cage and how often, which dove sits on the eggs and which does the feeding, when the babies are given

OUR CLASSROOM DOVES

We have two adult white doves. The girl's name is Ruby and the boy's name is Prince. They make strange noises. So if you hear something, don't be afraid, it's probably just the doves.

CARING FOR THE DOVES

The person in charge of the pets makes sure the doves have a half a bowl of dove seeds and a half a bowl of water every day. Do you want to know why we give them a half a bowl? They sling their food everywhere, and if they only have half a bowl, they don't make as big of a mess. However, on the week-end, we give them a full bowl of food and water so they won't run out.

The person in charge of the pets also has to make sure the dove's cage is clean. The paper at the bottom of the cage must be changed daily or it will become real hard to clean and it gets really stinky!! This is a messy job, but someone has to do it!!

BABY DOVES

The momma bird lays eggs. The momma and daddy take turns sitting on it and keeping it warm so it will hatch. It takes the eggs 14 days to hatch. The parents also take turns feeding the babies. When the babies are five weeks old we give them away. Usually the momma bird has started laying new eggs before we give the babies away!

away, and when the next cycle of egg-laying begins.

- The text is illustrated nicely with drawings of the two doves.

- Although there is no formal ending to the brochure as a whole, each section does end naturally.

Writing Standard 3:
Language Use and Conventions

This piece meets the Language Use and Conventions Standard for second grade.

Style and Syntax

The style of this piece is straightforward and informative. The writing exhibits a range of syntactic patterns, and there is even a rhetorical question to keep the reader engaged. Stylistically, the piece mirrors the kind of brochure writing aimed at elementary school students, though clearly a second grader is doing the writing.

Vocabulary and Word Choice

This piece contains words typical of a second-grade vocabulary. Some of the words are more appropriate to oral language than to written language ("stinky" and "momma and daddy"), but the overall use of language is quite good. Notice the precise verb "sling." This is not a piece of writing that encourages a technical vocabulary because its purpose is to inform and explain. Therefore, the writing, by necessity, avoids complicated wording.

Spelling

The piece has been edited and published, so there are no spelling errors.

Punctuation, Capitalization and Other Conventions

The piece has been edited and published, so the few errors that do exist are beyond expectations of second-grade students.

(For more on Language Use and Conventions see page 182.)

Getting Things Done: Functional and Procedural Writing

In the real world, words have the power to alter the course of events. As children grow older and more experienced, they come to understand author's craft and use language with enormous care, explicitness and empathy, so their words help readers do what the authors want them to do. Whether children are writing directions to their house, a recipe for a birthday cake, the procedures to recreate a scientific experiment or the steps toward creating special effects on a computer, the writing and thinking challenges children face are similar.

By the end of the year, we expect second-grade students to produce narrative procedures that:

◆ establish a context for the piece;

◆ identify the topic;

◆ show the steps in an action in enough detail to follow them;

◆ include relevant information;

◆ use language that is straightforward and clear; and

◆ frequently use pictures to illustrate steps in the procedure.

Second-Grade Writing Standard 1:
Habits and Processes

Second-Grade Writing Standard 2:
Writing Purposes and Resulting Genres

◆ Sharing Events, Telling Stories: Narrative Writing

◆ Informing Others: Report or Informational Writing

◆ Getting Things Done: Functional and Procedural Writing

◆ Producing and Responding to Literature

Second-Grade Writing Standard 3:
Language Use and Conventions

◆ Style and Syntax

◆ Vocabulary and Word Choice

◆ Spelling

◆ Punctuation, Capitalization and Other Conventions

"HOW TO CARVE A JACK-O-LANTERN"

Writing Standard 2:
Writing Purposes and Resulting Genres

Functional and Procedural Writing

This is a good example of a child's ability to produce a narrative procedure. It provides a reader with a clear sense of the steps involved in carving a jack-o'-lantern. It represents functional writing that meets the standard for second grade. (To see this same topic treated adequately by students at other grade levels, see page 279.)

◆ Ginny establishes a context for the piece ("One day after school") and sets a narrative frame for the procedure ("I went to the supermarket to buy a pumkin").

◆ After identifying the topic in the title, Ginny shows the steps in the procedure by using clear, straightforward details ("big ones and little ones," "skiny ones and fat ones," "dug the seeds out," "two2 triagels") and appropriate transition words and phrases ("So," "When I got home," "After," "Then" and "Next").

◆ The piece has an implied closure in the final step: the lighting of the candle in the pumpkin.

Writing Standard 3:

Language Use and Conventions

This piece meets the Language Use and Conventions Standard for second grade.

Style and Syntax

Ginny uses sentences that are direct and explanatory, typical of procedural writing. Sentence patterns are typical of literary language ("They had big ones and little ones they had skinny ones and fat ones") as well as of oral language.

Vocabulary and Word Choice

Ginny makes word choices that show a vocabulary large enough to exercise options ("supermarket" instead of *store*, "triagels" instead of *holes*). She uses words for numbers as well as showing the number ("two2 triagels") and uses shapes ("triagels," "squer," "banana" and "zigzags") to describe the pumpkin face.

Spelling

Ginny correctly spells most words, especially high-frequency words. She also uses logic to spell unfamiliar words, writing "pumkin," an accurate reproduction of the way many people pronounce the word *pumpkin*.

Punctuation, Capitalization and Other Conventions

Ginny uses periods at the end of sentences and capitalizes correctly, beginning all sentences with a capital letter and consistently capitalizing the personal pronoun *I*.

(For more on Language Use and Conventions, see page 182.)

HOW TO CARVE A JACK-O-LANTERN

One day after school I went to the supermarket to buy a pumkin. They had big ones and *pumpkin
little ones they had skiny ones and fat ones. I did not know skinny
wich one to get. So I got which
the the big and fat one. When I got home I got a knife and cut the top off. After I cut off the top

I got a pan and dug the seeds out of the pumkin pumpkin
and put them in the pan. Then I got a pencil and drew two2 triagels for the triangles
eyes and a squer for the square
nose. And a banana for the mouth and five5 zigzags for the teeth. Next I cut them all out and put the candle in the middle of the pumkin and lit the candle. pumpkin

*Translation of phonetically spelled words

Toni

How to Publish a Story. If you want to Publish
a book hears how. First start with Prewriting talk to
*here's
a neighbor ore look in the back of you folder.
or   /your
Next Draft get your pencil and start writing you
/your
story. Then go to Responese Group and listen carefully
Response
so that you wantsay somthing else thats not in the
won't   something   that's
story. Next go to Revise you use a blue pencil to
do that you circle words you think that iu uncor
incorrectly
elly and cross out some of the words that you have
in there so many times. And add more to it. Then

*Translation of phonetically spelled words

"How to Publish a Story"

Writing Standard 2:
Writing Purposes and Resulting Genres

Functional and Procedural Writing

In this piece of functional writing, Toni provides a very thoughtful description of the writing process from prewriting through publishing. She clearly understands the different steps and describes each of them — if somewhat generally — for the reader. Some of the directions are almost elliptical ("First start with Prewriting talk to a neighbor ore look in the back of you folder"). Presumably, the neighbor or the back of the folder would provide help to Toni on generating ideas for writing.

This degree of generality, no doubt, comes from her assumptions about the reader's familiarity with classroom rules about the writing process. Such assumptions about the reader's knowledge are common throughout what is otherwise a very informative piece. The writing meets the standard for a narrative procedure in second grade.

◆ Toni begins with a title and then a conversational "If you want to Publish a book hears how."

◆ She names and capitalizes all the steps of the process, and she uses transition words to lead the reader from one to the next. She describes some of the steps more fully than others. For example, to draft, she tells the reader to get a pencil and "start writing you story." On the other hand, she gives a good deal of precise information about how to revise ("use a blue pencil" and "circle words you think that iu

go to the Edit table and you trade your papers with
your partner you check you partners paper and they
　　　　　　　　　　　　your　partners
check your's and you sighn your name at the top and
　　　yours　　　　　sign
go to the teacher she says you have done a good
job and she sighn her name at the top. Finally you
　　　　　signs
may Publish your book get the half sheet of papper
　　　　　　　　　　　　　　　　　　　　　　　paper
and start copying one of you ruff Drafts and after
　　　　　　　　　　　　　　rough
you finish every page write the number and if you
had done the hole book right and had looked
have　　　　whole　　　　　　　　　have
at the Publish sheet you will be ready to staple.

uncorrelly and cross out some of the words that you have in there so many times").

◆ All the information is relevant to this seven-step process and is articulated in straightforward language.

Writing Standard 3:
Language Use and Conventions

This piece does not meet the Language Use and Conventions Standard for second grade because of problems with capitalization and end punctuation. However, it does have some notable features.

This piece contains a variety of sentence structures, but the sentences are not always coherent. Toni tries to embed the names of the steps ("Draft") but does not manage to find a way to both announce the step and describe it. She links sentences by transitions, which carry the reader through the piece, a strategy common to this genre.

Her vocabulary is typical of second-grade oral language. She names each stage of the writing process, and she demonstrates familiarity with language associated with the process ("ruff Drafts").

The spelling is somewhat uneven ("sighn," "papper"). She misuses several words ("hears" for *here's* and "ruff" for *rough*), but these are errors in usage, not in spelling. Toni almost consistently controls for capital letters at the beginning of all other sentences and for end punctuation. However, as she moves through each of the steps ("Prewriting," "Revise"), she has difficulty naming each step (which she capitalizes) and then attaching that particular step to a sentence unit.

(For more on Language Use and Conventions, see page 182.)

Producing and Responding to Literature

Second-grade students produce and respond to the literature they are reading or that they hear read. They write in the genre of texts they read, and they write about texts also. They write about books, elaborating on various aspects that interest them. As part of their genre studies, they read and write in particular genres. They understand the range and possibilities of literary genres. Over time, they can give examples of poetry, memoirs, letters, songs, brochures and other specific kinds of writing. They discuss what they see in these forms and can show their grasp of the forms by reproducing them in their own writing. When they respond to literature, they mark text they find notable (perhaps using Post-it Notes™) and comment on their ideas in class discussions. They can see a bigger idea or theme at work and collect evidence of that theme.

Producing literature

By the end of the year, we expect second-grade students to:

◆ write stories, poems, memoirs, songs and dramas — conforming to appropriate expectations for each form;

◆ write a story using styles learned from studying authors and genres; and

◆ write poetry using techniques they observe through a study of the genre.

Responding to literature

By the end of the year, we expect second-grade students to:

◆ provide a retelling;

◆ write letters to the author, telling what they thought or asking questions;

◆ make a plausible claim about what they have read (for example, suggesting a big idea or theme and offering evidence from the text);

◆ write variations on texts they have read, telling the story from a new point of view, putting in a new setting, altering a crucial character or rewriting the ending; and

◆ make connections between the text and their own ideas and lives.

Second-Grade Writing Standard 1:
Habits and Processes

Second-Grade Writing Standard 2:
Writing Purposes and Resulting Genres

◆ Sharing Events, Telling Stories: Narrative Writing

◆ Informing Others: Report or Informational Writing

◆ Getting Things Done: Functional and Procedural Writing

◆ Producing and Responding to Literature

Second-Grade Writing Standard 3:
Language Use and Conventions

◆ Style and Syntax

◆ Vocabulary and Word Choice

◆ Spelling

◆ Punctuation, Capitalization and Other Conventions

"Necklace or Sky"

Writing Standard 2:
Writing Purposes and Resulting Genres

Producing Literature

Stella's sample is an excellent example of a child's ability to produce literature that fulfills a reader's expectations for poetry. It provides evidence that she can develop a sense of metaphor and sustain a comparison to a degree that is impressive for a second grader. The piece clearly meets the standard for producing literature for second grade.

◆ The sample develops a description of the sky, comparing it to a necklace and consistently maintaining the imagery.

◆ The sample uses poetic techniques Stella may have observed in descriptive poems and employs a striking metaphor ("The Sun is a gold ball hanging … ").

Writing Standard 3:
Language Use and Conventions

This piece meets the Language Use and Conventions Standard for second grade.

Style and Syntax

Stella employs four descriptive, declarative sentences. Additionally, she uses an introductory prepositional phrase followed by a "there is" construction ("In the gold ball there is a blue stone"). She effectively begins one sentence with "And" ("And the blue stone is made of the sky itself"), much in the manner of many poets.

Vocabulary and Word Choice

Stella uses effective word choices to convey meaning (clouds like "links" in a chain, clouds as "Soft" and cottony). She also selects words that reveal a vocabulary large enough to create imagery that is particularly effective ("chain of soft cotton links").

Spelling

She correctly spells all words used in this piece.

Punctuation, Capitalization and Other Conventions

She begins all sentences with a capital letter and uses periods at the end of all sentences. Additionally, she separates "soft cotton clouds" from the rest of the sentence by using a comma. Such use of punctuation suggests that Stella understands the function of commas in poetry is to facilitate reading, underscore meaning and set up repetition.

(For more on Language Use and Conventions, see page 182.)

> Necklace or Sky
>
> The Sun is a gold ball hanging from a chain of soft cotton links. The links are made of clouds, soft cotton clouds. In the gold ball there is a blue stone. And the blue stone is made of the sky itself.
>
> By
>
> Stella
>
> 2nd grade

"Today I whent to Thathers"

Writing Standard 2:
Writing Purposes and Resulting Genres

Producing Literature

This piece of expressive text was an entry in Miles' notebook. It is a fine piece of writing and demonstrates his attention to detail ("windows and PeeP holes with Small stiks For window sills"), his syntactic maturity ("we started to Bild Stik aFterstiK") and his remarkable ability to step back from the text and reflect on the significance of the event he is writing about ("Butwe rillY bilt a frendshiP"). This piece meets the standard for a piece of literature produced at second grade.

◆ The piece seemingly is a straight-forward account of two boys who are building a shelter.

◆ The piece begins with an initiating event ("I whent to Thathers") and a reaction ("I had a grat time"). Then Miles details building the shelter in very precise language ("made windows and PeeP holes with Small stiks For window sills").

◆ In the last line, Miles distances himself from the story and surprises the reader by concluding that what the boys were really building was not a shelter but a friendship. This final observation is completely unexpected, though not discordant.

*Today I Went to Thatchers. I had a great time. Me and Thatcher built a shelter for a program. Miss Taylor found a good spot, and we started to build stick after stick. Finally, we had a den, but me and Thatcher made windows and peepholes with small sticks for window sills. Finally, we put the leaves on the walls to keep it warm in the shelter. We built a bird watching place. But we really built a friendship.

*Translation of phonetically spelled words

Writing Standard 3:
Language Use and Conventions

This piece does not meet the Language Use and Conventions Standard for second grade because of the number of spelling errors. Still, it is simply a notebook entry, which is really a first draft and not a polished piece. It does have some notable features, however.

The sentences in this piece are crafted nicely and represent a range of syntactic patterns. Of particular note are "we started to Bild Stik aFterstiK" and the simple phrasing of the final thought, "Butwe rillY bilt a frendshiP." Transitions lead a reader through the piece.

The vocabulary is appropriate, given the topic, and there are several precise word choices ("PeeP holes" and "window sills"). The spelling is good for rough-draft writing at second grade. Those words that are misspelled can be read easily. Miles controls for beginning capitalization and end punctuation.

(For more on Language Use and Conventions, see page 182.)

"My Terrible Horrible No good Very Bad Day"

Writing Standard 2:

Writing Purposes and Resulting Genres

Responding to Literature

Josh's sample is an example of a child's ability to respond to literature by imitating a text the child has read. He creates a variation on Judith Viorst's *Alexander and the Terrible, Horrible, No Good, Very Bad Day*. It is an example of work that meets the standard for a response to literature for second grade.

◆ Josh retells the story using his own experiences, mirroring to some degree the chain of unfortunate happenings portrayed in the model.

◆ The piece begins with a standard narrative account but then introduces a list of events similar to those in the story Josh is imitating.

My Terrible Horrible No good Very Bad Day By: Josh

one day when I got up I went in to the livig [*living] roomand jumped and landed onded [on] my sisters [sister's] skate Board and the skateBoard hit the Door I went flyingBach wards [backwards] and hit the edG [edge] of The cofee [coffee] table it hert [hurt].

We went rollerSkateing [rollerskating] I got hert [hurt] were [where] I went rollerskating They had viedo [video] Games I Put a Qurter [quarter] in one of Them it took my money.

*Translation of phonetically spelled words

Writing Standard 3:

Language Use and Conventions

This piece does not meet the Language Use and Conventions Standard for second grade. Josh makes too many mistakes with punctuation, and he does not use capital letters (except for *I*) systematically.

Josh uses simple declarative sentences with the exception of one introductory adverbial clause. He uses "and" for transitions, but the piece includes little substantial detail.

He uses words from a common speaking vocabulary. He also uses words that indicate he was able to select appropriate words for the situation — "skateBoard," "edG of The cofee table" and "viedo Games." Josh correctly spells most words, although some errors exist, such as using a single consonant in "cofee" and not adding a silent *e* on the ending of the word *edge*.

(For more on Language Use and Conventions, see page 182.)

"Owl Moon"

Writing Standard 2:
Writing Purposes and Resulting Genres

Responding to Literature

This sample is a good example of a child's ability to respond to literature. The class read the picture book *Owl Moon* by Jane Yolen and discussed the language in the book. Each student then copied a quote from the book and explained why that language was meaningful. This writer was able not only to respond to words from the text, but also to connect a quotation to the overall theme of the book. The piece meets the standard for response to literature in second grade.

♦ The student begins with a quotation from the story and names the title and author, providing the context.

♦ The student connects the quotation to the story by a selective retelling ("Because The boy was happy becaus he got to go owling and hes been wonted to go owling for a long time and he finally got to go").

♦ The student makes a personal response to the happy feeling of the character in the story by stating, "When other Kids are happy that maKes me happy."

♦ The student makes a claim ("I liKe it Because it maKes me feel good"). This claim is supported by a summary of the story and its theme ("you don't haf't to have words to go owling but you haf't to have hope to see an owl").

> <u>Owl Moon</u>
> When you go owling
> you don't need words, or worm
> [*worms]
> or any thing, but hope. This
> [anything]
> is the booK of <u>Owl Moon.</u>
> This booK is written by
> Jane Yolen. I liKe that
> phrase Because The boy
> was happy becaus he got
> [because]
> to go owling and hes been
> [he's]
> wonted to go owling for a
> [wanting]
> long time and he finally
> got to go.

*Translation of phonetically spelled words

Writing Standard 3:
Language Use and Conventions

This piece does not meet the Language Use and Conventions Standard for second grade. The writing does not provide evidence of an appropriate level of control for spelling and capitalization.

The writer uses a variety of sentence structures, mimicking those in the picture book. In addition, there are very complex constructions, such as "When other Kids are happy that

When other Kids are happy that maKes me happy. I liKe it Because it maKes me feel good Because you dont haf't [have] to have words to go owling but you haf't to have [have] hope to see an owl.

maKes me happy," a sentence that begins with an adverbial clause. There is one run-on sentence (the one that begins "I liKe that phrase Because The boy was happy ... ").

The vocabulary is consistent with the level of language in the picture book. Most of the sight words in the piece are spelled correctly. In one case, the writer leaves the final *e* off *because,* but in all other cases the word is spelled correctly. An apostrophe is omitted from "hes." The spelling of "haf't" instead of *have to* may reflect the child's dialect. Also, the writer uses the wrong verb ending when writing "wanted" instead of *wanting*.

The writer is consistent in capitalization after every period. However, the writer capitalizes "Because" three times when no capital letter is called for. The writer uses an apostrophe correctly in "don't" and incorrectly in "haf't." Other conventions the writer uses are capitals for proper nouns and underlining for a title.

(For more on Language Use and Conventions, see page 182.)

Second-Grade
Writing Standard 3: Language Use and Conventions

Second graders should be developing fluency as writers, producing longer, more detailed texts and crafting stories to achieve an effect, as their control over the conventions of language increases. Some of their sentences still echo their oral language patterns, while others show their awareness of literary style and other generic forms. Conventions appear more regularly:

> **Second-Grade Writing Standard 1:**
> *Habits and Processes*
>
> **Second-Grade Writing Standard 2:**
> *Writing Purposes and Resulting Genres*
>
> ◆ Sharing Events, Telling Stories: Narrative Writing
>
> ◆ Informing Others: Report or Informational Writing
>
> ◆ Getting Things Done: Functional and Procedural Writing
>
> ◆ Producing and Responding to Literature
>
> **Second-Grade Writing Standard 3:**
> *Language Use and Conventions*
>
> ◆ Style and Syntax
>
> ◆ Vocabulary and Word Choice
>
> ◆ Spelling
>
> ◆ Punctuation, Capitalization and Other Conventions

Periods, capital letters, quotation marks and exclamation points frequently are used correctly.

Style and Syntax

Children meeting standards use a variety of sentence structures by the time they leave second grade. The simple sentences that beginning writers relied on because of the difficulties of forming words have evolved into more complex sentences. By using a variety of sentence structures, second-grade writers show their ability to handle subordination of thought by subordination of structures. While punctuation of such sentences may be erratic or uneven, the sentences themselves show children's increasing proficiency in realizing their thoughts in writing. As children experience greater variety of language in books, speech patterns should be augmented by the more writerly structures we expect in specific genres.

Using one's own language
By the end of the year, we expect second-grade students to:

◆ use all sentence patterns typical of spoken language;

◆ incorporate transition words and phrases; and

◆ use various embeddings (phrases, modifiers) as well as coordination and subordination.

Taking on language of authors
By the end of the year, we expect second-grade students to:

◆ use varying sentence patterns and lengths to slow reading down, speed it up or create a mood;

◆ embed literary language where appropriate; and

◆ reproduce sentence structures found in the various genres they are reading.

Vocabulary and Word Choice

Using one's own language
By the end of the year, we expect second-grade students to:

◆ use words from their speaking vocabulary in their writing, including words they have learned from reading and class discussion; and

◆ make word choices that reveal they have a large enough vocabulary to exercise options in word choice.

Taking on language of authors

By the end of the year, we expect second-grade students to:

◆ make choices about which words to use on the basis of whether they accurately convey the intended meaning; and

◆ extend their writing vocabulary by using specialized words related to the topic or setting of their writing (for example, the names of kinds of trees if they are writing about a forest).

Spelling

Second-grade writers on target for meeting standards are beginning to control for spelling. That is, they correctly spell words that they have studied, words that they encounter frequently as readers and words that they regularly employ as writers. They also should spell correctly some high-frequency words with unpredictable spelling patterns that must be memorized (for example, *of, have, the*). At the same time, their incorrect spellings become less random because a clear logic is at work (for example, *used to* is frequently spelled as *yousto*). Some inflectional endings (for example, *-ed, -ing, -ed*), word families and high-frequency words are becoming more automatic.

By the end of the year, we expect second-grade students to be able to:

◆ use a discernible logic to guide their spelling of unfamiliar words, making incorrect spellings less random;

◆ produce writing in which most high-frequency words are spelled correctly;

◆ correctly spell most words with regularly spelled patterns such as consonant-vowel-consonant, consonant-vowel-consonant-silent *e* and one-syllable words with blends;

◆ correctly spell most inflectional endings, including plurals and verb tenses; and

◆ use correct spelling patterns and rules most of the time.

In addition, we expect these students to:

◆ use specific spelling strategies during the writing process (for example, consult the word wall to check a spelling, think about the base and prefixes and suffixes they know); and

◆ engage in the editing process, perhaps with a partner, to correct spelling errors.

Punctuation, Capitalization and Other Conventions

Children should leave second grade with a good sense of how beginning capitalization and end punctuation are applied conventionally, though they may continue their creative use of capital letters (for example, "the dog was HUGE") and exaggerated punctuation (for example, "he bit me!!!!!").

Second graders meeting standards may not have consistent control over punctuation, but they show their understanding by incorporating all the commonly used punctuation marks to some degree in their writing.

By the end of the year, we expect second-grade students to:

◆ use capital letters at the beginnings of sentences;

◆ use periods to end sentences;

◆ approximate the use of quotation marks;

◆ use capital letters and exclamation marks for emphasis;

◆ use question marks; and

◆ use common contractions.

"Sports"

Writing Standard 3:
Language Use and Conventions

This piece is a simple, informational report on sports in France that meets the standard for Language Use and Conventions. The report itself does not meet the standard for Writing Purposes and Resulting Genres because it is a simple list, with one- or two-sentence elaborations for each sport and no conclusion.

Style and Syntax

The piece is made up almost entirely of simple sentences with subject and verb constructions. There does appear to be one compound sentence in the piece (the one that begins "The race goes up and down ... "), though Patricia uses a period rather than a comma to mark the end of the first clause. The first word after the period is not capitalized, whereas every other word following a period has been capitalized. It is reasonable, therefore, to infer that Patricia meant to write a compound sentence but did not use appropriate punctuation. The overall style of the piece, although somewhat choppy, is reflective of many pieces of informational text.

Sports

Auto racing first began in France.
One of the biggest sports is Auto racing.
The Auto race last 24 hours one day and
one night. A nother grate sport
*lasts   another   great
is the bike race. The race covers
4,023 Km (2,500 mi) The race
goes up and down mountains.
and They'll evih do it at the
even
hottest time of the year.
A nother grate sport is
another   great
Soccer. Soccer is the biggest game
in fance.
France

*Translation of phonetically spelled words

Vocabulary and Word Choice

Patricia uses vocabulary appropriate for the topic, and her word choice adequately conveys information to the reader. The translation of 4,023 kilometers to 2,500 miles is an example of one writer's attempt to be precise and convey data meaningfully.

Spelling

The spelling almost uniformly is correct. *Great* ("grate"), *even* ("evin") and *another* ("A nother") are misrepresented, but they are easily readable. In the last sentence, the last word is both a misspelling and a capitalization error.

Punctuation, Capitalization and Other Conventions

There are no other capitalization errors in this piece beyond the use of a capital *A* in "Auto race" — a logical error given that auto racing is the name of a specific sport. Patricia uses parentheses correctly and also punctuates a contraction correctly. There is end punctuation for each sentence except the one ending with a parenthesis.

Third Grade

Third Grade

"Reading to learn," in fact, becomes a reality in third grade, when students are capable of doing independent research from sources they choose themselves.

Confident Readers and Writers

Third grade is a pivotal year in literacy development. Students who have reached reading and writing standards for kindergarten, first grade and second grade should be confident readers and writers by the time they enter third grade. Most third graders are comfortable with the conventions of language — and they are, by the end of third grade, making use of reading and writing for their own purposes. They can find out about a topic independently and then state matter-of-factly what they learned.

Students who enter third grade without this confidence will need to catch up. As in earlier grades, "summer learning loss" is a handicap among children who do not read during summer vacation. At this point, most students lose not only accuracy and fluency when they don't read, but also new vocabulary and concepts. These students face an even more severe challenge if they are still carrying an accumulated learning deficit from the previous summer.

Moreover, these literacy deficits may snowball into social and emotional problems as well. Third graders are keenly aware that they all should be reading well — and they know that real textbooks will be coming their way in fourth grade. Third graders who do not bounce back and make progress will need intensive intervention to help them catch up.

Reading and Writing: What to Expect

Most third graders are discerning readers and writers, picking up details in a nonfiction book such as the Wright Group's *Whales* or a fiction book such as Avon Books' *Ramona Quimby, Age 8*. They read thoughtfully, comprehending shades of meaning. When they talk and write about books, they reveal a deep understanding of the text — making comparisons among books, questioning authors' perspectives, interpreting the significance of stories and identifying characteristics of particular authors. Frequently, these responses are very personal.

Third graders can read stories they enjoy as well as serious, nonfiction books. Nonfiction reading builds third graders' vocabularies and introduces them to major concepts they will study in more depth in later grades. Students may read more than one book about the way plants grow, the American Revolution or Egyptian pyramids, for example; these books challenge them with new words and important ideas that they can use in their writing. Students also may read fiction and nonfiction books on the same topic and then

compare the real and imaginary worlds. For a science unit on insects, for example, students may raise live crickets for a few weeks, read about crickets in nonfiction texts and the fiction book *The Cricket in Times Square,* and write about what they have learned.

"Reading to learn," in fact, becomes a reality in third grade, when students are capable of doing independent research from sources they choose themselves. Through their reading, they can become experts on topics that interest them, taking notes about what they read, composing elaborate narratives and writing lengthy reports.

Most third graders communicate in writing with teachers, parents and friends, for example,

by composing songs and plays. They write longer pieces, take on harder topics and embed their writing with more details than do students in earlier grades. They use language to paint a picture or set a mood. They play with language and make conscious word choices. They use their imaginations to create a believable world and develop characters, and then they dramatize this world for others. The connection between reading and writing is stronger in third grade. When students discover a literary feature or technique used by a favorite author, for example, they try it in their own writing. They read to each other and to younger children; in doing so, they enhance their sense of themselves as readers.

Literacy is a more social and practical endeavor in third grade. Like adult readers, most third graders are eager to talk about what they are reading and learning — and apply it to their own work. They frequently use their new knowledge to elaborate on reports and narratives.

Developing Literacy Habits

Third graders should read widely, from fiction and nonfiction books, and in depth. Their readings should include author studies, in which students read and compare several works by a favorite author, and genre studies, in which students read and compare several works in a particular genre, such as folk tales, mystery stories or poetry. Most third graders notice a stunning array of nuances about language, style and effect when they read. Structured author and genre studies enable students to articulate and categorize their observations as well as sharpen their skills at interpreting, analyzing and synthesizing what they read.

Most reading should be done independently. Third graders can learn to select books they can read on their own — and most like extended time for curling up with a good book. Independent and assisted reading become more rich sources of new vocabulary than in previous grades, where the texts are easier. However, third graders still need to hear their teacher read books aloud to them. Like younger students, third

graders expand their vocabularies and learn the ebb and flow of language by listening to good literature. *For examples of the kinds of books third graders should read, see* **Leveled Books to Read for Accuracy and Fluency,** *page 192, and* **What Books Should Third Graders Read?,** *page 204.*

Third graders also should write daily. Classroom time and access to response partners should help students harness their budding creativity — and their genuine pleasure in writing and language. Third graders can write poems, plays and stories as well as real-world pieces, such as letters, lists, surveys, posters, complaints and songs. They enjoy hearing their writing read aloud. The way words sound — the way they say words themselves — delights third graders.

Third graders also should be expected to stretch themselves when they write. They can experiment further with writing narrative accounts, responses to literature, reports and procedures. Students who are especially fluent show their originality by trying new ways to engage readers. They revise their first drafts on their own, as well as with feedback from classmates and adults.

By third grade, students no longer use drawings as a key element to convey meaning. They may use drawings to illustrate their stories or charts and diagrams to add information to their reports — but the main story, now, is in their writing.

> Like adult readers,
> most third graders are
> eager to talk about
> what they are reading and
> learning — and apply it
> to their own work.

Third-Grade
Reading Standard 1: Print-Sound Code

I n third grade, students' decoding of the print-sound code should become automatic across the whole span of language. Throughout third grade they should continue to learn about words — roots, inflections, suffixes, prefixes, homophones and word families — as part of vocabulary growth. Each book they read presents new words that they should be able to figure out using their knowledge of word structures.

Third-Grade
Reading Standard 1:
Print-Sound Code

**Third-Grade
Reading Standard 2:**
Getting the Meaning

◆ Accuracy

◆ Fluency

◆ Self-Monitoring and
    Self-Correcting Strategies

◆ Comprehension

**Third-Grade
Reading Standard 3:**
Reading Habits

◆ Reading a Lot

◆ Literature

◆ Discussing Books

◆ Vocabulary

Carey

Reading Standard 1:
Print-Sound Code

◆ Decoding of the print-sound
   code should become automatic
   across the whole span of
   language

While reading *Beezus and Ramona,* Carey clearly is able to decode the print-sound code in more complex texts. Carey reads fluently, decoding more difficult words as she comes to them almost automatically. Words such as *exasperating* do not faze her. Carey pauses, rereading when necessary, to say the words clearly and with the correct emphasis.

The images and commentary in the reading section of this book refer to reading performances available on the CD-ROM.

Read-Aloud Books

Buck, Pearl S., *The Big Wave*

Cleary, Beverly, *Dear Mr. Henshaw*

Dahl, Roald, *Danny the Champion of the World*

Dahl, Roald, *James and the Giant Peach*

Dalgliesh, Alice, *The Courage of Sarah Noble*

Fleischman, Paul, *Joyful Noise: Poems for Two Voices*

Forbes, Esther, *Johnny Tremain*

Garland, Sherry, *The Lotus Seed*

Gipson, Fred, *Old Yeller*

Heide, Florence Parry, *The Shrinking of Treehorn*

Lewis, C.S., *The Chronicles of Narnia* (series)

Lewis, C.S., *The Lion, the Witch and the Wardrobe*

Lowry, Lois, *Number the Stars*

MacLachlan, Patricia, *Sarah, Plain and Tall*

MacLachlan, Patricia, *Skylark*

Marton, Jirina, *You Can Go Home Again*

Polacco, Patricia, *Pink and Say*

Rawls, Wilson, *Where the Red Fern Grows*

Rylant, Cynthia, *Waiting to Waltz: A Childhood*

Silverstein, Shel, *Lafcadio: The Lion Who Shot Back*

Viorst, Judith, *If I Were in Charge of the Words and Other Worries*

Yolen, Jane, *Encounter*

Young, Ed, *Lon Po Po: A Red Riding Hood Story from China*

Level O Books

Albert Whitman, The Boxcar Children Series, Warner, *The Boxcar Children*

Avon Books, Cleary, *Beezus and Ramona*

Avon Books, Cleary, *Henry and Beezus*

Avon Books, Cleary, *Ramona Quimby, Age 8*

Dell, Yearling Books, Coerr, *Mieko and the Fifth Treasure*

Dial Books for Young Readers, Flournoy, *The Patchwork Quilt*

Random House, Bullseye Books, Ackerman, *The Night Crossing*

Scholastic, Little Apple, Hurwitz, *Class Clown*

Scholastic, Engel, *We'll Never Forget You, Roberto Clemente*

Wright Group, Wonder World, Boon, *Whales*

A Level O Text

Beverly Cleary

RAMONA QUIMBY, AGE 8

"It's a rare thing to be hailed by audience and critics alike. In Mrs. Cleary's case, everyone seems delighted." *The New York Times*

RAMONA QUIMBY, AGE 8

long enough—she hoped—to make her feel carsick. Ramona was going to ride the bus, because changes had been made in the schools in the Quimbys' part of the city during the summer. Glenwood, the girls' old school, had become an intermediate school, which meant Ramona had to go to Cedarhurst Primary School.

"Ha-ha yourself." Beezus was too excited to be annoyed with her little sister. "Today I start high school."

"*Junior* high school," corrected Ramona, who was not going to let her sister get away with acting older than she really was. "Rosemont Junior High School is not the same as high school, and besides you have to walk."

Ramona had reached the age of demanding accuracy from everyone, even herself. All summer, whenever a grown-up asked what grade she was in, she felt as if she were fibbing when she answered, "third," because she had not

12

THE FIRST DAY OF SCHOOL

actually started the third grade. Still, she could not say she was in the second grade since she had finished that grade last June. Grown-ups did not understand that summers were free from grades.

"Ha-ha to both of you," said Mr. Quimby, as he carried his breakfast dishes into the kitchen. "You're not the only ones going to school today." Yesterday had been his last day working at the check-out counter of the Shop-Rite Market. Today he was returning to college to become what he called "a real, live school teacher." He was also going to work one day a week in the frozen-food warehouse of the chain of Shop-Rite Markets to help the family "squeak by," as the grown-ups put it, until he finished his schooling.

"Ha-ha to all of you if you don't hurry up," said Mrs. Quimby, as she swished suds in the dishpan. She stood back from the sink so she would not spatter the white uniform she wore

13

Third-Grade
Reading Standard 2: Getting the Meaning

Accuracy

By the end of the year, we expect third-grade students to be able to:

◆ independently read aloud unfamiliar Level O books with 90 percent or better accuracy of word recognition (self-correction allowed).

Fluency

Third graders' growing fluency is displayed mainly in the more mature texts they are able to read easily.

By the end of the year, we expect third-grade students to:

◆ independently read aloud from Level O books that they have previewed silently on their own, using intonation, pauses and emphasis that signal the meaning of the text;

◆ easily read words with irregularly spelled suffixes (for example, *-ous, -ion, -ive*);

◆ use the cues of punctuation to guide themselves in getting meaning and fluently reading aloud from the increasingly complex texts they read; and

◆ use pacing and intonation to convey the meaning of the clauses and phrases of the sentences they read aloud.

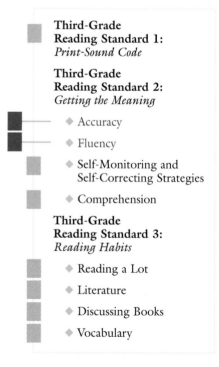

Leveled Books to Read for Accuracy and Fluency

Level O books include a variety of chapter books, often extending into a series. Fiction books have more sophisticated development of plot and character than books at previous levels, allowing students to explore concepts, ideas, setting, characters, craft and genre in more depth than ever before.

Level O expository books are more detailed; they are thick with information and longer than books at previous levels. They have real scientific or historical content.

Andrea

Reading Standard 2:
Getting the Meaning

Accuracy

In this sample, Andrea reads with 99 percent accuracy. She misses only a few words, and she handles irregularly spelled words with ease. Words such as *spoil, breakfast, stomach* and *quivery* do not give her pause. In addition, Andrea does not stumble over compound or hyphenated words such as *talking-to* or *carsick* (which was hyphenated because it fell at the end of a line in the text Andrea was reading). Andrea has difficulty with the word *intermediate* but attempts to sound it out. In one instance, she left out the word *high*, and in another, she put the incorrect stress on the word *accuracy*. Overall, these mistakes do not interrupt the flow of Andrea's reading.

Fluency

Andrea also reads fluently. For the most part, she uses the punctuation clues to measure her delivery and changes her voice to signal the character speaking "ha-ha" and the slightly taunting "*junior* high school." ▶▶

A Third-Grade Running Record*

> SC = Self-correction
> O = Omitted the word
> R = Repeated the word
> T = Told a word

Book Title: <u>*Ramona Quimby, Age 8*</u>

Page 11:   The First Day of School

Ramona Quimby hoped her parents would forget to give her a little

talking-to. She did not want anything to spoil this exciting day.

"Ha-ha, I get to ride the bus to school all by myself," Ramona [SC school, R]

bragged to her big sister, Beatrice, at breakfast. Her stomach felt [R]

quivery with excitement at the day ahead, a day that would begin

with a bus ride just the right length to make her feel a long way

from home but not

Page 12:   long enough — she hoped — to make her feel carsick. Ramona was

going to ride the bus, because changes had been made in the

schools in the Quimbys' part of the city during the summer.

Glenwood, the girls' old school, had become an intermediate [T]

school, which meant Ramona had to go to Cedarhurst Primary [R]

School.

"Ha-ha yourself." Beezus was too excited to be annoyed with her

little sister. "Today I start high school."

"*Junior* high school," corrected Ramona, who was not going to let

her sister get away with acting older than she really was. "Rosemont [SC]

Junior High School is not the same as high school, and besides you [O]

have to walk."

Ramona had reached the age of demanding accuracy from everyone, [accúracy]

even herself. All summer, whenever a grown-up asked what grade

she was in, she felt as if she were fibbing when she answered,

*For more on running records, see page 21.

New Standards

Self-Monitoring and
Self-Correcting Strategies

Andrea automatically falls back to self-correcting strategies as needed, such as sounding out or rereading.

(For more on Self-Monitoring and Self-Correcting Strategies, see page 196).

Comprehension

Gauging comprehension by such a short reading is difficult. Typically, third-grade students will read several chapters of a chapter book before they have gathered sufficient information to discuss character development and motivations, plots and subplots, style or use of language, and connections to their own lives. However, Andrea clearly gets the general gist of this reading — Ramona is excited because she will be riding the bus, and she doesn't want her sister trying to get away with acting older.

(For more on Comprehension, see page 198.)

"third," because she had not

Page 13: actually started the third grade. Still, she could not say she was in

the second grade *SC/was* ⌐ R since she had finished that grade last June. Grown-

ups did not understand that summers were free from grades.

"Ha-ha to both of you," said Mr. Quimby, as he carried his break-

fast dishes into the kitchen. "You're not the only ones *SC who/whose* going to

school today."

3 errors = 99% accuracy

(Word count: 293)

Authors' Perspectives

" Our fourth grade teacher read to us for a half an hour after lunch everyday. I still recall resting my head on my desk and staring out the window into the trees while her voice created the daydreams and visions of the stories in my mind.

"Many of my elementary teachers had the policy of reading to us in the morning and at the beginning of the afternoon session. How I loved that time. I'd wait with dread as they turned each page for fear it was time to stop. "

From G. Robert Carlsen and Anne Sherrill,
"Literature and the Human Voice," Voices of Readers,
How We Come to Love Books (Urbana, Ill.:
National Council of Teachers of English, 1988), p. 3.

Self-Monitoring and Self-Correcting Strategies

In third grade, children are deepening their self-monitoring strategies and are beginning to analyze the author's strategy as a way of figuring out what a passage means. They use these strategies most overtly when they read challenging texts that require them to stretch beyond their range for accuracy and fluency.

By the end of third grade, we expect students to:

◆ monitor their own reading, noticing when sentences or paragraphs are incomplete or when texts do not make sense;

◆ use their ear for syntax to help figure out the meaning of new words;

◆ infer the meaning of words from roots, prefixes and suffixes, as well as from the overall contextual meaning of what they are reading;

◆ analyze the relations among different parts of a text; and

◆ raise questions about what the author was trying to say and use the text to help answer the questions.

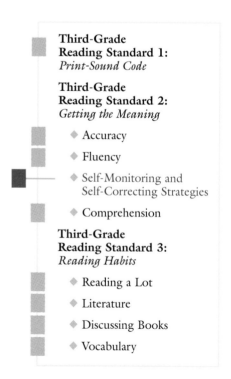

Priscilla

Margaret

Reading Standard 2:
Getting the Meaning

Self-Monitoring and
Self-Correcting Strategies

While reading *Class Clown,* Priscilla automatically falls back on her self-correcting strategies to decipher more irregularly spelled words, such as *studies* (she corrects to a short /*u*/ sound) and *straight* (with its vowel digraph* and silent *gh*). If Priscilla were encouraged to think about contextual clues, she most likely would figure out the word *initials,* which she attempts unsurely.

Margaret demonstrates she can decode automatically as she reads *Henry and Beezus.* She has trouble with the word *looked* but uses a strategy to say it correctly. She knows the multiple sounds that *ed* can make — a /*t*/ sound, a /*d*/ sound or "sometimes makes *e-d*."

*A digraph is a combination of two letters that, together, make one sound, which is different from either of the letter sounds alone. Consonant digraphs include letter combinations such as *ch, ph, sh, th* and *wh*. Vowel digraphs include combinations such as *ea* in *eat, ay* in *day, oi* in *oil* and *oa* in *coat*.

Comprehension

Third-grade books are more complex than second-grade books. They often have chapters and cannot be read in one day. There frequently are subplots as well as plots. Characters develop, there is more detail and figurative language is used. So it is more difficult to summarize the more complicated story. In nonfiction texts, concepts with subordinate and coordinate structures are presented in complex and compound sentences. The conceptual content of texts, and children's background knowledge in relation to that content, starts to become important at this stage.

Third-Grade Reading Standard 1: *Print-Sound Code*

Third-Grade Reading Standard 2: *Getting the Meaning*
- ◆ Accuracy
- ◆ Fluency
- ◆ Self-Monitoring and Self-Correcting Strategies
- ◆ Comprehension

Third-Grade Reading Standard 3: *Reading Habits*
- ◆ Reading a Lot
- ◆ Literature
- ◆ Discussing Books
- ◆ Vocabulary

In third grade, the distinction between texts children read independently or with a partner and those that adults read to them is no longer a primary consideration with respect to the comprehension component of the standard. Now, the levels of complexity do not always differ, so our expectations for comprehension are generally the same for independent reading and being read to.

By the end of third grade, we expect students to continue to demonstrate the comprehension capabilities they used in second grade. In addition, we expect them to:

- ◆ capture meaning from figurative language (for example, similes, metaphors, poetic images) and explain the meaning;

- ◆ cite important details from a text;

- ◆ compare one text to another text they have read or heard; and

- ◆ discuss why an author might have chosen particular words.

In addition, when engaging with narratives (whether fiction or nonfiction), we expect third graders to:

- ◆ say how a story relates to something in real-life experience;

- ◆ explain the motives of characters; and

- ◆ discuss plot and setting.

Further, when they read informational texts, we expect third graders to:

- ◆ use the structure of informational text to retrieve information;

- ◆ analyze the causes, motivations, sequences and results of events;

- ◆ understand the concepts and relationships described;

- ◆ use reasoning and information from within and outside the text to examine arguments; and

- ◆ describe in their own words what new information they gained from a nonfiction text and how it relates to their prior knowledge.

Finally, we expect third graders to be able to:

- ◆ follow instructions or directions they encounter in the more complicated functional texts they now are reading.

Jennifer Karson and Third-Grade Students

Reading Standard 2:
Getting the Meaning

Comprehension

In this segment, the children read and follow the directions for making origami animal finger puppets. Alison begins by reading the instructions: "You can make five animal puppets with the same basic pattern. A small piece of paper, about 2 inches x 2 inches, will make a decorative cap for a pen or a pencil and a large piece [of] a hat. See facing page."

The teacher then asks the students, "What does it mean by 'See facing page'?"

Dzemal shows that he understands by pointing to the page opposite the one Alison just read from and saying, "Because it faces it."

The teacher guides the children throughout this exercise by asking questions to check for understanding. "What should I do first, do you think?" the teacher asks.

Having read Step 1 to themselves already, Melanie, Alison and Del'Lana respond in unison, "Fold it in half."

The teacher presses for further understanding by asking, "How does it say to fold in half and unfold?"

Melanie answers, "It's like a diamond."

The teacher guides the group by asking, "So, how should I hold my paper?"

Demonstrating that they get it, they answer in unison, "Sideways."

The teacher asks, "And what's the next step?"

Alison answers, "Unfold!"

The children then read Step 3: "Fold the top corners down."

The teacher says, "Which way do the arrows go? I'm not sure I understand."

Dzemal answers, "You have to put both of them down here like this."

The teacher asks the children, "How should I find out if I should make it exactly [even]?"

Melanie refers to the text and says, "What it is trying to say is, well, you see those arrows, like that, you just bring it down. Like and then it turns into a diamond, and it has a little space around the middle."

Demonstrating that he knows to follow the directions in sequence, Youngnam adds, "And then after that you just like saying … ." When the teacher pushes for evidence, Youngnam refers to the text, saying, "Because it says right here, 'Fold the bottom corner up … as shown to make ears.'"

Nearing completion, the teacher asks, "Now what does it say?"

Del'Lana reads, "Fold bottom up! All the way to here. And fold top corner forward." She refers to the words on the instruction sheet once again. "Oh, now I get it! It's this one!" she announces. Getting up from her seat to lean over the table and show her classmates, she says, "You see it from here? It says, '9, now put it a little bit up.'"

With the teacher's encouragement, the children check to see if their folded paper matches the illustration. Their satisfaction with themselves is evident in their smiles, and the segment ends with the children discussing what kinds of faces they will draw on their puppets.

These children are learning how to read and follow directions. They demonstrate that they can handle this type of text by reading each step in turn and carrying out the instructions successfully. They talk and repeatedly refer to the text as they move through the steps and help one another make sense of the words and illustrations.

While the specific words encountered in these instructions pose no problem to these students, this genre requires a different type of comprehension and close attention to detail. The children demonstrate that they can use the structure of this informational text to retrieve information and understand the concepts and relationships described.

Third-Grade
Reading Standard 3: **Reading Habits**

At third grade, children can do most of their reading on their own. But being read to is still important for a variety of reasons — for example, it exposes children to the rhythms and patterns of written language read aloud and to examples of language that may be different (for example, more literary) than what children typically choose for their independent reading. A read-aloud is also an important occasion for deep discussion of books.

As children's reading matures, learning how to read is only part of the literacy picture. By third grade, students should begin to study literature for its own sake, not simply because it helps them learn to read (although it also does that). Reading literature helps build good reading habits by reinforcing the interest and pleasure that reading holds. For these reasons, our third-grade standards set forth specific expectations for literature.

Reading a Lot

The reading habits we expect to see in third grade are similar to those we expect to see in second, but they are more rigorous because the texts students encounter are increasingly complex. As before, third graders should read across a range of genres. The more difficult books they now read typically present more full realizations of the genres than books they read in second grade.

We expect third-grade students to:

◆ read 30 chapter books a year, independently or with assistance, and regularly participate in discussions of their reading with another student, a group or an adult;

◆ read and hear texts read aloud from a variety of genres, including narrative accounts, responses to literature (written by other students and found in book blurbs and reviews), informational writing, reports, narrative procedures, recountings, memoirs, poetry and plays;

◆ read multiple books by the same author and be able to identify differences and similarities among them;

◆ reread some favorite books, or parts of longer books, gaining deeper comprehension and knowledge of author's craft;

◆ read their own writing and the writing of their classmates, including pieces compiled in class books or placed on public display;

◆ read the functional and instructional messages they see in the classroom environment (for example, announcements, labels, instructions, menus, invitations) and some of those encountered outside school;

◆ listen to and discuss at least one chapter read to them every day; and

◆ voluntarily read to each other, signaling their sense of themselves as readers.

**Third-Grade
Reading Standard 1:**
Print-Sound Code

**Third-Grade
Reading Standard 2:**
Getting the Meaning

◆ Accuracy

◆ Fluency

◆ Self-Monitoring and Self-Correcting Strategies

◆ Comprehension

**Third-Grade
Reading Standard 3:**
Reading Habits

◆ Reading a Lot

◆ Literature

◆ Discussing Books

◆ Vocabulary

Literature

Children's literature includes stories, poems, plays, autobiographical writing and some nonfiction. By third grade, students should recognize and be able to evaluate and discuss literary qualities and themes of the children's literature they read. They talk and write about similarities they see in different books by the same author; differences in similar books by different authors; genre features; and the effects of author's craft including content, point of view, word choice, plot, beginnings and endings, and character development. They interpret themes across works and authors, usually through identification with story characters.

We expect third-grade students to:

◆ read good children's literature every day;

◆ have worthwhile literature read to them to model the language and craft of good writing;

◆ discuss underlying themes or messages when interpreting fiction;

◆ read and respond to poems, stories, memoirs and plays written by peers;

◆ identify and discuss recurring themes across works;

◆ evaluate literary merit and participate informatively in peer talk about selecting books to read;

◆ examine the reasons for a character's actions, accounting for situation and motive;

◆ read multiple books by the same author and be able to identify differences and similarities among them;

◆ recognize genre features, understand differences among genres and compare works by different authors in the same genre; and

◆ note and talk about author's craft: content, point of view, word choice, plot, beginnings and endings, and character development.

Discussing Books

Third-grade book discussions are likely to vary widely, attending to themes and content, to author's craft, and to inferred meanings of the text. Third graders also should be extending their ability to talk "accountably" in all of the ways described in second grade.

In discussions of their reading, we expect students finishing third grade to be able to:

◆ demonstrate the skills we look for in the comprehension component of Reading Standard 2: Getting the Meaning;

◆ note and talk about author's craft: word choice, beginnings and endings, plot, and character development;

◆ use comparisons and analogies to explain ideas;

◆ refer to knowledge built during discussion;

◆ use information that is accurate, accessible and relevant;

◆ restate their own ideas with greater clarity when a listener indicates noncomprehension;

◆ ask other students questions requiring them to support their claims or arguments; and

◆ indicate when their own or others' ideas need further support or explanation.

**Jennifer Karson and
Third-Grade Class**

Reading Standard 3:
Reading Habits

Discussing Books

◆ Refer to knowledge built during discussion

◆ Use information that is accurate, accessible and relevant

The students in this class have just finished jotting down their thoughts about connections between what they know about Japanese culture (from their recent study of Japan) and their current reading of the novel *The Big Wave* by Pearl S. Buck. The teacher asks the children to share entries in their Japan schema. Sara replies, "My Japan schema is that in Japan there are … tsunamis [big waves]."

When the teacher requests another entry, Erica answers, "Respectfulness! And my connection to *The Big Wave* is 'Jiya respected the old man for his kindness.'"

After charting Erica's response, the teacher continues, "Who thinks they have another one?"

Josephine answers, "Japanese people wear wooden shoes. And my connection from *The Big Wave* is that Setsu wore wooden shoes when she saw Jiya."

Adding relevant information to this comment, another student calls out, "I want to tell Josephine that, um, the wooden shoes that Setsu wore are called clogs."

Alison continues with another connection between life in Japan and the picture of Japanese life from the book *The Big Wave:* "Fish, rice, green tea and vegetables. And my connection is 'All these foods were in the book when Japanese people ate.'"

Demonstrating a culture of accountable talk, a boy extends this comment and says, "I can build off of what Alison said because mine was kinda like hers. I said, 'In Japan many people eat rice and healthy foods. In *The Big Wave*, in Kino's home, they ate a lot of rice and healthy foods.'"

Dana adds another idea: "Obeying parents. Kino and Setsu has to obey the parents."

When called upon, Dzemal concludes this segment by adding "[The] sea. Kino, Jiya and the father fear the sea."

The children in this class demonstrate strategies for discussing books by referring to knowledge built together during previous social studies lessons and by making connections to the text currently under discussion. They point to specific relevant examples from the book, citing characters and scenes. One student adds information that is accurate, accessible and relevant when she names the wooden shoes as "clogs."

Vocabulary

We expect third-grade students to:

◆ learn new words every day from their reading;

◆ recognize when they don't know what a word means and use a variety of strategies for figuring it out (for example, ask others, look at the context, find the word in use elsewhere and look for clues there);

◆ know meanings of roots, prefixes and suffixes;

◆ talk about the meaning of most of the new words encountered in independent and assisted reading;

◆ notice and show interest in understanding unfamiliar words in texts that are read to them;

◆ know how to talk about what nouns mean in terms of function (for example, "Water is for drinking"), features (for example, "Water is wet") and category (for example, "Water is a liquid");

◆ know how to talk about verbs as "action words"; and

◆ talk about words as they relate to other words: synonyms, antonyms or which word is more precise.

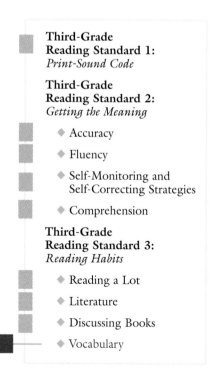

Third-Grade Reading Standard 1:
Print-Sound Code

Third-Grade Reading Standard 2:
Getting the Meaning

◆ Accuracy

◆ Fluency

◆ Self-Monitoring and Self-Correcting Strategies

◆ Comprehension

Third-Grade Reading Standard 3:
Reading Habits

◆ Reading a Lot

◆ Literature

◆ Discussing Books

◆ Vocabulary

What Books Should Third Graders Read?

Beyond leveled texts, which are used for practice-reading, teaching, and testing for accuracy and fluency, third graders should read widely from a variety of texts.

Many excellent fiction and nonfiction books do not appear on any leveled text lists. Classroom libraries should include a wide range of classic and modern books that will satisfy readers with various reading abilities and interests. Third graders need books at their own reading levels and books above their reading levels to stretch and challenge them.

Third-grade classrooms also should include books that teachers can read aloud to students. Third graders need to hear books to learn new vocabulary and more sophisticated syntax.

There are many lists of recommended titles, including the Newbury and Caldecott Award winners, *The Read-Aloud Handbook* by Jim Trelease, *Books to Build on: A Grade-by-Grade Resource Guide for Parents and Teachers (Core Knowledge Series)* by E.D. Hirsch, and the *Elementary School Library Collection: A Guide to Books and Other Media*. The American Library Association also recommends titles.

Students' Perspectives

Sometimes instead of a middle I have a conflict. Some of my stories have more interesting words than others, I used to write silly stories. Now I am taking my writing more seriously. My handwriting used to be sloppy now it is alot neater.

I am really happy my writing has improved, and gotten better.

Third-Grade
Writing Standard 1: Habits and Processes

To become proficient writers, children should write a lot. By writing a lot, we mean that children should write every day; that the writing time should be uninterrupted; and that they should always have a way of preserving what they have written — a place in the classroom, a box, a folder, a notebook. Children should have access to

**Third-Grade
Writing Standard 1:**
Habits and Processes

**Third-Grade
Writing Standard 2:**
*Writing Purposes and
Resulting Genres*

◆ Sharing Events, Telling
Stories: Narrative Writing

◆ Informing Others: Report
or Informational Writing

◆ Getting Things Done:
Functional and
Procedural Writing

◆ Producing and
Responding to Literature

**Third-Grade
Writing Standard 3:**
*Language Use and
Conventions*

◆ Style and Syntax

◆ Vocabulary and
Word Choice

◆ Spelling

◆ Punctuation, Capitalization
and Other Conventions

what they already have written; they need to revisit and revise their writing and also to reflect on their growing sense of what good writing is.

Third graders on target to meet the standard know how to decide what to write about and how to learn more about the topics they select. They have facility in extending a piece of writing and can say more or edit out whole sections for effect. Literate third graders understand the concept of audience. They know when to stop and share their writing. They count on their classmates to listen, tell them what they do not understand, ask questions that will help clarify or add details that will make the writing more meaningful to others. Proficient third-grade writers keep writing even when they do not know how to spell a word. They know that they can come back to the spelling problem, get help from teachers or peers, and make the corrections that will make the writing understandable to the audience.

The writing habits and processes we expect in third grade are similar to those we expect in second grade. What differs is the work students produce. Third graders write longer, more complex and more varied pieces than they did in second grade, showing their deepening understanding of genres and their increasing control of written language and its conventions.

We expect third-grade students to:

◆ write daily;

◆ generate their own topics and spend the necessary amount of time to revisit and refine their writing;

◆ extend and rework pieces of writing (for example, turn a paragraph from a memoir into a fully developed piece);

◆ routinely rework, revise, edit and proofread their work;

◆ over the course of the year, polish 10 or 12 pieces for an audience in and beyond the classroom;

◆ write for specific purposes of their own (for example, writing a thank-you letter, writing a birthday card for a parent or friend);

◆ consciously appropriate specific elements of a favorite author's craft to refine the quality of their own work; and

◆ apply criteria (both public and personal) to judge the quality of their writing.

Grandpa
By Jenny

My grandpa has white skin, short white hair, black eyes and he's tall. He takes me to fun places and he makes me laugh. He lives in China with my grandmother. He takes care of me alot when I was small but now I am in America and hes in China so I cant see him anymore, but I can still call him. He somtimes took me to restraunts.

My favorite food in the restraunt were the biscuits. They are long and

skinny. In hot summer days me and my grandpa took walks aroud the block. Sometimes we watch pink, blue and some other different colored clouds pass by our house. and watch birds fly pass by us. I like my grandpa alot.

(P.2)

"Grandpa"

Writing Standard 1:
Habits and Processes

Jenny's piece comes from her third-grade writing folder. Because Jenny is a third grader, she produces longer, more complex pieces of writing than students in earlier grades do, and her collection of work contains fewer pieces (the work on a single piece might extend over several days or longer). In particular, those pieces she revised took time to reshape and polish. Jenny obviously considers writing important, and she invests time and energy in getting it right. She takes notes on suggestions from response partners. She is careful to correct spelling and to punctuate her final drafts. The collection as a whole provides evidence of meeting the standard for third-grade Writing Habits and Processes.

"Grandpa" is an informational piece about Jenny's grandfather. It begins with a physical description of the grandfather ("white skin, short white hair, black eyes and he's tall"). It goes on to say that he and Jenny used to visit fun places and that he made her laugh. Jenny explains that she no longer sees her grandfather because he remained in China when she moved to America. She closes the piece by saying that she likes her grandfather a lot.

Only once does Jenny lose control of the piece — she digresses about biscuits — though she does have problems with verb tenses ("takes" for *took* and "watch" for *watched*). This piece, done in September of her third-grade year, shows Jenny is a very thoughtful writer who is able to communicate her feelings to the reader (she obviously cares a great deal for her grandfather) by providing details.

(For more of Jenny's collection, see page 255.)

Third-Grade
Writing Standard 2: Writing Purposes and Resulting Genres

Third graders meeting standards have a well-defined sense of themselves as writers. They know their strengths as poets, as fiction writers, as memoir writers, as experts about various nonfiction forms. They can talk knowledgeably about their writing and about the strategies of their favorite published writers.

Once these third graders plan what to write about, often drawing inspiration from notebooks, they can choose from several genres a form that will allow them to develop effectively what they have to say.

Sharing Events, Telling Stories: Narrative Writing

In a typical third-grade narrative, the student shows a developing sense of story. Autobiographical pieces — frequently memoirs — are drawn from important memories, and their significance often is described. Fictional narratives sometimes make use of the traditional problem/resolution structure seen in many of the stories students have read. Often these narratives express how a character (or the writer) feels — that is, they tell the internal story and offer the author's reflections or commentary.

Building on the skills they developed in second grade, third-grade writers are able to infuse their stories with mood and to create pace and tension. They use details carefully to create believable worlds in which their events unfold naturally, and they employ dialogue to reveal character, to advance the action and to provide readers with important understandings.

By the end of the year, we expect third-grade students to produce narrative accounts (fictional or autobiographical) that:

- orient or engage the reader (set the time, indicate the location where the story takes place, introduce the character or enter immediately into the story line);

- create a believable world and introduce characters through the precise choice of detail;

- create a sequence of events that unfolds naturally;

- provide pacing;

- develop a character, often by providing motivation for action and having the character solve the problem;

- develop the plot or tell about the event by describing actions and emotions of the main characters, including descriptive details, using dialogue and other story strategies;

- add reflective comments (especially in an autobiographical narrative); and

- provide some kind of conclusion.

"When my Puppys Ranaway"

Writing Standard 2:
Writing Purposes and Resulting Genres

Narrative Writing

This piece is an example of a controlled narrative account that is capable of causing an emotional response from some readers. It includes many of the characteristics of narrative writing; specifically, it builds a believable story line by creating a sequence of events that occurs quite naturally. It meets the standard for narrative writing in third grade.

◆ The piece engages the reader by establishing the time of day, implying time of year and introducing characters ("ONE night when the air was warm" and "I was in bed").

◆ The piece includes a number of characters and develops the emotion of these characters ("She had a worried exspression on her face," "I worried all through school" and "Her eyes started to fill with tears").

◆ The piece creates a believable world through Alex's choice of detail ("I wuldn't go to sleep," "I thought maybe if I went outside" and "I went to my room and cried").

◆ The piece creates a sequence of events that unfolds naturally ("ONE night … I went into … I opened The back door … I … woke up my dad … The next day … I got home from … ").

When my Puppys Ranaway

ONE night when the air was warm, my puppys were sleeping on the back porch. Me and my sisters were getting ready for bed. When I was in bed. I read a chapter from my Nancy Drew book. When I finished the chapter I turned out my lamp. I wuldn't go to sleep.

I went into the living room. I saw my mom geting ready to walk out the door. I asked "where are you going"? "Just for a drive" she replied. She had a worried exspression on her face.

I knew somthing was wrong. I thought maybe if I went outside and played with my puppys. I would forget about moms worried exspression and go to sleep.

When I opened The back door, I excpected my puppys Maggie and Tucker to jump up on me. They didn't come at all. I called, they still didn't come.

Now I knew somthing was wrong. I went and woke up my dad, he said moms got it under control I thought mom had taken them to the vet because somthing was really wrong. Dad wouldn't tell me anything else. I went to my room and cried. Thats all I rembered about that

◆ The piece adds reflective comments ("I knew somthing was wrong").

◆ The piece provides a conclusion by solving the problem ("I've got over them leaving because … "). ▶▶

night because I fell asleep.
The next day I still worried.
I worried all through school.
When I got home from me
and my mom made a snack for
sisters.
I asked my mom, "so were are
the puppys"? Her eyes started to
fill with tears as she answered
my question with 3 words "I don't
know", she burst into tears. So did I.
She hugged me. If we never find
them I am sure they will have
a good home.
I went outside and sat in moms
rocking chair. I cried some more.
Mom came out I got up. She
sat down and motioned me by waving
her hand to come and sit on her lap.
I went over and cried on her
shoulder.
After dinner that night we went
looking for them, we couldn't find them
at all.
My dad after work each day went
to the pound to see if they had
picked them up. They didn't at all.
I've got over them leaving because
mom says we can get 2 new puppys
very soon.

Writing Standard 3:
Language Use and Conventions

This piece meets the Language Use and Conventions Standard for third grade.

Style and Syntax

Alex uses a variety of syntactic patterns, including introductory adverbial clauses, to address the time of events or to show passage of time. She uses transitions to keep the story grounded in the sequence of events ("When," "Now," "The next day" and "After"). She also embeds literary language by replicating story elements effectively (the initial nighttime setting, the mother's evasive reply to child's question, the father's offhanded response that the mother had "it under control," and the crying of child and mother).

Vocabulary and Word Choice

Alex uses words that show familiarity with literary language ("ONE night when the air was warm," "moms worried exsression" and "Her eyes started to fill with tears"). She also shows the result of effective word choices in the use of precise and vivid words ("worried all through school" and "she answered my question with 3 words").

Spelling

Alex spells nearly all words correctly but consistently pluralizes *puppy* by adding *s* rather than changing the *y* to *i* and adding *es*.

Punctuation, Capitalization and Other Conventions

Alex demonstrates a clear sense of paragraphing, even though she does not indent in the traditional style. She uses quotation marks when writing dialogue. She approximates the use of a comma to separate two independent clauses ("I called, they still didn't come"). She uses a comma to set off an introductory dependent clause ("ONE night when the air was warm, my puppys were sleeping on the back porch") and uses apostrophes correctly and consistently in all contractions.

(For more on Language Use and Conventions, see page 230.)

"My Sad Trip To the Doctors Office"

Writing Standard 2:
Writing Purposes and Resulting Genres

Narrative Writing

This narrative illustrates Kendall's familiarity with a demanding writing strategy. The sample is actually a story within a story. At one level, Kendall describes a trip to the doctor's office to get a shot. While waiting there, her mother tells her a story to alleviate her boredom. What is interesting about the parallel stories is the way Kendall uses the emotional impact of the story to carry her through the pain of getting a shot. This is a sophisticated strategy, and given that Kendall is a third grader, she carries it off nicely.

Nevertheless, the piece obviously is driven by the plot. Kendall does not do much to develop character or provide detail about events or settings. So the piece is not as balanced as it might have been had she drawn more from personal experience. This writing meets the standard for narrative writing in third grade.

◆ The story weaves together two narratives and successfully creates a unified ending.

◆ Kendall creates a context for both the story (a visit to the doctor's office) and for the story within the story (the mother telling a story to distract her child).

◆ The events of these parallel stories unfold naturally and reflect her

careful planning to merge the two story lines at the end of the piece.

◆ The piece adequately details Kendall's emotions ("I was pretty bored," "I hoped that she had something for me to do" and "I was so scared that I could barley feel my shot!"). We also know a little about the narrator's character

— she says a prayer for Alex at the end of the piece.

◆ The writer uses dialogue as a segue between the two stories. The line "'Shawn, you may come in with Kendall now'" brings the reader back into the story that began in the doctor's waiting room.   ▶▶

My Sad Trip To the Doctors Office
By: Kendall

I was about 8 year's old and I was waiting in the the doctors office waiting for my doctor. I was pretty bored so I asked my mom if she had something for me to do. She said, "I'll look but I'm not sure."Crossing my fingers I hoped that she had something for me to do because by now I was about to die of boredness. Lucky for me she pulled out a couple of piece's of paper with a little story on it. I wondered what in the world it was. Then my mommy asked me, " Do you want to hear a story?" I nodded my head yes. And that's where our story begins...

One cool Summer day a little boy named Alex was riding his bike in the drive - way, practicing his tricks. He was practicing tricks like no hands, no feet, even no hands and no feet. But most of all with his eyes closed, and that's the scary part. It is scary because his dad thought that Alex was having fun and he would be out there for a while-so he closed the garage door. Right after he pushed the button and went inside, there went Alex, eyes closed headed for the garage. Just then his bike slid into the garage. . . . . .

plop! Alex was stuck under the garage and couldn't breath. He was yelling for help as loud as he could at that moment. His dad came running out of terror screaming, " Where are you and what is the matter!?" By the time his father got there there was Alex lying there dead. His father drove him to the hospital but the doctor said, "I'm sorry your son is dead."

"Shawn, you may come in with Kendall now."" All right." I was so scared that I could barley feel my shot! That night after my mom kissed me good night I said a prayer that Alex was happy in heaven and would have a good life up there.

Vocabulary and Word Choice

The vocabulary of this piece comes from language appropriate for third grade. The most descriptive words used are those that describe bicycle tricks ("no hands and no feet," etc.), and these also seem to come from oral language. The phrase "running out of terror" is a bit awkward but highly evocative.

Spelling

This is a published piece and so has been edited for spelling errors.

Punctuation, Capitalization and Other Conventions

The piece demonstrates Kendall's control for capital letters and punctuation as well as quotation marks and ellipses. This level of correctness is to be expected in an edited piece by a third-grade writer.

(For more on Language Use and Conventions, see pages 230.)

Writing Standard 3:
Language Use and Conventions

This piece meets the Language Use and Conventions Standard for third grade.

Style and Syntax

This writing exhibits a full range of syntactic patterns. The author uses both transition words ("Then") and other more sophisticated structures ("By the time") to signal changes in time. The sentences themselves have clausal embeddings, some of them quite elegant ("Crossing my fingers I hoped"). The text has both the rhythms of natural speech and the language of authors ("And that's where our story begins... ").

Informing Others: Report or Informational Writing

Reports are a favorite form of writing for many third graders, who love looking things up or going places and writing down what they have seen. Third-grade reports can be expected to sound "authorial" — that is, they sound like the kinds of nonfiction third graders are reading and approximating. Many third-grade reports are drawn from classroom research efforts and, especially in science, are a combination of observation and data drawn from textbooks. They are most successful when the reports are on a topic that the child actually knows something about firsthand.

By the end of the year, we expect third-grade students to produce reports that:

◆ introduce the topic, sometimes providing a context;

◆ have an organizational structure that is useful to the reader;

◆ communicate big ideas, insights or theories that have been elaborated on or illustrated through facts, details, quotations, statistics and information;

◆ use diagrams, charts or illustrations appropriate to the text;

◆ have a concluding sentence or section; and

◆ employ a straightforward tone of voice.

"Horses"

Writing Standard 2:
Writing Purposes and Resulting Genres

Report or Informational Writing

In "Horses," Gwen uses an authorial tone, blending her own knowledge of and experiences with horses with material gathered from a variety of sources. Throughout the report, Gwen's stance clearly is that of one who is an authority on horses; in fact, in her conclusion, she asserts, "I like horses and I know a lot about them."

Gwen uses an organizational structure typical of children's informational texts — headings followed by anywhere from one to 13 sentences. This model typically does not incorporate transitional devices that lead from one topic to the next, and Gwen does not include them either. While she uses printed sources of information for her report, she blends this information throughout the report with her own observations and interpretations ("Don't give a young horse too much oatmeal, it makes them too hyper" and "If you thought , like I did that the Wild stallion was really dangerous you were wrong"). This piece meets the standard for report writing in third grade.

◆ The sample explains why Gwen chose to write on the topic of horses by relating her own interest in and experiences with horses at camp.

Horses
by Gwen

Why I Chose This Animal
I chose horses because I like to ride them. I also like to pet them. At the camp I go to everybody gets to have horses back riding lessons. Horses are so beautiful and fun to ride.

Horse Families
A mother or female horse is called a mare. A father or male horse is called a stallion. A foal is a baby horse.

Markings
A star is a little white diamond on the forelock. The forelock is a horses forehead. A race is a white line down the middle of the horses face. A blaze is kind of like a race but wider. If the white line on it face spreads out to its eyes it is called a white face. A small amount of white on its muzzle is called a snip. A muzzle is a horses mouth.

Breeds and Color Coats
Icelandic and Shetland ponies are very small when they are full grown. Chestnuts are red-brown and Roans have white hairs on their brown coat. Cream is a rare color. Rare means you don't see the color cream very much. Brown horses are brown all over. Blacks are black all over. Piebalds have black and white spots. Skewbalds are brown and white. Duns are a sandy brown with black manes and tails. Palominos have a yellowish coat and a shiny mane and tail. Grays have black and white hairs that make the color gray. Bays are brown with black manes,tails,and legs. Whites are white all over.

Breeds I Like
I like thoroughbreds because they are such a pretty brown. I like Arabians because their different coats are very beautiful and they're one of the oldest horses. I like Morgans because they have a beautiful reddish-brown coat. I like Lipizzaners because their white coats are so very pretty. I like Icelandic and Shetland ponies because they are so very cute, pretty and small.

◆ Gwen uses headings to organize the piece, providing the reader with a structure to follow. Within each topic, she uses definitions to ensure that the reader understands all the terminology.

◆ The ideas in this report range from horse origins and survival to feeding and breeds. Each idea is elaborated on with facts, definitions, and sometimes, personal experiences or comments.

◆ The conclusion refers to the opening ("I like to ride them") and expresses a wish to own a horse.

Horses from Different Countries
Hocaidos are from Japan, Sumbas are from Indonesia, and Pintos are from America.

Horse Movement
A horse can walk, trot, canter, and gallop. A trot is kind of like a skip. A canter is like a fast skip. And a gallop is like running.

Friendly Horses
Horses can be great friends. Some horses can be dangerous. Most horses are are very lovable.

Foals
Baby horses are called foals. When a foal is ready to be born, the mare(the mother horse) lies down. As soon as the foal is born it struggles to break out of the membrane sack. When the foal breaks out of the sack it breathes on it's own. In about less than a minute the foal tries to get up and walk on it's own. Foals are born with their hooves first and head last. They drink their mother's milk until they're nine to ten months old.

How Long a Horse Lives
They live about 12 to 14 years.

Horses Habitat
You usually find horses in a barn. Some horses are wild. You can find horses on ranches too.

What Horses Eat
Horses eat hay, grass, barley and oats. The best food for a tired horse is oatmeal. Don't give a young horse too much oatmeal, it makes them too hyper. Horses love carrots, apples, molasses and sugar cubes. A block of salt gives the horse important minerals and makes them thirsty so the will drink enough water.

The Most Dangerous Horse
The most dangerous horse is the Percheron. Some people cannot pronounce that so they call them war horses. It is only dangerous if it is a wild horse. If it is wild it can kill you in 7 to 8 minutes. If it is trained it is nice like any other horse.

The Fastest Horse
The fastest horse is the wild stallion. If you thought , like I did that the Wild stallion was really dangerous you were wrong. A wild stallion can kill you but it could take up to one hour.

The First Horses
The first horses were no bigger than a fox and looked like a donkey. They had short tails and small ears. These horses lived millions of years ago, but now they are extinct. The only way we knew there were horses like that was because the first humans (our ancestors) painted these horses on ancient cave walls. These horses lived in North America and over the years they changed into the horses we know now.

Horse Survival
Most horses live on farms or ranches, but some horses are wild. Wild horses can survive hard weather and they graze on hills, marshes and grasslands. These days wild horses are very rare. People work to keep these wild horses free.

My Description of a Horse
A horse is a mammal because it has fur, drinks milk and their babies are born alive. They have four legs and hooves. They have beautiful long manes and tails.

I like horses and I know a lot about them. I like to ride them and they're so beautiful! Their coats are beautiful, I wish I had a horse of my own!

Writing Standard 3:
Language Use and Conventions

This piece does not meet the Language Use and Conventions Standard for third grade because it depends too much on short, simple sentences. It does have some notable features, however.

Throughout the piece, Gwen uses appropriate vocabulary, carefully defining words that may not be part of the reader's vocabulary (technical language). Gwen confidently handles specialized vocabulary.

Gwen makes an effort to spell all specialized vocabulary in the report correctly. There are several errors in punctuation, largely the omission of commas with initial dependent clauses and the use of apostrophes ("it's" instead of *its*). Gwen uses capital letters for proper nouns, although there are some inaccuracies ("the Wild stallion").

(For more on Language Use and Conventions, see page 230.)

"ROALD DAHL Biography"

Writing Standard 2:
Writing Purposes and Resulting Genres

Report or Informational Writing

Gwen's biography is a good example of a third-grade report. It was done as part of an author study on Roald Dahl. Although some of the phrases may have been lifted from various sources, these phrases are embedded in text that clearly has been written by a third grader. Furthermore, Gwen conveys a genuine interest in the subject ("I really like the books he writes" and "He also makes his storys funny, I even laghf sometimes"). She shows a familiarity with report writing by using pictures with labels to accompany the writing. This piece meets the report writing standard for third grade.

- ◆ The writing is organized coherently, with each paragraph dedicated to a single overarching idea. The first paragraph announces the topic, the second covers the subject's parents, the third discusses his siblings, etc.

- ◆ The report looks across Roald Dahl's works. For example, Gwen explains the commonality of death or dying in a number of books.

- ◆ At the conclusion of the report, the voice of a third grader comes through again ("I want to read all of his books, but I'm not there yet!").

- ◆ The pictures, with labels, add to the information in the report.

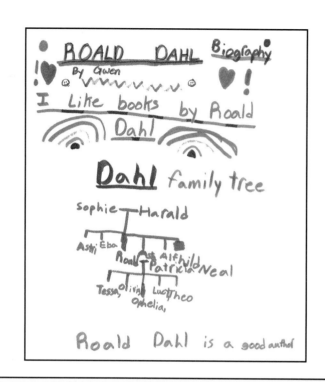

Writing Standard 3:
Language Use and Conventions

This piece does not meet the Language Use and Conventions Standard for third grade because of syntactic problems. For example, some sentences do not express complete, well-developed thoughts ("He wrote at least 19 children's books if not more," "Roald Dahl wrote a lot of wonderful stories for children but died in 1990"). This piece does have some notable features, however.

The style and syntax of this piece read like a blend of information drawn from encyclopedias and other resources that engage a third grader. It is difficult to be certain how much influence they had on this piece of writing, which is typical of elementary school reports. However, some sentences seem drawn from oral language patterns ("For example, a lot of people died in Roald Dahl's family, like his dad, so in all most every book he wrote, some one dies, or someone is all readdy dead"). Overall, the piece uses a variety of sentence patterns.

The vocabulary, in turn, is drawn from oral language and copied directly from published materials. Because the topic does not call for it, there are no technical words.

The piece is marred by several misspellings (for example, "writeing," "storys" and "explans"). The misspellings are consistent; that is, the same word is misspelled the same way throughout the document.

Overall, the punctuation in this piece is quite good. Gwen correctly punctuates sentences and controls for the use of parentheses, underlining of titles and several comma usages.

(For more on Language Use and Conventions, see page 230.)

> Then in 1960 after writeing books for adalts, he started writeing storys for children.
> His first two novels were: James and the Giant Peach and Charlie and the Chocolate Factory, which were both made into movies.
> For the ideas for his storys he wrote about things that hapened in his life but used different charicters. For example, a lot of people died in Roald Dahl's family, like his dad, so in all most every book he wrote, some one dies, or someone is all ready dead. Like in The B.F.G. (one of the books he wrote) Sophie (the little girl) is an orphan.
> I really like the books he writes. He makes up words like in The B.F.G., but somewere in the story he all ways explans them. He also makes his storys funny, I even laghf sometimes.
> Roald Dahl wrote a lot of wonderful stories for children but died in 1990.

> You can still find his books at a book store or library and read his storys.
> Most of his ideas for those storys came frome dreams or storys he told to his children.
> I want to read all of his books, but I'm not there yet!

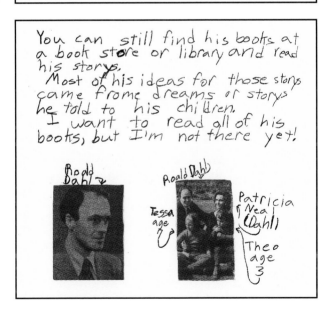

Getting Things Done: Functional and Procedural Writing

Third graders typically know a lot about the subjects that capture their interest and are good at doing a great many things. Given the opportunities, they work on computers, they earn merit badges, they care for pets, they ride bicycles, they use the library — theirs is a world that requires expertise. And their expertise constantly is being expanded by reading materials that detail how to do new things — play soccer, start a stamp collection, make cookies. Functional materials are important elements in developing third graders' own skills and in sharing their skills with others.

The process of explaining the steps in how to do something has strong real-world applications. Third graders should be able to take a process apart, look at the steps involved and explain to someone else how to do it. Third graders often produce brochures that explain how to do something and minimanuals that detail more complicated processes.

By the end of the year, we expect third-grade students to produce functional writings that:

◆ engage the reader by establishing a context for the piece;

◆ identify the topic;

◆ provide a guide to action;

◆ show the steps in an action in considerable detail;

◆ include relevant information;

◆ use language that is straightforward and clear; and

◆ may use illustrations detailing steps in the procedure.

How to Change Schools
by Tucker

You know, I have changed schools alot, and I have decided to tell you kids that haven't changed schools before what it's like. Well, it's not easy. You have to change styles of work. You have to learn new rules, and worst of all you have to leave old friends and make new ones. I have gone to three different schools in four years, so I have gone through this experience plenty of times

and I am O.K. about it. p.2

The first step is changing styles of work. For example, one school might say you need to have five items for a proper heading on your paper and your new school says three. You have to be willing to forget the old ways and practice the new ones.

The second step is to learn new rules. At one school if you sign a conduct folder three or more times in a week,

"How to Change Schools"

Writing Standard 2:
Writing Purposes and Resulting Genres

Functional and Procedural Writing

This student sample is a fine example of procedural writing. In this piece, Tucker shows strong organizational abilities and an understanding of his audience. This piece of writing provides the reader with a very clear sense of the steps that may be involved, at least for this third-grade student, in moving from one school to another. He has carefully crafted a procedure, which he has thought about. The sample represents procedural writing that meets the standard for third grade.

◆ Tucker engages the reader by identifying the topic and establishing a personal context (see title and first sentence).

◆ Tucker organizes the piece appropriately by showing the steps in detail. He establishes three areas of discussion (changing styles of work, learning new rules and making new friends) and organizes the piece around them.

◆ He takes into account the needs of readers who someday may have to change schools and provides directions for them, giving them a specific guide in clear, straightforward language.

◆ Each step contains considerable detail ("For example," "At one school" and "This is the easiest part").   ▶▶

you would lose free time ^p.3
on Friday afternoons. At your
new school, if you sign a teacher
book three times in a day
you would have to call your
parents right then! So, you
might have to practice more
self control.

    Last of all, you have
to make new friends. This
is the easiest part of change
because alot of the people are
nice. If ^you are nice to them

by sharing and joining in ^p.4
at games, they will want to
be your friend.

    In my opinion changing
schools can be good because you
learn how to change what
you do and how you do it.
But best of all you end up
with more friends than before.

Writing Standard 3:
Language Use and Conventions

This piece meets the Language Use and
Conventions Standard for third grade.

Style and Syntax

Tucker uses a conversational tone that
is appropriate for his readers ("You
know," "you kids," "Well, it's not easy"
and "O.K."). In addition, he uses
conventional transitions for this five-
paragraph essay ("first step," "second
step" and "Last of all") and elaborates
on his examples appropriately.

Vocabulary and Word Choice

Tucker uses words from an extensive
speaking vocabulary and employs specific words that characterize certain
rules from different schools.

Spelling

Tucker correctly spells all words,
including some difficult words such as
"practice" and "opinion."

Punctuation, Capitalization and
Other Conventions

Tucker displays outstanding skills
in correct use of punctuation and
capitalization.

    (For more on Language Use and
Conventions, see page 230.)

"How to do ballet Positions"

Writing Standard 2:
Writing Purposes and Resulting Genres

Functional and Procedural Writing

This wonderfully illustrated piece of functional writing manages to explain how to assume the five positions in ballet. The overall tone is lively and conversational, and the illustrations are integral to understanding the instructions. Whether the analogous information is original or not ("1st position Kind of looks like a V" and "3rd position Kind of looks like a T on its side"), its presence further elaborates on both the text and the drawings and provides the reader with very helpful information.

This piece is further remarkable for Gwen's useful tips ("1st and 2nd position are preety easy but 3rd, 4th, and 5th are preety hard for beginners. One little thing I have to tell you, 3rd, and 4th position are not used very much in ballet"). This piece represents functional writing that meets the standard for third grade.

◆ This piece provides a very explicit set of directions that, if followed, could allow a reader to assume and teach the positions.

◆ The piece begins by announcing Gwen's intent ("I'm going to tell you how to do the five ballet positions") and establishing her expertise ("When I was younger my ballet techer helped me learn all five ballet positions").

◆ Each position is illustrated and described fully, with the illustration playing a very important role ("put your heels together like this").

◆ The language is straightforward and clear, and Gwen goes a long way toward making the reader feel that learning the five positions is not an insurmountable task ("All you do is") and later explaining that though positions three, four and five are relatively difficult, the third and fourth positions are not used frequently. She also shows the similarities and differences in the positions so that a reader can easily believe that understanding one position makes learning another fairly simple.

◆ There is no extraneous information in this writing; it is lucid and coherent. ▶▶

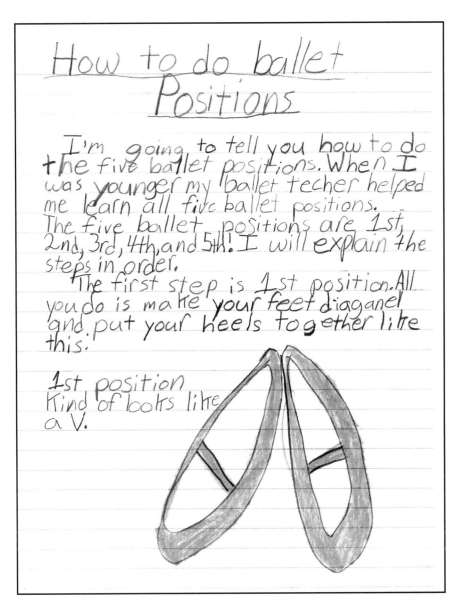

How to do ballet Positions

I'm going to tell you how to do the five ballet positions. When I was younger my ballet techer helped me learn all five ballet positions. The five ballet positions are 1st, 2nd, 3rd, 4th, and 5th! I will explain the steps in order.

The first step is 1st position. All you do is make your feet diaganel and put your heels together like this.

1st position
Kind of looks like a V.

Writing Standard 3:
Language Use and Conventions

This piece meets the Language Use and Conventions Standard for third grade.

Style and Syntax

The writing has a style and range of sentence patterns appropriate for this genre. Sentences are relatively short, but they need to be short so that the reader is not confused. Meaning is further enhanced through transitional elements. Occasionally, Gwen does have syntax problems ("The foot thats sideways put that heel in the middlle"), but such problems are rare and do not inhibit meaning or take away from the overall sense that this is a well-written piece. When she drops into a conversational style (see the last paragraph), the sentence structures are more complex.

Vocabulary and Word Choice

Gwen uses vocabulary appropriate for the task and subject at hand, in this case the specialized vocabulary of learning something about ballet. Although the language she employs is relatively simple, the simplicity is appropriate for teaching another child how to do something.

Spelling

All the words in this text are spelled correctly except "diaganel," "preety," "middlle" and "techer."

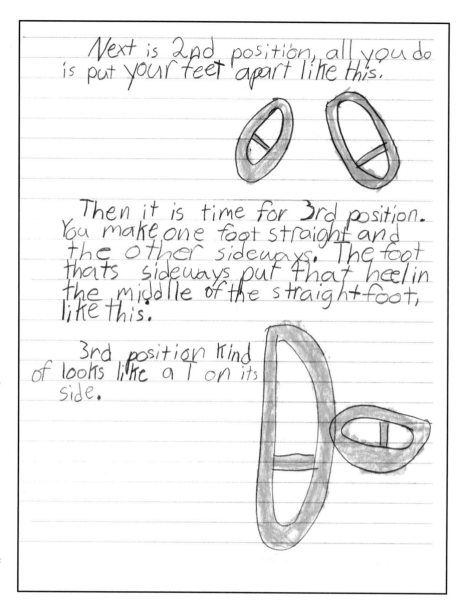

Punctuation, Capitalization and Other Conventions

Although there are several punctuation problems, most of these are comma errors. Gwen uses capital letters at the beginning of sentences and punctuation at the end, and she uses contractions, uppercase letters and lowercase letters correctly. One contraction ("thats") is not punctuated, and "ballet" in the title should be capitalized. Otherwise, this piece shows good control for conventions.

(For more on Language Use and Conventions, see page 230.)

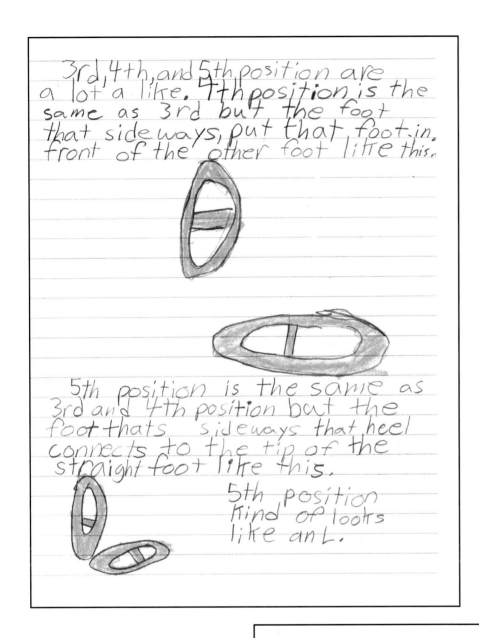

3rd, 4th, and 5th position are a lot a like. 4th position is the same as 3rd but the foot that sideways, put that foot in front of the other foot like this.

5th position is the same as 3rd and 4th position but the foot thats sideways that heel connects to the tip of the straight foot like this.

5th position kind of looks like an L.

1st and 2nd position are preety easy but 3rd, 4th, and 5th are preety hard for beginners. One little thing I have to tell you, 3rd, and 4th position are not used very much in ballet. When you have learned the 5 positions of ballet you can go teach your friends!

Producing and Responding to Literature

The literature that third graders write reflects what they have learned in their genre studies of poetry, memoir, fiction and nonfiction. They have developed a repertoire of writing strategies and can identify specific elements of particular genres. They read and understand the variety of possibilities within a genre, and they discuss what strategies an author has used and whether these strategies work. All of this knowledge contributes to their writing repertoire.

When third graders evaluate literature, they are able to refer to the text and make assertions about big ideas, find commonalities across texts, develop interpretive hunches and run these hunches by others during book talks, and elaborate on their evaluation of the text. Because they write themselves, third graders are able to make discerning comments about literature, attending both to stylistic elements and overall effectiveness of a piece.

Producing literature

By the end of the year, we expect third-grade students to be able to:

◆ write stories, songs, memoirs, poetry and plays — conforming to appropriate expectations for each form;

◆ produce a piece that incorporates elements appropriate to the genre after engaging in a genre study; and

◆ build on the thread of a story by extending or changing the story line.

Responding to literature

By the end of the year, we expect third-grade students to be able to:

◆ support an interpretation by making specific references to the text;

◆ provide enough detail from the text so the reader can understand the interpretation;

◆ go beyond retelling;

◆ compare two works by an author;

◆ discuss several works that have a common idea or theme; and

◆ make connections between the text and their own ideas and lives.

Third-Grade Writing Standard 1:
Habits and Processes

Third-Grade Writing Standard 2:
Writing Purposes and Resulting Genres

   ◆ Sharing Events, Telling Stories: Narrative Writing

   ◆ Informing Others: Report or Informational Writing

   ◆ Getting Things Done: Functional and Procedural Writing

   ◆ Producing and Responding to Literature

Third-Grade Writing Standard 3:
Language Use and Conventions

   ◆ Style and Syntax

   ◆ Vocabulary and Word Choice

   ◆ Spelling

   ◆ Punctuation, Capitalization and Other Conventions

"Turtle"

Writing Standard 2:
Writing Purposes and Resulting Genres

Producing Literature

"Turtle" is an excellent example of a student-written poem. The piece of writing suggests Emma has internalized poetic elements through reading and studying, and she uses several to describe a swimming turtle. "Turtle" is a piece of literature that meets the standard for third grade.

The piece displays short line lengths, probably in imitation of poems Emma has read. She develops imagery through effective use of descriptive action words ("swoops," "blends," "glides" and "sways") and through use of similes ("cloud white/as/winter snow" and "Water clear/as/lenses").

Writing Standard 3:
Language Use and Conventions

This piece does not meet the Language Use and Conventions Standard for third grade because of inconsistencies in capitalization and lack of any punctuation. It does have some notable features, however.

Emma employs simple phrases in short line lengths, ending with a statement that repeats the first line to create a closed circle. She uses words that are natural to a speaking vocabulary. She also uses words in unusual groupings that are poetic ("blends water" and "Wheat glides"). She has created some striking similes as well, especially "Water clear/as/lenses." All words are spelled correctly.

(For more on Language Use and Conventions, see page 230.)

Emma

Turtle

turtle swims
through clear water
clear
blue sky
swoops down
blends water

Wheat glides
through the water
It sways in the sky
cloud white
as
winter snow
sun orange
as
Australia's Orange
Water clear
as
lenses
Turtle swims

"Putting Things in Box's"

Writing Standard 2:
Writing Purposes and Resulting Genres

Producing Literature

This sample displays Gabrielle's rather amazing ability to create a piece of literature that looks like prose but reads like poetry. This piece of writing provides the reader with the sense that the writer has read widely and internalized a number of highly effective literary techniques. Gabrielle produces a piece of literature that meets the standard for third grade.

The writing occurred immediately after hearing the teacher read pieces that contained a lot of repetition. This piece represents Gabrielle's understanding of repetition as a literary device. It also meets the third-grade standard for a response to literature.

◆ The piece effectively uses the repetition of phrases to heighten what is perhaps a sense of alienation ("half the night," "half the afternoon," "throwing out" and "sit behind box's"). The parallel structure created by this repetition is quite sophisticated.

◆ By moving from a first-person point of view ("my parents") to a third-person perspective ("they spent") to a universal you ("You would go to bed") and finally back to the original first person, the piece suggests a sense of uncertainty and loneliness.

It was strange my parents were up half the night putting things in box's half the night wrapping things in newspaper half the night sealing it with special sealing tape they spent half the afternoon packing, half the afternoon cleaning out old shelfs and closets throwing out forgotten garbge, thowing out old junk and baby toys. You would go to bed in a bare room all alone ~~and your bed creaks your bed g~~ as your floor moans. the walls are brighter than before, Higher than before, newer than before. it was different diffrent lights diffrent space, diffrent life. I would sit behind box's writing I would sit behind box's reading I would sit behind box's ~~eating and it~~ drawing. ~~it was~~ ~~toatley~~ ~~all all alone~~

Writing Standard 3:
Language Use and Conventions

This piece does not meet the Language Use and Conventions Standard for third grade because of problems with spelling and punctuation, capitalization and other conventions. It does have some notable features, however.

The piece employs literary syntactic patterns, including the piling up of parallel phrases and clauses. Gabrielle initially uses long sentences, which are followed by short and partial ones to create a feeling of abandonment and loneliness.

Gabrielle uses words natural to a speaking vocabulary but creates a poetic effect by using everyday words in a stylistic manner. She correctly spells most words or approximates correct spelling ("diffrent" for *different*). She shows evidence of understanding the addition of *s* to make a plural ("shelfs") and exhibits an awareness of the apostrophe ("box's") without understanding how to use it.

Gabrielle uses some end punctuation but omits periods at the ends of several sentences. She uses the capital *I* correctly throughout and capitalizes the first word of a sentence if there is a period before it. She also uses commas correctly to indicate phrases in a series.

(For more on Language Use and Conventions, see page 230.)

"Wilfred Gorden McDonald Patridge"

Writing Standard 2:
Writing Purposes and Resulting Genres

Responding to Literature

Emily's sample shows how a third grader responds in several ways to a piece of literature. While the sample is not a full-blown "composition," it shows one way a student can demonstrate a response to literature that meets the standard for third grade.

◆ The piece expresses Emily's understanding of the book by making a number of specific references to the text ("Wilfreds friend Nancy" and "he took a basket and filled it with some of his memories").

◆ She begins with a straightforward summary of the plot, told in narrative form. However, she goes beyond retelling to recount her personal connection to the story, ending with the difference between the book's ending and real life, where her great-grandmother "could never remeber the past again."

Writing Standard 3:
Language Use and Conventions

This piece meets the Language Use and Conventions Standard for third grade. Although there are some spelling errors, the overall quality of the other elements of this standard offsets concerns raised because of misspellings.

> Emily
> Wilfred Gorden McDonald Patridge
>
> This is a story about a little boy who changes his friend's life. Wilfreds friend Nancy has lost her memory but Wilfred doesn't know what memory means. So Wilfred goes around asking people what a memory is. The people gave many answers. Wilfred decided to bring back Miss Nancy's memory so he took a basket and filled it with some of his memories. When Miss Nancy holds Wilfreds memories she sadenly rembers her past.
>
> Miss Nancy reminds me of my great-grandmother MeeMaw who had Alsimers disease. She lost her memory like Miss Nancy and she didnt even know my mom or herself. The only difference was that my great-grandmother could never remeber the past again.

Style and Syntax

Emily uses transitions such as "so," but she also uses more sophisticated linkages ("like Miss Nancy" and "The only difference"). She uses a variety of sentence patterns to show the relationships among ideas and demonstrates control over subordinate phrases and clauses that are used appropriately to show such relationships ("When Miss Nancy holds Wilfreds memories she sudenly rembers her past").

Vocabulary and Word Choice

Emily uses words that are generally part of a third grader's speaking vocabulary but also uses some words that are specialized or technical ("Alsimers").

Spelling

There are five spelling errors ("sudenly," "rembers," "remeber," "diseas" and the specialized word "Alsimers").

Punctuation, Capitalization and Other Conventions

Emily uses capital letters at the beginning of sentences and for all proper names. Likewise, she uses end punctuation correctly. She sometimes correctly uses the apostrophe for possessives ("friend's" and "Miss Nancy's") and in contractions.

(For more on Language Use and Conventions, see page 230.)

"The Outcast of Redwall"

Writing Standard 2:
Writing Purposes and Resulting Genres

Responding to Literature

This is an edited piece of third-grade writing, a variation on the book report, in which Miles recommends the book *The Outcast of Redwall* by Brian Jacques to another reader. It demonstrates his ability to determine the "big idea," or theme, of the book (friendship and love) and to refer to specific incidents in the text that relate to that theme. Although he does not specifically compare this work with another, Miles does identify the book as part of a body of work from an author ("This well-known author has finally made a book" and "he is writing a new book"). This piece meets the standard for a third-grade response to literature.

◆ The writing incorporates the style of a published book review that Miles probably has read in book club promotions ("This book is a must for every library"). He uses a common rating system for books, movies, restaurants, etc. ("I rate this book ********").

◆ Miles supports an interpretation by making specific references to the text ("Later Veail has a difficult decision to make. Should he … ").

◆ He provides enough detail from the text so that the reader can understand the interpretation ("Veail has two parts of evil in him and these parts lead him to murder and to be outcast").

◆ The writing goes beyond merely retelling the story; Miles refers to specific incidents in the text without giving a plot summary. He refers to specific vivid images from the book without revealing too much to the intended audience (potential readers) ("I still remember the section in which … " and "I can still see him walking").

The Outcast of Redwall
By Brian Jaques

This well-known author has finally made a book that noone can resist or not love. This tale of friendship and love will bring tears to even the youngest readers. This book is a must for every library; pravtae, public or government.
I still remember the section in which Sunflash returned to Salamanston, a true badger lord. I can still see him walking across the hot sands to Salamanstrom. I remember Veail Six Claws difficult decision Veill's father was evil so Veail has two parts of evil in him and these parts lead him to murder and to be outcast. But Veaill also has good parts...Later Veail has a difficult decision to make. Should he join the ones who outcast him or join his evil father and his murdering band
I suggest this book to readers young and old. It should be read immediatly. Also, Brian Jacques is open for letters and quite soon he will be opning a fan club and also he is writing a new book.
The Outcasts of Redwall has certainly brought a new dimension to book writing.I rate this book ********
       Miles
           reporter

Writing Standard 3:
Language Use and Conventions

This piece meets the Language Use and Conventions Standard for third grade.

Style and Syntax

Miles uses a variety of syntactic patterns including complex sentences. He also uses some unusual literary constructions such as the retained adjectives in "This book is a must for every library; pravtae, public or government."

Vocabulary and Word Choice

Miles uses both literary language ("This tale of friendship and love") and his own language ("Brian Jacques is open for letters"). He uses the specialized vocabulary appropriate to the book review ("well-known author," "to readers young and old" and "new dimension to book writing").

Spelling

Familiar high-frequency words are spelled correctly, as are many words not frequently used by third graders ("government," "outcast" and "dimension"). He spells words with inflectional endings correctly.

Although this is an edited final copy, there are a few errors in spelling ("noone," "pravtae," "immediatly" and "opning"). Some may be typing mistakes, as Miles used a word processor to copy his handwritten response.

Punctuation, Capitalization and Other Conventions

Miles uses capital letters and periods correctly. He attempts some advanced punctuation marks — the semicolon and the ellipsis — although he omits some end punctuation marks and puts a period where a question mark should be.

(For more on Language Use and Conventions, see page 230.)

Third-Grade
Writing Standard 3: Language Use and Conventions

Control of conventions is an important issue for third graders who want their writing to be read appropriately. By the time they finish the primary grades, young authors have several "writerly" techniques at their command. With their emerging mastery of the conventions of writing comes a growing sensitivity to the audience with whom they are trying to communicate. They can use direct quotations to produce dialogue; they can write an engaging lead that will hook a reader; they can bring conflicting opinions and contrasting views to life; and they can build a sense of anticipation or suspense that keeps the reader interested. Third graders recognize the relationship between syntax and having readers read with the correct expression. They are able to explore a variety of syntactic patterns to create rhythm and tone that support meaning in their writing. They are equally adept with word choice — often reaching for words that they only partly control but that reflect a desire to give their writing substance and style.

Style and Syntax

Students meeting standards when they leave third grade have a strong "sentence sense." They use more "writerly writing," modeling and responding to the increasingly complex kinds of reading they are doing. Their style and syntax show an awareness of the choices a writer makes to produce a particular effect (for example, suspense) or to produce a certain kind of reading (getting the expression correct). Their writing reads like many of the books they hear in class, and they often embed borrowings, such as refrains or phrasings, from familiar books.

Using one's own language

By the end of the year, we expect third-grade students to:

- use appropriately a variety of syntactic patterns (for example, equal weight in compound sentences, subordination in complex sentences) to show relationships of ideas;

- incorporate transitional words and phrases appropriate to thinking; and

- embed phrases and modifiers that make their writing lively and graphic.

Taking on language of authors

By the end of the year, we expect third-grade students to:

- use varying sentence patterns and lengths to slow reading down, speed it up or create a mood;

- embed literary language where appropriate; and

- reproduce sentence structures from various genres they are reading.

Vocabulary and Word Choice

Using one's own language

By the end of the year, we expect third-grade students to:

- use words from their speaking vocabulary in their writing, including

Sidebar

Third-Grade Writing Standard 1:
Habits and Processes

Third-Grade Writing Standard 2:
Writing Purposes and Resulting Genres

- Sharing Events, Telling Stories: Narrative Writing
- Informing Others: Report or Informational Writing
- Getting Things Done: Functional and Procedural Writing
- Producing and Responding to Literature

Third-Grade Writing Standard 3:
Language Use and Conventions

- Style and Syntax
- Vocabulary and Word Choice
- Spelling
- Punctuation, Capitalization and Other Conventions

words they have learned from reading and class discussion; and

◆ make word choices that reveal they have a large enough vocabulary to exercise options in word choice (for example, more precise and vivid words).

Taking on language of authors

By the end of the year, we expect third-grade students to:

◆ extend their writing vocabulary by using specialized words related to the topic or setting of their writing (for example, the names of breeds of dogs if they are writing about dogs).

Spelling

Third graders typically are more focused on correct spelling than they were previously. They often can recognize when a word does not look correct. When they do not know how to spell a word, they look it up (given resources) or experiment until it looks right. By the end of third grade, we expect students' writing to be easy to read, with most words spelled correctly and errors limited to irregularly spelled and infrequently encountered words.

At the end of third grade, students should have a strong enough base of spelling knowledge that the rules are starting to make sense to them and they can catch on to spelling

instruction. That is, they have developed a layered understanding of how spelling works through experimenting with spelling patterns, generalizing from words they know how to spell and having had sufficient spelling instruction to draw on with confidence. These children use phonetic spelling correctly for regular and irregular words most of the time. They know and use word chunks, word families, spelling patterns and basic spelling rules to generate conventional or close-to-conventional spellings. They are learning to recognize how meaning influences spelling in combination with letter-sound correspondence (for example, *read* can be pronounced two ways, and the two words have different meanings; *read* and *red*, though they sound the same, have different spellings and meanings).

By the end of the year, we expect third-grade students to:

◆ notice when words do not look correct and use strategies to correct the spelling (for example, experiment with alternative spellings, look the word up in a dictionary or word list);

◆ correctly spell all familiar high-frequency words;

◆ correctly spell words with short vowels and common endings;

◆ correctly spell most inflectional endings, including plurals and verb tenses;

◆ use correct spelling patterns and rules such as consonant doubling, dropping *e* and changing *y* to *i*; and

◆ correctly spell most derivational words (for example, *-tion, -ment, -ly*).

Punctuation, Capitalization and Other Conventions

By the end of third grade, children should be using punctuation that makes sense, even if it is not always completely correct.

By the end of the year, we expect third-grade students to:

◆ use capital letters at the beginnings of sentences;

◆ use periods and other end punctuation correctly nearly all of the time;

◆ approximate the use of quotation marks;

◆ approximate the use of commas;

◆ use question marks;

◆ use capital and lowercase letters; and

◆ use contractions.

"Going to My Grandma's"

Writing Standard 3:
Language Use and Conventions

This piece is a simple narrative about a trip to "Grandma's." Although the narrative itself does not meet the standard for Writing Purposes and Resulting Genres, it does meet the standard for Language Use and Conventions. This writing is made up of 12 sentences, which are punctuated almost flawlessly. The writer spells all words correctly and uses capitals appropriately. In fact, the only errors are some problems with commas, which are to be expected in third grade.

Style and Syntax

The piece contains a range of syntactic patterns. In addition, there are transition words ("One day," "First," "Then") and introductory adverbial clauses ("When one of my cousins") to signal shifts in time. The piece also uses the language of oral speech ("I had fun").

Vocabulary and Word Choice

The vocabulary and word choice in this piece are adequate to convey meaning, although there is scant concrete detail ("a 5 ft. fish" and the exact number of eggs found by the cousins). The vocabulary, hence, is not very precise, but the overall feel of the writing, almost "bed-to-bed" in character, does not require much precision.

Spelling

There are no misspellings in this piece.

> Going to My Grandma's
>
> One day I went to my grandma's for Easter and my cousins were there too. First we went fishing. We caught a 5 ft. fish. Then it was time for the Easter egg hunt. When one of my cousins was done and my mom was done hiding the eggs we went outside and I found 10. Four of my cousins found 10 too. 3 of the rest of my cousins found 9 eggs. Next we ate our candy inside. Then my brother and I played with our cousins. One cousin gave me a frisbee and we played catch. I had fun. Then we went home.

Punctuation, Capitalization and Other Conventions

There are no punctuation errors (except for the comma problem in the compound-complex sentence and the need for a comma after "10" and before "too"). Not capitalizing "frisbee" (a brand name) is the only error in capitalization. The writer uses the apostrophe correctly and uses a period to mark an abbreviation ("ft.").

Collections

Collections of Student Writing

Individual pieces of student work accompany the New Standards Primary Literacy Standards, illustrating "how good is good enough" to meet the standards, grade by grade. In the classroom, however, teachers evaluate student work and progress over the course of a year or more. This section adds that dimension of time to student work. It contains several kinds of collections of student writing.

Growth Over One Year

These collections feature selected writing pieces of individual students over the course of one school year. For example, Melissa's collection includes six pieces that, taken together, provide a snapshot of Melissa's literacy development in kindergarten.

In reviewing these collections, it is important to pay special attention to each student's first piece, which shows the student's skill level at the beginning of the school year. The kindergarten and first-grade collections come from students who entered school with very different skills. The second-grade collection comes from a student whose writing did not meet first-grade standards at the start of the year. The third-grade collection comes from a strong student.

The point is, students with a wide range of skills can and will make noticeable progress over the course of a school year — if they are in very good writing programs, as the students whose work appears here are.

Growth Over Four Years

This collection shows the growth of a highly literate and imaginative writer throughout the primary years. In good writing programs, students with similar skills likely can show similar growth.

This collection is interesting, too, in demonstrating that students' phonetic and literary skills develop unevenly. But with much encouragement and many opportunities to practice, these skills even out, and students produce writing that is more polished.

One Assignment, Four Grade Levels

This collection shows how students at each grade level respond to the same assignment. In this case, the students are explaining a familiar task, carving a pumpkin into a jack-o'-lantern. Even a kindergartner can lay out the sequence of steps required to get the job done. But the progression of accumulated skills demonstrated grade by grade is remarkable. Year by year, students gain more control over their writing. The downhill slant of the kindergartner evens out by first grade. The first grader adds a title page and transition language. The second grader blends narrative and functional writing — and enlivens her piece with more sophisticated words, such as "supermarket," "banana" and "zigzags." The third graders produce revised works with illustrations that are synchronized carefully with the text. Their writing is confident and creative.

In the early primary grades, students have to work very hard simply to coordinate the dance between eyes and hands, pencils and paper. Nevertheless, beginning in kindergarten, students are remarkably able to make their meaning clear and compelling. Commentary on the student writing in these collections shows how they do it. The commentary explains how and why the student work meets the standards — or how and why it falls short.

Third Grade

First Grade

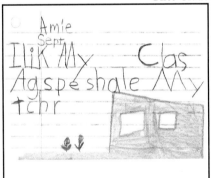

Third Grade

When The Stars Come Out

Dad just says straight out of the blue, "No." No, I can't have a puppy of my own. I remember the litter of puppies lying at my feet. One peered at me, licking my fingers and whimpering, nudging at me gently. I wanted that one. But Dad says no. My tears start as a trickle and then burn my eyes when Dad says no. He's wrong to say no. He doesn't know a thing about King Charles Cavelier spaniels and yet he says no.

I have a dream. I can picture it now. Dad comes back from canoeing and walk into my bedroom and hears a woof. That would be terrific. It's my dream. In my dream,. I run outside to meet the new snow. I watch my puppy snuffling the snowy trail of mouse. I laugh. He snuffles at me as if he's saying "oopsey." But it is just a dream. Now I look at my snow prints in the snow and hope that someday there'll be another pair right beside mine. Maybe someday my dog and I will make an angel in the snow.

And when it begins to get dark and it's time to come in, we'll go up to bed and watch the night. When the stars come out and the pink clouds leave, when my lights are long past out, my dog and I will be fast asleep.

By Evan

Kindergarten

Kindergarten

Second Grade

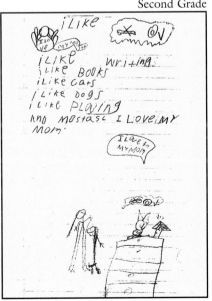

Third Grade

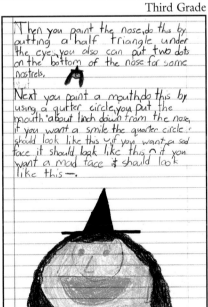

"Melissa's Collection"
Kindergarten Growth Over One Year

The six samples produced by this kindergarten student demonstrate remarkable growth over the course of a year. The student, Melissa, started kindergarten after one year in a prekindergarten program. Her kindergarten teacher provided time each day for students to engage in a writers' workshop, so Melissa generated her own topics, wrote regularly, worked with response groups, conferred with her teacher, and edited and polished selected pieces. Her remarkable growth as a writer is due in no small part to the quality of her instruction. The full collection of Melissa's kindergarten writing provides evidence of her meeting the Writing Habits and Processes Standard. One of the pieces in this collection is an example that meets the standard for kindergarten narrative writing, "I wit fihn," and a second piece, "Frags," is an example that is above the standard for informational writing.

Mid-September

The first sample, "ABCD … ," was generated in mid-September, about a week into the school year, after the teacher had distributed "writing journals" to the class and directed the students to write about anything they wanted her to read. The teacher's plan was to respond to these journals on a daily basis. Melissa's entry shows that she wanted her teacher to know that she knew some of the alphabet. As a writing sample this, of course, is limited, but it does demonstrate that Melissa has one of the basic tools of literacy.

November 5

*I   like   jelly   beans

*Translation of phonetically spelled words

The second sample, a simple piece of expressive writing dated Nov. 5, illustrates that Melissa understands to write from left to right across the page (we could probably infer the left-to-right ordering from the alphabet sample, but we could not be certain). Melissa's sample also shows that she is attempting letter-sound correspondence (she has represented *like* with the beginning and ending sounds, though the ending sound is represented by the letter *c* rather than by the actual ending consonant). Melissa relies heavily on beginning and ending consonant sounds to represent whole words. She still is not creating word boundaries, and whether her writing could be read by another person, even someone who is knowledgeable about phonetic spelling, is doubtful.

January 22

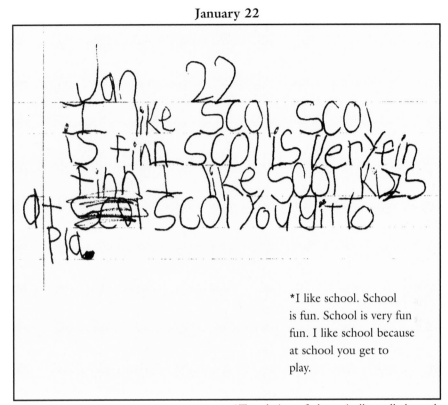

The third sample, dated Jan. 22, shows that Melissa continues to spell phonetically while beginning to spell some words correctly. There are word boundaries and a left-to-right, top-to-bottom ordering. There is evidence that Melissa can use both uppercase and lowercase letters. Her writing clearly can be read by another person. The message contains a total of 21 words, although only 12 different words actually are represented (some are repeated). Of these, seven are spelled correctly. Those words not spelled correctly still can be read because they are spelled phonetically. Melissa's sample also demonstrates her awareness of punctuation (she uses a period). The sample represents the kind of expressive writing typical of kindergarten and first-grade writers. Notice the repetition ("scol is finn scol is very fin"), which is commonplace as young writers attempt to "write more." ▶▶

*I like school. School is fun. School is very fun fun. I like school because at school you get to play.

*Translation of phonetically spelled words

February/March

*nurse's

hat

*Translation of phonetically spelled words

The fourth sample contains 30 different words, 15 of which Melissa spells correctly and 10 of which Melissa uses more than once. This is an early sample of a polished (revised) piece. That is, Melissa designed a cover for the piece, gave it a title and made several revisions to clarify her meaning. She did not copy the piece over because her teacher allowed for less than perfect copy. This sample actually lacks a certain coherence. It begins with an assertion about a preference of Melissa's ("I like a nrsis hat") followed (inferentially) by the cause for this preference ("Wn I groo up Im goown to b a nrs"). Following this attempt to set a context for the piece, Melissa describes a sequence of events about trying on hats after the teacher read a story to the class about hats. The piece shows Melissa's awareness of both the apostrophe (though she uses it to make plurals rather than possessives) and the period (though she employs only one, which marks the end of the sample).

We like hat's Melissa
I like a ▮ nrsis ▮ hat
                nurse's
Wn I gnoo up Im
when   grow   I'm
goown to b a hrs We got
going   be   nurse
to tri on hat's Wns day
        try   hats   Wednesday
and tnn mrs John rid iss
        then   read   us
a story ibat hat's aftr We
                about   hats   after
rid the story
hY rid the story
        she   read
Wns. day We go to trion
Wednesday   got   try
▮ hat's.
        hats

April 7

The fifth sample, dated April 7, at first might appear to represent a step backward because Melissa misspells more words. However, this 37-word message repeats fewer words — only five appear more than once. (She spells seven words correctly.) The message is significantly more complex than what Melissa wrote in January, and her vocabulary is more advanced. The writing now more closely approximates Melissa's oral language — she is confident enough as a writer not to inhibit her word choice. Correctly spelling words like *cousin*, *adventure*, *caught* and *roly-poly* would require more understanding of orthographic rules than would be reasonable to expect from kindergarten writers.

This is an example that meets the standard for narrative writing at the end of kindergarten. It has an initiating event ("I wit fihn wit mY ciznn's and mY ilcl Erll and mY dad"), a reaction to the event ("it wizs andvihr!") and then the subsequent events ("we clild hil … we oalso coct 2 fih … we wrr fiidn roolepoles").

(See page 72 for a more complete analysis of this student work.) ▶▶

April 7
*I went fishing with
my cousins and my
Uncle Earl and my dad.
It was an adventure!
We climbed hill. It was
fun! And we also
caught 2 fish. On our
way back we were
finding roly-polys.

*Translation of phonetically spelled words

May 6

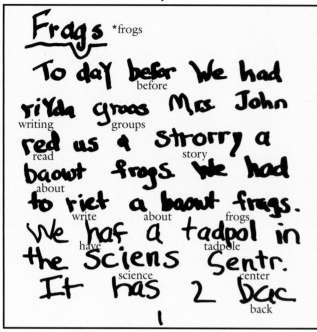

Frags *frogs

To day befor We had
riYda groos Mrs. John
red us a strorry a
baowt frogs. We had
to riet a baowt frags.
We haf a tadpol in
the Sciens Sentr.
It has 2 bac

writing
groups
read
story
about
write   about   frogs
have   tadpole
science   center
back

1

ligs and wen it
has 2 frunt ligs
its tal disupirs
and it can not egt
wen its maot is
chajn. Then the
scknn gets to little
and the frogs pol
off thrr scknn an

legs
when
front   legs
tail   disappears
eat
when   mouth
changing
skin   too
pull
their   2   skin

2

*Translation of phonetically spelled words

thaa eyt it. Saum
af the frogs bloo
baubools. Frogs lad
eggs that look like
jele and the fish eyt
some but some
hach to tadpoos.
It gros bigr and
bigr and bigr.

they   eat   some
blow
bubbles   laid
jelly   eat
hatch   tadpoles
grows   bigger
bigger   bigger

3

The sixth piece, dated May 6, is quite remarkable and clearly exceeds the kindergarten standard. It is a well-developed report of information — which in itself far exceeds what would be reasonable to expect in kindergarten. Moreover, it is well punctuated. Periods for the most part come where they belong, although there are several run-on sentences. There is control for the use of uppercase and lowercase letters — all sentences start with capital letters, and the teacher's name is capitalized. The title of the piece is underlined. There is even a period at the end of the term of address ("Mrs.").

There is one tense mistake — a shift from the present to the past ("frogs lad [laid] eggs") toward the end of the piece. She spells 28 of the words correctly. She also organizes her writing in coherent sections. Melissa begins by setting the context for the piece and then establishes her expertise — how she knows this information.

Then she discusses the tadpole's metamorphosis — the emergence of front legs, the disappearance of the tail, the change of the mouth, the disappearance of the skin. Next, she switches to remarking on frog behaviors — blowing bubbles, laying eggs, eating skin. Finally, she tells us about the eggs hatching to tadpoles and the growth of these tadpoles. This piece exceeds expectations for kindergarten report writing.

"A I⊗ʌ's Collection"
Kindergarten Growth Over One Year

This collection of seven samples was drawn from the portfolio of Alex, who was enrolled in a bilingual program and lived in a monolingual family. The bilingual program had a very strong daily reading and writing workshop. Alex's starting point is more typical of children entering kindergarten than Melissa's (see page 236). It is also important to know that unlike Melissa, Alex did not attend a prekindergarten program.

September 7

The first entry, dated Sept. 7, is a simple picture of familiar objects — a house, a cloud and grass. The teacher instructed the class to write a story, and Alex drew a response. There are a few details in the drawing. The house has windows and a door with a handle. To the right of the house is a plant or a small tree.

Eleven days later, Alex still is drawing in response to an invitation to write. His second drawing, however, is much more detailed. This time, the house has windows with windowpanes and a chimney with smoke coming out. There is a sun with beams. The drawing also includes a person with facial features and hair. ▶▶

September 18

September 28

Ten days later, Alex's writing has undergone an amazing transformation. Although drawing is still an important part of writing for him, he has begun to incorporate into the text random letters with which he is familiar. Alex demonstrates an awareness of segmentation when he uses dashes and arrows and "happy faces" between some letter groups. He also demonstrates an awareness that writing is not part of the picture — it is separate — and that it moves from left to right and top to bottom.

November 28

On Nov. 28, Alex again produces writing that illustrates dramatic growth, with a Christmas list made up of five items. Each item is preceded by a number followed by a period. All the items are written in capital letters, and the spelling indicates that he is aware of letter-sound correspondence. Each word begins and ends with the appropriate consonant and includes internal vowels. The spelling is so logical that this piece can be read easily by another person.

*1. Blocks
2. Shoes
3. Bicycle
4. Books
5. Colors

*Translation of phonetically spelled words

In the next sample, done in March, Alex's writing undergoes another change: A whole story emerges in text form and is supported by the illustration. The spelling of the piece is somewhat problematic, although for the most part initial sounds are represented correctly, and the word "two" is spelled consistently. The lengths of the spaces between words are uneven, and he reverses several letters. He ends the piece with an exclamation point. Initially, this writing may seem somewhat disappointing because the spelling in the December piece was so much easier to read. However, December's sample simply listed five words. In this sample, he is telling a story, and the story requires many words, some of which are unfamiliar to him.

March

*A doctor came by to take a person to the hospital too. It's too late.

*Translation of phonetically spelled words

In April, Alex's spelling once again is more controlled, but the text is more a label than a story. He again reverses some of the letters, but he represents the initial and final consonants more consistently and uses three lowercase letters. The spacing between words is more regular. ▶▶

April

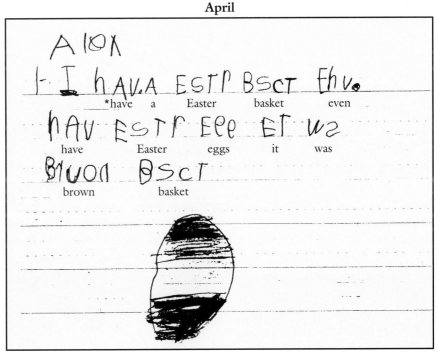

*have a Easter basket even
have Easter eggs it was
brown basket

*Translation of phonetically spelled words

May

*Woman and a girl
went to the pet store. The
car smoked a lot. The
car and it broke.
The dog is scared.

*Translation of phonetically spelled words

Alex's collection presents a snapshot of growth from September to May that is fairly typical of many kindergarten students. He has learned a great deal as a writer, but his growth has not always been smooth and predictable. He backslid when he attempted more challenging tasks, and sometimes he lost control of even simple things, such as maintaining equal spacing between words. But that is how children usually grow as writers. At the end of kindergarten, Alex is not nearly as fluent as Melissa (the writer of the other kindergarten collection), nor does he control for spelling or conventions as well as she does, but he did not enter kindergarten with the same background. He nevertheless is well on his way, and if his growth during first grade is as continuous as his growth during kindergarten, he likely will meet the standard for writing at the end of first grade.

The last sample, done in May, is again a narrative and is the longest piece to date with 20 words. In this sample, Alex spells five high-frequency words ("AnD," "A," "GirL," "TO" and "car"), and the text for the most part is readable. As he does in all of his writing, Alex represents words consistently ("TA" is always *the*), even if they are represented incorrectly, and he is very aware of periods — there are 10 of them scattered throughout this piece. The space between words is fairly regular, though he uses a dash once instead of a space. The letters are both lowercase and uppercase, but there are clearly more of the latter. The story is carried by the text but is supported by a very detailed drawing.

"Amie's Collection"
First-Grade Growth Over One Year

This collection of student work was produced by Amie, a first grader who wrote daily in a writer's workshop. She had to generate her own topics, take comments and suggestions from other writers, and polish a certain number of pieces during the year. The full collection of Amie's work provides evidence of meeting the Writing Habits and Processes Standard. Furthermore, the third sample, "On Saturday," is an example that meets the standard for narrative writing. The last sample, "How To Tacke A Test," is an example that meets the standard for functional writing for first grade.

September

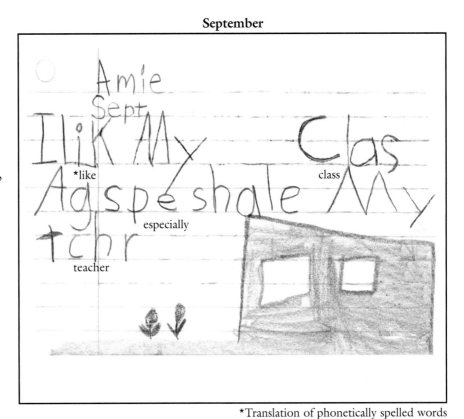

*Translation of phonetically spelled words

Amie wrote the first sample, "I Lik My Clas," on the first day of school. She spells four of the seven words phonetically, and she spells the other three words correctly, controlling for word boundaries and demonstrating left-to-right and top-to-bottom movement. Her message can be read — although "Agspeshale" may give readers some problems. A picture accompanies the text, though it is doubtful whether the picture ties to the text. ▶▶

September 9

Amie

Sept. 9

I hav sic in My iys and it is Cold jtvid My iys and i hav Medusen for My iys

*I have sick in my eyes, and it is conjunctivitis. My eyes and I have medicine for my eyes.

*Translation of phonetically spelled words

The second sample, "I hav sic in My iys," written on Sept. 9, just one week after the first sample, shows significant growth on Amie's part. This 19-word sample has seven words spelled correctly. Clearly, the picture and text are related. Like the first piece, this sample shows that Amie understands letter-sound correspondences because she represents sounds with letters — at least with beginning and ending consonants — and she uses common English letter sequences. Vowels are commonplace throughout this sample, and most of them are determined logically. Again, the vocabulary is well beyond Amie's range as a speller *(conjunctivitis* and *medicine)*. In this piece, the picture clearly illustrates the text, and Amie, like many first graders, is focusing on herself and her experiences as subjects for expressive writing.

December 14

In the third sample, written on Dec. 14 and titled "On Saturday," growth in Amie's writing is of a different order of magnitude altogether. Amie's development over four months is stunning (by contrast, her development is less impressive over the next four months). The piece comprises 115 words, 22 of which are repeated. She begins the piece with a setting in time ("On Saturday") and holds it together with a series of transition words ("And frust," "Then," "And," etc.). It is a long list of events built around what Amie did and saw on a Christmas outing with her family. It contains specific details and a gradual winding down of events before its close ("The End"). In fact, the ending is reminiscent of the bed-to-bed narrative style typically affected by writers in the second grade in which they convey a whole litany of events. Amie controls for the use of capital letters at the beginning of sentences and periods at the end. She also uses a capital letter for the name of a day of the week.

(See page 113 for a more complete analysis of this student work.) ▶▶

Amie
On Saturday

On Saturday I went to
look at the lights. And frust
[*first]
my mom and dad told me
thet we wur going. Then
[that] [were]
I got on my cot. Then
[coat]
we wet to look at
[went]
the lights. On the the
Strets we sol ol uv the
[streets] [saw] [all] [of]
pepul thet wur on that
[people] [that] [were]
stret. had bels, and ajuls, and
[street] [bells] [angels]
cande cangs. And I sol lights
[candy] [canes] [saw]
most uv the time. And I
[of]
sol Sunt clos to. And he
[saw] [Santa] [Claus] [too]
gav me a culurfol camde
[gave] [colorful] [candy]
cang. Then we sol mor
[cane] [saw] [more]
uv lights. Then I went
[of]
home. And wocht some tvi
[watched]
Then I went to get
my doll. Then I went
to slep. Then I had a
[sleep]
drem. Then I woc up!
[dream] [woke] [up]
The End

*Translation of phonetically spelled words

New Standards

March 29

> 1 | March 29
> Amie
> About My Perens
>   *parents
> Yesterday my
> dad got glassis.
>   glasses
> Today my mom
> is geting new glassis.
>   getting   glasses
> and biger ones.
>   bigger
> My dad Has his
> so he can read
> and drive beter.
>   better

*Translation of phonetically spelled words

> 2 | My mom is geting
>   getting
> new one bcus her
>   ones   because
> old one are reel
> old ones   real
> old and rustey.
>   rusty
> They both
> can see beter.
>   better
> my mom cud
>   could
> are rety see.
> already
> But she still wants
>   wants

> 3 | new one. and
>   ones
> my dad cud
>   could
> arerty see.
> already
> That's a boate
>   about
> my peren.
>   parents
> The End

The fourth piece, dated March 29, contains 67 words with only 11 misspelled. Amie titles this piece "About My Perens" and writes about her father and mother getting new glasses. She explains the reasons for these new acquisitions — the father gets them to read and drive better; the mother gets them because hers are "old and rustey." Amie explains, however, that her parents already can see — without glasses, it is assumed. This piece is not as impressive as the December one, but the spelling is more developed. She correctly spells "Yesterday" and "Today," as well as many other words. Her misspellings are logical ("glassis" for *glasses,* "biger" for *bigger* and "beter" for *better*). She controls for capital letters at the start of sentences and periods at the end. She even uses an apostrophe correctly in a contraction ("That's").

April 13

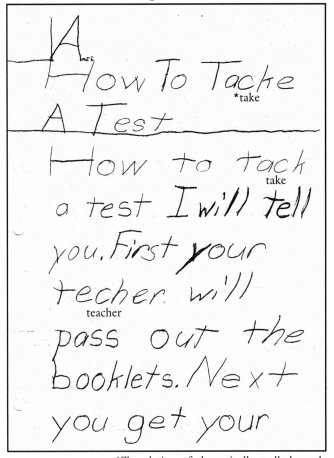

A we E
How To Tacke
A Test
  *take

How to tack
            take
a test I will tell
you. First your
techer will
      teacher
pass out the
booklets. Next
you get your

2
pennsels redey
pencils   ready
for your test.
Then you open
your book when
your seayel is
          seal
brok en. Then
you read the
instruchches.
       instructions
to your self.
      yourself

*Translation of phonetically spelled words

The fifth piece is dated April 13 and titled "How To Tacke A Test." It shows a writer well on the way to controlling for correct spelling. The development around the issue of author's craft is less easy to determine. This is clearly a piece of functional text, appropriate for first grade. The sample has 74 words with some repetitions. The only misspellings ("tacke," "tack," "pennsels," "instruchches," "closs," "Findley," etc.) are words that might give a first grader problems. This writing sample explains how to take a test. It outlines a series of general instructions that range from passing out the test booklets to finishing the test and stretching. It contains a picture — not wholly detailed — that shows student tests (and chairs) distributed around the four sides of a table. (See page 126 for a more complete analysis of this student work.) ▶▶

3| hen you mark your anser.
answer

Then aften you are fineshed
finished

with chopter one. Your techen
teacher

will closs your book. Findley you strech.
close   Finally
stretch

4) Thats the way to tack a test.
that's   take

"Nora's Collection"
Second-Grade Growth Over One Year

This collection of student work illustrates one student's growth over the course of a year. The student, Nora, started second grade with a fairly limited understanding of writing. Her original sample gives no indication that she is capable of meeting the expectations set out for the end of first grade, but her writing is typical of what many students bring to second grade. By the end of the year, however, Nora's writing indicates that she has begun to make real improvement as a writer: She has moved from simple listing to constructing a focused account.

September

*playing

*most of all

*Translation of phonetically spelled words

The first piece, done in September, is a basic list of what Nora likes and loves. The writing is justified to the left margin and is made up entirely of one-clause units. Of the six ideas expressed, five of them are made up of only three words — two in which the subject and predicate are the same. This pattern is fairly typical of first-grade writing and is familiar to readers of easy books. Most of the words are spelled correctly. The last idea breaks the pattern. The clause begins with a qualifying phrase ("and mostasl"), and the verb changes from "Like" to "Love." This modification in the wording of the last idea is very common in books written for emergent readers, and it is, therefore, possible to infer that Nora modeled her writing on these early books. ▶▶

October

I love

MY Mom AnD DaD
I Like MY BRathr brother
I Love grandma
I Lev in 300 E. 3n
live

*Translation of phonetically spelled words

December

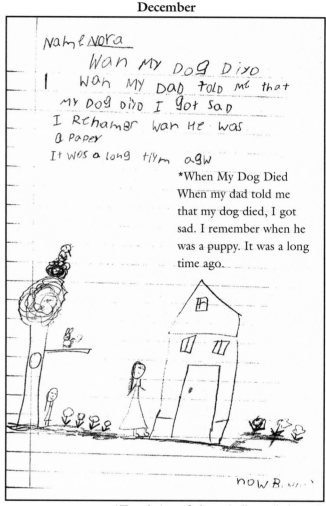

Nam£ NoRa
Wan MY DoG DiYD
I Wan MY DaD told M£ that
MY DoG DiYD I got Sad
I Rchambr wan He was
a PaPeY
It Wos a long tiYm agw

*When My Dog Died
When my dad told me
that my dog died, I got
sad. I remember when he
was a puppy. It was a long
time ago.

*Translation of phonetically spelled words

The second sample, completed in October, is a good deal like the first. The subject again is the author's feelings for people. The last idea breaks the pattern. The writing is justified to the left margin, the syntax is single-clause units and the spelling is mostly correct. The drawing that accompanies the writing clearly is attached (as it was in the first sample) to the meaning of the piece — it is illustrative. Both drawings are fairly detailed — note the expressions on the faces of the characters.

The third piece, produced in December, shows Nora's emerging sense of story. This piece is titled "Wan MY Dog DiYD," and she moves from relying on single-clause units to using a variety of syntactic patterns. The first sentence actually is made up of two dependent clauses and one independent clause; the second sentence is made up of one dependent and one independent clause; the final sentence is a single independent clause. The spelling in this piece is not as controlled as it was in the previous samples; Nora consistently misspells *when* ("Wan") along with several other words. The text is made up of an initiating event, a reaction and an associated memory ("I RenamBr wan He was a PaPeY"), and another reaction. The drawing, again, is quite detailed, though it does not illustrate the text.

Mid-January   **March**

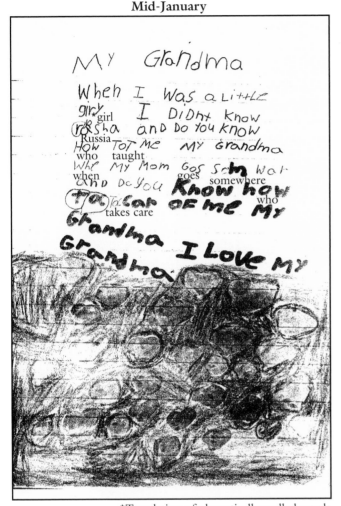

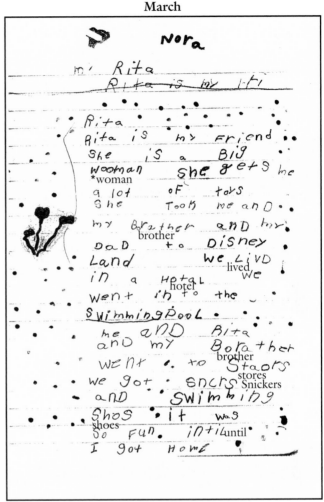

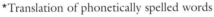

*Translation of phonetically spelled words   *Translation of phonetically spelled words

The fourth piece, done in mid-January, is titled "My Grandma." Nora begins the piece by setting a context for the writing ("When I Was a LittLe giry I DiDnt Know Rasha anD Do You Know How ToT Me My Grandma"). She then explains that when her mother goes somewhere, her grandma takes care of her. She concludes with "I Love MY Grandma" almost as a summary statement, an affection that grows naturally as the result of these two things the grandmother does for her. Nora gets herself into a problem with syntax when she tries to use "anD Do You Know" a second time because this phrase does not fit into her sentence production. So the text reads "Whe My Mom Gos Som war anD Do You Know ... ." The spelling in this fourth sample does not pose a problem for readers familiar with phonetic spelling. The misspellings are logical, and many words are spelled correctly.

The fifth sample, written in March, is substantially longer than the other pieces. It has a title and a narrative structure. Nora begins by introducing the subject of the piece, Rita, who is "my Friend" and "a Big wooman" who "gets me a lot oF toyS." She then recounts a trip to Disneyland that she took with Rita, her dad and her brother. She tells about four separate things that happened on the trip: living in a hotel, going into the swimming pool, going to stores, and getting Snickers and swimming shoes. Nora ends the piece with a concluding reaction ("it was so Fun intiL I got Home"). With the exception of the last sentence, the whole text is made up of simple sentences. The spelling in this piece is much improved; she misspells only eight words. The writer's drawings disappear, though the page is decorated.

▶▶

Late Spring

aDventures
Rita   anD me   anD   my
Bra+her   have ??(?.?..?)
*brother
aDventures   We go   to
Stors   We go to Ritas
stores
Haws   We go   to
house
toys aras   we go   to the
Toys "R" Us   we
. Paro
park
Eat   gaPan FooD
Japanese
anD   a+tr +hat   We
after
go get   iccrc?m
ice cream
anD   then   We go
Home   anD   tomoroN
tomorrow
is   a   Nyou DaY
new
So   I'll   Be sing
seeing
Her   tomo6ow
tomorrow

*Translation of phonetically spelled words

Nora's samples show that she has grown considerably as a writer during the second grade. Her writing demonstrates that she has developed a sense of storytelling. She relies primarily on text rather than on pictures to convey meaning, and when she uses art, it generally illustrates the text. She knows that text is generated by paragraphs rather than at the margins. She is able to recount a series of events. She also embeds details in these accounts and gives her work a title.

The final sample, done in late spring and titled "aDventures," recounts the activities of Rita, Nora and Nora's brother. The opening sentence establishes the subject of the piece — the agents and the actions. Then Nora details seven specific things the trio has done together. The writing is in part reminiscent of the style of the first two samples, and at first, it might appear that Nora no longer is developing as a writer. "We go to Stors we go to Ritas Haws We go to toys aras we go to the Parc" is a simple and undiscriminating list of things Nora, Rita and Nora's brother do. However, the last two sentences are more complicated structures ("We eat JaPan FooD aftr that We go get iccreem anD then we go Home and tomoroW is a Nyou Day so I'll Be sing Her tomarow"), and the piece begins with a context-framing remark. This piece also has a picture; though this particular drawing is small, it clearly ties to the text (Nora asleep waiting for "a Nyou Day"). The spelling is still uneven — she misspells 10 words — but as in the previous sample, some difficult words are spelled correctly.

"*Jenny*'s Collection" Third-Grade Growth Over One Year

These five pieces come from the portfolio of Jenny, a third-grade student. She writes routinely in a writer's workshop and is an enthusiastic author who is serious about revising and editing. Of the five pieces in this collection, three are attempts to produce fiction, and two are nonfiction efforts that draw upon a recurring theme in Jenny's writing — her family and coming to America.

Jenny's growth as a writer seems, at first, less dramatic than that of younger writers. There is good reason for this. Much of what young writers learn is already in place by third grade. Now, growth becomes a deeper understanding of craft, a willingness to take on and work through a demanding topic, or the ability to expand the length of a piece by emphasizing a central moment or a character description. So what happens at third grade is a refinement rather than the more dramatic moves — from pictures with random letters to letter strings and words to phrases to sentences — typically seen at kindergarten and first grade. Yet, if we look closely at the piece she wrote on Sept. 14 and the piece she wrote on May 8, we will see that refinement, too, can be dramatic.

September 14

Grandpa

By Jenny

My grandpa has white skin, short white hair, black eyes and he's tall. He takes me to fun places and he makes me laugh. He lives in China with my grandmother. He takes care of me alot when I was small but now I am in America and hes in China so I cant see him anymore, but I can still call him. He somtimes took me to restraunts.

My favorite food in the restraunt were the biscuits. They are long and

P1.

The first sample is "Grandpa," an informational piece about Jenny's grandfather. It begins with a physical description of the grandfather ("white skin, short white hair, black eyes and he's tall"). It goes on to say that he and Jenny used to visit fun places and that he made her laugh. Jenny explains that she no longer sees her grandfather because he remained in China when she moved to America. She closes the piece by saying that she likes her grandfather a lot.

Only once does Jenny lose control of the piece — she digresses about biscuits — though she does have problems with verb tenses ("takes" for *took* and "watch" for *watched*). This piece, done in September of her third-grade year, shows Jenny is a very thoughtful writer who is able to communicate her feelings to the reader (she obviously cares a great deal for her grandfather) by providing details. ▶▶

December

skinny. In hot summer days me and my grandpa took walks aroud the block. Som-etimes we watch pink, blue and some other different colored clouds pass by our house. and watch birds fly pass by us. I like my grandpa alot.

(P.2)

(1.)

Santa is missing

One night 2 little elves were sitting ~~playing~~ by the fire testing toys for Christmas. Each elf was given a job. Judy was given the job to watch all the dogs and cats for presents. Lily was given the job to (her assistant was flower) check the toys for presents. Sudd-nly their was a knock at the door. One of the little elves came and said "Santa is Missing!!!!!!" They went outside their house and went down 40 stairs, to go to Santa's house. All the elves looked

(2.)

for Santa, but no sign of him. Judy and Lily got on the sleigh and went to go see if Santa was around. But no sign of him anywhere. The elves did not know that when Santa was testing his sleigh late last night he fell off because ~~when he was pulling the~~ while he was testing the sleigh, the reindeer's thought it was Christmas, but it really wasn't, so they took off. But after a while they noticed that Santa wasn't on the sleigh

The second piece, "Santa is missing," is a fiction story written in December. The plot has a problem/solution structure. (Santa is missing, and it's the day before Christmas Eve.) The main characters are Judy and Lily, two elves, and Flower, Lily's assistant. To find Santa, the elves go outside and look. Ultimately, they discover a small cottage and find Santa inside. They take him home and get him "some hot coaco and a wet towel." Santa is revived and, real-izing that he has not missed Christmas, exclaims, "'This is my best present!'"

③

anymore. So they went back home. Then one of the elves that were guarding the door walked up to Lily and said "I didn't even see him last night." "Hmmm......" said Judy "This is quite a mystery." said Lily. "You bet" said Judy. "Lets go outside and look for Santa." Said Flower "Ok" said the other elves. "I'll lead the way." said Flower. They walked a long way until they came upon a small cottage.

④

"Let's go inside and see if there are some hot cocoa." said some of the little elves, because I'm freezing!" All the elves agreed. They explored the whole cottage. When they were in the basement they saw an old man dressed just like Santa Claus. "Hey, that's Santa Claus! said one of the littles elves. Flower "Let's go take him home. I'll go get some hot cocoa and a wet towel." said Mrs. Claus.

⑤

When they got home Santa woke up and told them his story about how he got there. "So I walked and found the cottage and rested in it." "At least it is still one day before Christmas." said Mrs. Claus. "This is my best present!" said Santa and they all gave him a big hug.

The END

Although this plot has several gaps — it's not clear why the reindeer ran off and left Santa — the story line is relatively coherent. The dialogue lets the writer inject some thoughts that otherwise would be difficult to communicate to the reader ("'This is quite a mystery.' said Lily. 'You bet' said Judy"). Often, the details provided ("Judy was given the job to watch all the dogs and cats for presents") distract the reader rather than add information. But, with all its limitations, the story has charm, and its very length represents a challenge for third-grade writers. ▶▶

February

My Great,Great Grandfather
By:Jenny

The last place I could remember was in a pleasant mansion.While I was young I lived upon my mothers milk for I had no teeth and could not eat anything else. In the afternoon I took naps in my crib and at night I lay sound asleep by her. My life was always like that until the age of 4. My mother was sick. I had to go to the nursery room. It was in late December and snow was falling,outside. I was cold. I could only make myself a little warm under the covers on my bed, because I didn't know how to make a fire in the fireplace. Then the door opened. In walked my grandfather. "Have

The third piece, "My Great,Great Grandfather," was written in February and is especially interesting because of all that Jenny attempts as a writer. The piece begins with recollections from Jenny's early childhood, before she was four. The wording here clearly imitates written language ("I lived upon my mothers milk") rather than oral language. The story then shifts in time.

One night when her mother was ill, Jenny was in a nursery, and she was cold and couldn't sleep. She was comforted by a story her grandfather told about her great-great-grandfather. He was wounded in the Civil War, and an older man, Mike, saved him. Later, they both were captured by marauders. The great-great-grandfather ultimately was released, but what happened to Mike was unknown. The great-great-grandfather's story was passed down in the family, and Jenny's grandfather was following the tradition in the piece. (This part of Jenny's piece parallels Patricia Polacco's *Pink and Say*, so much so that it is safe to assume that Jenny is familiar with this book.) Jenny's piece, then, has a story-within-a-story structure, which she brings off effectively.

There is quite a bit of literary language ("In the afternoon I took naps in my crib and at night I lay sound asleep by her," "I moved a little closer to him so I could hear him better while he told his story," "he could carry large and powerful guns," "But before he closed the door behind him, he whispered softlyto me. 'Sweet dreams.' And then he left"). The syntax, the vocabulary ("maruaders,"

"flutter") and the detail ("He lay on the grass wide eyed opened to see if someone would come and help him") are quite impressive. If the story has problems, they are the contrived dialogue and the holes in the grandfather's story, e.g., why was the great-great-grandfather released?

nothing to do?" he asked me. "Yep." I said shivering. "Well,let me tell you a story while you try to go to sleep." He made the fire very warm in the fireplace. I moved a little closer to him so I could hear him better while he told his story. "When your great,great,grandfather was 21,he went to the Civil War. He was very brave in the war and proved himself that he could carry large and powerful guns because he was so strong. One day he got injured very badly.He got shot in the arm and leg and he couldn't walk nor move a bit. He lay on the grass wide eyed opened to see if someone would come and help him. Well,his hopes came true. Across the river came a young man a little older than him. "Whats the matter with you?"he asked "Can't you move a bit?" "Nope." said

▶▶

Bob.(That's your great,great,grandfather.)

"I'm Bob." I'm Mike." "Why don't I take you to my so we can rest a little bit? Sure if you can carry me."Bob said. Bob fell asleep on the way and woke up in a comfortable bed under a quilt. Feeling warm,he opened his eyes. "Where am I? Your in my house."said Mike.After a few days later I could walk."We got to get back to the war."said Mike.After we put on our uniforms,we set off. Half way we ran into two maruaders on their horses. They reached for us and took us to a place where the slaves stayed

After a year or two,I was let free. I didn't know what happened to Mike. Well, I had a happy life after all. I told this story to Mary,then Mary told it to her son William,William told it to his grand daughter you. Jenny. My eyes started to flutter as he said his last sentence. "And that was the story of your great,great,grandfather in the Civil War." He took one last look at me. I was asleep. Then he walked out of the nursery room. But before he closed the door behind him, he whispered softlyto me. "Sweet dreams." And then he left.

The End

The **"SUPER MAN" piece,** also done in February, is not as impressive as the other fiction pieces. The story, again, has a problem/solution structure. (The hero is weak, and the solution is the "mysterious kind of medicine called the SUPER MAN. Shot.") There is not much of a plot beyond the hero's getting the shot, growing full of energy and muscles, and being able to fly. Jenny gives no information about the hero's flight other than "He did many interesting things." At the end, she tells us that the hero "could do this again and have another adventure.But that's another story."

The story is told in the third person and is the thinnest piece in this collection, with little to recommend it other than the effective use of repetition in the opening lines ("Once there was a man that was very weak.He had weak legs, a weak will, and he was very thin"). This kind of story, a variation of the action hero genre, is typical of the kinds of stories elementary school writers enjoy producing. As students develop characters more fully, these stories will take on some depth, but even writers in middle school continue to be fascinated by this genre. This piece is included here because even a writer as talented as Jenny might attempt the form. Moreover, the piece shows that student writing, like adult writing, will be uneven. Few writers are equally good in many genres.   ▶▶

February

Jenny

Once there was a man that was very weak. He had weak legs, a weak will, and he was very thin. His name was Chad Laisure. He was 21 years old and he wanted to get stronger and fatter So one day he went to the hospital to get a mysterious kind of medicine called **the SUPER MAN. Shot.** When the nurse motioned him in one of the rooms she said "You'll have to get a shot if you want to take this kind of medicine." But before he had time to say OK,

②

the nurse ~~t~~ pulled a sherenge out
of a drawer and filled it with
SUPER Man. After the nurse pulled the
sherenge out of his skin, he started to feel tired. Oh well, it's 9:30
allready so he drove home and went
to sleep. When he woke up in the m-
orning, he felt ᴸⁱᵏᵉ ʰᵉ ʷᵃˢ full of energy. He
looked down at his hands and arms.
He had grown much ~~fatter~~ and his
body was now filled with muscle. After
breakfast, he took the medicine again. This
time, he started to fly. He flew for abo

③

ut 4 hours. While he was flying, he got
lost, and found his back home again. He
did many interesting things while he was
flying. Before he went to sleep he thought that he could do this again and
have another adventure. But that's another
story.

February 8

My Trip To Fort Worth
The Story of Jenny
Jenny ought to be my first name
but my mother and father calls me
Jen. I was living in China, and my
my family only knew a little bit
of english. One day while I was
playing on the slide, I glanced at
my parents. They were sitting on a
wooden bench. Their faces were urgent
and it like as if that they were
having a serious conversation. Two
weeks later   my mommy said

that our family would be going to
America tomorrow. "Grandma, Grandpa, Uncle, and
Auntie aren't coming with us. It's just
you, me, and daddy," said my mom. I
started to cry because I didn't want
to leave, and I'd miss my grandma
grandpa and aunts and uncles. "You'll
go to school in America, but that
doesn't mean you'll never get
to see your other relatives. We will
still see them someday. replied my mom.

The final sample is another informational piece on Jenny's family that she began on Feb. 8. "My Trip To Fort Worth" tells how Jenny learns that her immediate family is moving to America. This whole sample later is embedded almost unchanged into her May 8 revision titled "Starting A New Life" (see pages 268–272). She worked extensively on the final draft.

The revision draft (pages 264–268) makes clear the extent of changes between the first draft and the final piece. Jenny's arrows, cross-outs and insertions reflect a writer who is not afraid of "re-visioning." ▶▶

Revision Draft

Titles for my story

The Day I Came to America

Leaving China

Starting A New Life

My Trip To Fort Worth

The Diary of Jenny

~~Jenny~~ ought to be my ~~first~~ name
but my mother and father calls me
~~Bǎo Bǎo that means baby in Chinese~~
~~I~~ I was living in China, and my
~~my~~ family only knew a little bit
of ~~English~~. One day while I was
playing on the slide, I glanced at
my parents. They were ~~sitting~~ on a
wooden bench. Their faces were urgent
and it ~~like~~ as if ~~that~~ they were
having a serious conversation. Two
weeks later, my ~~mommy~~ said

~~that~~ our family would be going to
America ~~soon~~. "Grandma, Grandpa, Uncle, and
Auntie aren't coming with us. It's just
you, me, and daddy, said my mom. I
started to cry because I didn't want
to leave and I'll miss my ā dí, ā pó
and my hǎo mā mā
~~and my uncles, my aunts.~~ "You will
go to school in America, but that
doesn't mean ~~you~~ you'll never get
to see your other relatives. We will
still see them someday replied my mom

---

she told me that we would not
only go there, but we would
stay there, and people will
call me Jen. My mom explained
that American's wouldn't
understand our language, so we're
very different from American
people."Your father and I have
decided Jen is a good American
name for you," She said.
'nǎo mā mā means good mommy
because she always wore a smile
on her face. and she was never angry at me.

ā diá is a Chinese word for grandpa.
ā pó is a Chinese word for grandma.
Why I would miss my other
relatives is because my
ā diá. gave me almost everything
(he spoiled me a lot.)
I want.
She took me to the park everyday to ride
Across the street from my house,
little airplanes, little motor cars, and boats
there was a park and my
hǎo mā mā is what I call my babysitter.
My babysitter takes me there, too.
grandma takes me there too.

While I watched my mommy and daddy pack, I thought a lot about how America would be like. Who would spoil me? Who will take me to the pork? Who will wear a smile for me? I had so many questions to ask and think about! At dinner I couldn't eat anything. All I thought about was America. America. The word got stuck in my mind all day. Even at night my eyes were wide open staring at

the ceiling. I believed that I would never go to sleep tonight, but after 1 hour I fell into a restless doze. My dad had gone in another plane and he already arrived in America when my mom and I were still on the plane. It was a very long flight to America. Once in a while, I would always think about my dia and po and what was going on at their house

Once again the questions came back into my mind. Who will spoil me? Who will take me to the park? Who will wear a smile for me? I opened my mouth to ask the questions but no sound came out of my mouth, so I closed my mouth and remained silent. That night my mommy told me how great America was going to be, but I still missed my home town, especially my relatives and my

hǎo mā mā.

After my mom and I joined my dad, my mother said, turn to page 2

A smile spread across my face and I then had a new life to began

Two years later in kintergarten, things were going pretty well. I didn't know America was so interesting but I always thought about my Āgā and my Āpó and my hǎo mā mā once in a while. I always would think about the questions too. Who will spoil me?

Who will take me to the park?

Who will wear a smile for me?

I always remembered what

mother said "You will go to school in

America, but that dosen't mean

you'll never get to see your other

relatives. We will still see them someday."

Now my name is changed to Jenny, but

my parents still call me Jen since I've head

that name for a long time in America.

May 8

Starting A New Life
By: Jenny

ought to be my name but my

mother and father calls me Băo Băo (that

means baby in Chinese.) I was living

in China, and my family only knew a

little bit of English. One day

while I was playing on the slide,

I glanced at my parents. They

were sitting on a wooden bench.

Their faces were urgent and it

looked as if they were having a

serious convorsation. Two weeks

later, my mommy said our family

would be going to America soon.

She told me that we would not only go there, but we would stay there, and people will call me Jen. My mom explained that American's wouldn't understand our language, so we're very different from American people. "Your father and I have decided Jen is a good American name for you," she said. "Grandpa, grandma, uncle, and auntie aren't coming with us. It's just you, me, and daddy," said my mom. I started to cry because I didn't

want to leave, and I'd miss my ā diá, ā pó, and my hǎo mā mā. Ā diá is a Chinese word for grandpa. Ā diá gave me almost everything I want. (He spoiled me alot.) Ā pó is a Chinese word for grandma. She took me to the park everyday to ride. little airplanes, little motor cars, and boats. Hǎo mā mā is what I call my babysitter. My babysitter takes me there too. Hǎo mā mā means good mommy because she always wore a smile on her face.

By comparing the early piece, the revision draft and the final piece, the reader realizes that "Starting A New Life" is a very carefully planned piece of writing. Jenny begins by telling the reader about her name; later, she explains that her name was changed when she moved to America; at the end, she returns to the issue of her name change.

In addition to using her name to thread through and conclude her writing, Jenny uses repetition for emphasis. The three questions ("Who would spoil me? Who will take me to the park? Who will wear a smile for me?") are the essence of what worried Jenny the most about leaving China. She sets up these questions by explaining that her grandfather "spoiled [her] alot," her grandmother took her "to the park everyday" and her babysitter always "wore a smile on her face." So when Jenny asks her questions, she also is asking who will be like her grandfather (and give her "almost everything"), like her grandmother (and take her to the park) and like her babysitter (and smile for her). This strategy is very effective and very sophisticated, and she handles it quite well.

Jenny also does several other things well. She provides some concrete details ("while I was playing on the slide … . They were sitting on a wooden bench. Their faces were urgent and it looked as if they were having a serious convorsation"), she embeds some Chinese words, she reveals internal conflict ("I thought alot about," "The word got stuck in my mind," "I believed that I would never go to sleep,"

▶▶

While I watched my mommy and daddy pack, I thought alot about how America would be like. Who would spoil me? Who will take me to the park? Who will wear a smile for me? I had so many questions to ask and think about! At dinner I couldn't eat anything. All I thought about was America, America. The word got stuck in my mind all day. Even at night my eyes were wide open staring at the ceiling. I believed that I would never go to sleep tonight, but after 1 hour I fell into a restless doze. My dad had gone in another plane and he already arrived in America when my mom and I were still on the plane. It was a very long flight to America. Once in a while, I would always think about my ā diá and ā pó and what was going on at their house. Once again the questions came back into my mind. Who will spoil me?

"Once again the questions came back into my mind") and she uses language that does not sound like speech ("While I watched my mommy and daddy pack, I thought"). "Starting A New Life" is a long piece (eight pages) and is accomplished both in style and story. In it, Jenny overcomes many weaknesses. She uses dialogue effectively, and the details she provides illuminate rather than distract the reader. As an end-of-the-year effort, it represents dramatic refinement.

Who will take me to the park? Who will wear a smile for me? I opened my mouth to ask the questions but no sound came out of my mouth, so I closed my mouth and remained silent. That night my mommy told me how great America was going to be, but I still missed my home town, especially my relatives and my hǎo mō mā. After my mom and I joined my dad, my mother said "You will go to school in America, but that dosen't mean you'll never get to see your other relatives. We will still see them someday," replied my mom. A smile spread across my face and I knew I had a new life to begin. Two years later in kintergarten, things were going pretty well. I didn't know America was so interesting, but I always thought about my ā diá and my ā pó and my hǎo mā mā once in a while. I always would think about the questions too.

▶▶

Who will spoil me? Who will take me to the park? Who will wear a smile for me? I always remembered what mother said. "You will go to school in America, but that dosen't mean you'll never get to see your other relatives. We will still see them someday!"

Now my name is changed to Jenny, but my parents still call me Jen since I've had that name for a long time in America.

"Evan's Collection"
Kindergarten through Third Grade
Growth Over Four Years

This collection of student work contains samples from each of four levels — kindergarten, first grade, second grade and third grade. The samples from kindergarten, first grade and second grade are all first-draft efforts drawn from Evan's notebook. The third-grade sample is a polished piece of text.

Evan is a remarkably talented writer, equally comfortable with poetry and prose. What also is apparent to anyone looking across all four samples is that Evan's control of form emerged much earlier than did his control of spelling. In fact, to someone not familiar with reading phonetic spelling, the kindergarten sample ("ZoM") is almost unintelligible.

Kindergarten

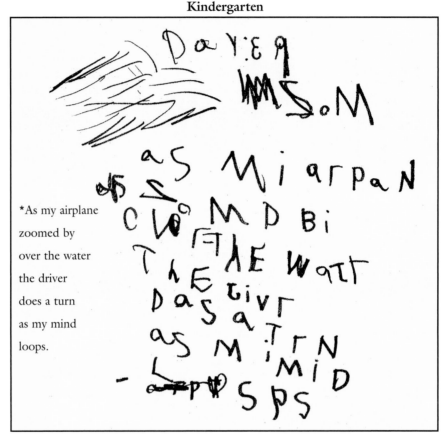

*As my airplane

zoomed by

over the water

the driver

does a turn

as my mind

loops.

*Translation of phonetically spelled words

This kindergarten sample indicates that Evan knows quite a bit about print conventions. He understands that text moves left to right across a page and top to bottom down a page. He does not control evenly for space between words, but he does have a sense about line breaks. He gives his work a title and correctly spells two sight words ("as" and "ThE"). He represents words with initial and final consonants and embeds vowels occasionally, at least those that say their own name.

"ZoM" is quite a good piece of poetry. "ZoM" is onomatopoetic in the title; it occurs as a past-tense verb in the poem's second line. The poem presents two images. One is of a plane zooming by and heading out over water where the pilot does a turn. In the second image, Evan's mind is doing a loop, surprising the reader, who is expecting the image of looping to attach to the plane, not to the speaker's mind. The parallel images of the plane zooming and the mind looping give the reader a sense of a mind alive with movement, not frantic but graceful, like a plane seeming to meander slowly above the ocean. ▶▶

First Grade

The first-grade piece, "Sleep over," is another poem. Again, Evan demonstrates adroit use of line breaks, this time coupled with artful use of repetition. The final line of the poem plays with both a variation on the refrain and the meaning, which is underscored by printing the text somewhat smaller and separating it from the body of the poem for visual impact. The poem is constructed around three very joyful childhood images that take place during a sleepover — eating spaghetti, having a pillow fight and decorating for Christmas. Evan at first claims not to have been lonely during the visit but then in the last line comes back with the disclaimer that maybe he was lonely but "only one inch lonly."

As with the kindergarten piece, the surprise is that Evan so clearly can demonstrate control of form yet have difficulty with spelling. It is not that the spelling errors are problematic given Evan's age — they are not. It is just that the sophistication of the writing leads a reader to expect more control of spelling (not "slerped" for *slurped* and "was in't" for *wasn't*). Another sample from first grade underscores this mismatch of spelling and writing proficiency.

Sleep over
When we Slerped up hot spagety
*slurped   spaghetti

I was in't lonly
wasn't   lonely

When me and gregg had a piloow fight
pillow

I was in't lonly
wasn't   lonely

Whe We decerated christmas doow
decorated   door

I was in't lonly
wasn't   lonely

only one inch lonly
lonely

*Translation of phonetically spelled words

First Grade

"**I Wish**" is made up of three images that together capture Evan's desire for "amasing ikskovrings and in vanchris." His first wish is to sail into the strongest waves and almost tip over. His second wish is to have adventures and "to travll threuth trails with spibry wabas of stiks." His third wish is to run through fields and play tennis with his dad. The poem is wonderfully expressive of Evan's voice and provides the reader a very real sense of this particular first grader's daydreams.

In this work, Evan further demonstrates a novice understanding of spelling ("s alle" for *sail*, "waevis" for *waves*, and "amasing ikskovrings" for *amazing discoveries*). As with "Sleep over," however, the misspellings are logical, and it is pretty safe to assume this is a case of a student's understanding of and talent for writing completely outstripping his age-appropriate control of spelling.   ►►

*I wish we sail in
the strangest waves
of wind and almost tip
but tip three quarters.
I wish we go to islands
and find amazing discoveries
and adventures to travel
through trails with spidery webs
of sticks. I wish Dad will run through
the fields with us and play
tennis with us in the tennis courts.

*Translation of phonetically spelled words

Second Grade

> It is spring and I watch gregg
> swing ing and lung ing aubove me
> he grabs a *baer* than *anoher*
>   *bar   another
> My eye *faloed* his hand
>   followed
> I *kikt* the *dort* and *fast*
>   kicked   dirt   glowing fast
> away the sky, was *glowing*
> Deep Blue. *Pall* Blue.
>   pale
> all *tho* the grass was new
> although
> and *froh*
>   fresh
> *thar* was a august sun
> there
> a *Bech* sun
>   beach
> a *playgraoned* sun
>   playground
> but still I was not Happy
> I looked at all the *ater* *kids*
>   other
> jane.. John...

*Translation of phonetically spelled words

By second grade, Evan's talent for poetry is even more apparent. The untitled poem that begins "It is spring" tells about conquering fear and the elation that follows. Perhaps this work, more than any of the others, makes explicit the gap between Evan's achievement as a poet and as a speller. Consider the lines:

> he grabs a baer than anoher
> My eye faloed his hand
> I kikt the dort and fast
> away the sky, was glowing
> Deep Blue. Pall Blue.

A reader has to work not to be brought up short by misspellings. All of the misspelled words interrupt the flow of the reading: "baer" for *bar,* "faloed" for *followed* and "kikt" for *kicked.* Yet each of these misspellings is logical and not unreasonable for a second-grade student. It is the contrast between the power of the imagery and the level of spelling proficiency that again surprises the reader. One child watches while another makes his way across the monkey bars, one hand after the other. The first child kicks the dirt. The sky glows, deep blue and pale blue. Here is an image of challenge laid down, one boy to another. At the poem's end, the boy has picked up the challenge and made his way across the monkey bars until:

> I rech out with my top
> it tocht silid graond I stod
> up and saw the brods fling
> and falt like fling to

Evan's capacity to capture exaltation by comparing his emotion to the sense of flying is amazing. Many older, much more practiced writers could not begin

to express themselves as effectively. True, the spelling again is problematic, but Evan is, after all, only in second grade. What is significant across all of Evan's pieces is the dissonance a reader feels trying to accept the unevenness of Evan's proficiency. We continually are brought up short, asking how it is possible that someone whose thinking is so mature, whose knowledge about poetry is so extensive, can be such a poor speller.

And that is exactly the point of this collection. Children do not grow evenly. They grow in fits and starts. One competence may very well outstrip another. Fortunately, Evan's teacher knew this and did not force him to focus on spelling and did not require that he use only words he could spell correctly. Consequently, Evan could work at getting his thoughts down on paper and on trying to write poetry.

than I looked at the moncebars
                              monkey   bars

I wocked near her a tating
     walked   hesitating

I looked Back

than up at the scaty
then   scary

Bars

    next day

I walked to the monke bars
                    monkey

greeg vad nothing I grabed the
       said   grabbed

farsed bar it was cald
first

I reched for the next but
    reached

My feet lost hold I was

hainging by my hands
hanging

but I cept going
        kept

the next, the next,
one after another
              another

It seemed like a hower befor
It   hour   before
         last bar
I reched the other sid
reached

I rech out with my toe
reach   toe

It tacht silid graond I stod
touched solid ground

up and sed the brods fling
           birds   flying

and falt like fling to
felt   flying   too

Third Grade

When The Stars Come Out

Dad just says straight out of the blue, "No." No, I can't have a puppy of my own. I remember the litter of puppies lying at my feet. One peered at me, licking my fingers and whimpering, nudging at me gently. I wanted that one. But Dad says no. My tears start as a trickle and then burn my eyes when Dad says no. He's wrong to say no. He doesn't know a thing about King Charles Cavelier spaniels and yet he says no.

I have a dream. I can picture it now. Dad comes back from canoeing and walks into my bedroom and hears a woof. That would be terrific. It's my dream. In my dream,. I run outside to meet the new snow. I watch my puppy snuffling the snowy trail of mouse. I laugh. He snuffles at me as if he's saying "oopsey." But it is just a dream. Now I look at my snow prints in the snow and hope that someday there'll be another pair right beside mine. Maybe someday my dog and I will make an angel in the snow.

And when it begins to get dark and it's time to come in, we'll go up to bed and watch the night. When the stars come out and the pink clouds leave, when my lights are long past out, my dog and I will be fast asleep.

By Evan

The third-grade sample, "When The Stars Come Out," is an edited example of expressive writing. It is an excellent piece of writing, though perhaps not as remarkable as the second-grade poem. The piece begins with an image: a father denying his son's request for a puppy. Next, Evan remembers a particular pup that "peered at me, licking my fingers and whimpering, nudging at me gently." The precise word choice, as well as the syntax, reminds us that Evan is a poet who works in realms of images and rhythms. The same power of image, supported this time by repetition ("when") and by syntax that emphasizes the repetition, marks the final paragraph of this piece:

> And when it begins to get dark and it's time to come in, we'll go up to bed and watch the night. When the stars come out and the pink clouds leave, when my lights are long past out, my dog and I will be fast asleep.

Because this piece has been edited, we are not distracted by any spelling irregularities, and we can concentrate on the substance of the text. There is some discontinuity in the second paragraph. The dream sequence (the father returning and hearing the dog's bark) stops abruptly when Evan goes on to recount a snow scene with the dog. But even with this problem, this is particularly good writing for a third-grade student.

"The Jack-o'-Lantern Collection"
Functional Writing Growth Over Four Years

The following five pieces of writing demonstrate performances for the Writing Purposes and Resulting Genres Standard. Each one represents work that meets the standard for functional writing at each of four grade levels, kindergarten through third grade (there are two third-grade samples). By reading through the collection as a whole, one can see student writing proficiency increase across the grade levels.

The pieces were done in response to the same prompt: Explain the steps involved in carving a jack-o'-lantern to someone who does not know how. However, not all the pieces were done at the same time of the year. Two pieces, those at first and second grades, were done in October. Those at kindergarten and third grade were done in February. What is important to remember is that each of the texts as a whole represents a performance that meets end-of-year standards for functional writing. ▶▶

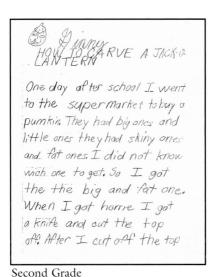

Second Grade

Third Grade

Third Grade

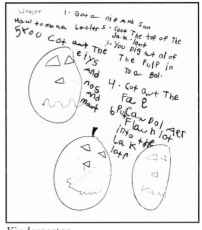

Kindergarten

First Grade

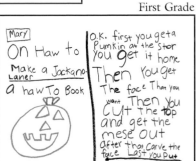

Kindergarten

*How to Make a
Jack-O'-Lantern
1. Get a knife and
spoon.
2. Cut the top off the
jack-o'-lantern.
3. You dig out all of
the pulp into a bowl.
4. Cut out the face.
5. You cut out the eyes
and nose and mouth.
6. Put candle or flash
light into the jack-o'-
lantern.

*Translation of phonetically spelled words

Kindergarten

This piece of writing is a good example of a kindergartner using writing to get things done by giving directions. Lindsey provides the reader a clear sense of the basic steps in making a jack-o'-lantern. The sample represents functional writing that meets the standard for kindergarten.

Lindsey begins by identifying and naming the materials one will need to carve the pumpkin ("1. Got a nif And Son"). She then sequences the steps from beginning to end, segmenting the steps by using numbers (1–6), so the reader can easily follow the directions.

Lindsey uses simple, short, almost choppy sentences. It is, however, easy to read this text and follow the directions, and relatively short sentences are often the norm in functional writing.

Lindsey makes deliberate choices to explain how to get this job done ("Coot The top of," "Dig owt ol of The PulP" and "Put CaNDol Aer Flowhlot into the Jak lotr") and to convey accurately the actions of the steps.

This piece of writing is an excellent example of a kindergartner showing control of her knowledge of letter-sound correlation. She represents

words by including beginning, ending and some internal consonant sounds along with internal vowels, although the vowels are not always the correct ones. There are also the beginnings of spacing between words, along with left-to-right and top-to-bottom directionality. Many sight words also are included in the writing and are spelled accurately ("And," "The," "You," "Put," "to" and "into").

Lindsey demonstrates awareness of conventions or punctuation at the beginning or ending of sentences.

This piece was written in February.

First Grade

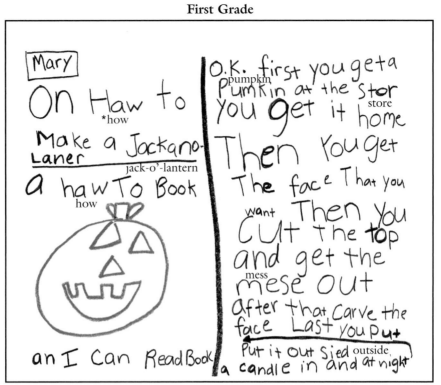

*Translation of phonetically spelled words

First Grade

Mary's sample is a rich example of a child's literacy development. It has been polished — that is, Mary worked on it to correct gross misspellings and a sequencing problem (see the editing arrow at the bottom right). It represents functional writing that meets the standard for first grade.

This piece of writing provides the reader a general sense of the steps involved in making (carving) a jack-o'-lantern. It begins by explaining to the reader where to get a pumpkin ("at the stor") and then sequences the steps from the beginning ("get The face That you want") to the end ("Put … a candle in and at night Put it out sied"). Although the detail is minimal ("get a Pumkin at the stor" and "get [carve] The face That you want"), the reader has a clear sense of the "what" of the process, though not exactly of the "how."

Mary demonstrates a familiarity with the genre by labeling the work as a functional work ("a haw To Book") and by ascribing a reading level to it ("an I Can Read Book"). She also creates a title page that is formatted and illustrated appropriately. She makes the text coherent through the use of transition words ("first," "Then" and "Last").

This piece does not meet the Language Use and Conventions Standard for first grade because Mary shows no awareness of end punctuation. It does have some notable features, however.

Mary uses an informal beginning ("O.K.") at the start of this writing sample, clearly connecting it to the patterns of oral language. At the same time, she uses transition words that obviously mark the piece's association with written text. This piece has varied sentence openers rather than a repeated sentence stem to scaffold ideas: The syntax is primarily a subject-verb patterning of simple sentences introduced by a variety of appropriate transition words.

Mary uses words from her daily vocabulary ("mese") as well as words familiar to the genre of directions ("first," "Then" and "Last"). Her work contains a large proportion of correctly spelled, high-frequency words and can be read by others because most of the perceived sounds are phonetically represented. Familiar words and word endings are spelled correctly. There are actually only six misspellings.

This piece was written in October.

▶▶

Second Grade

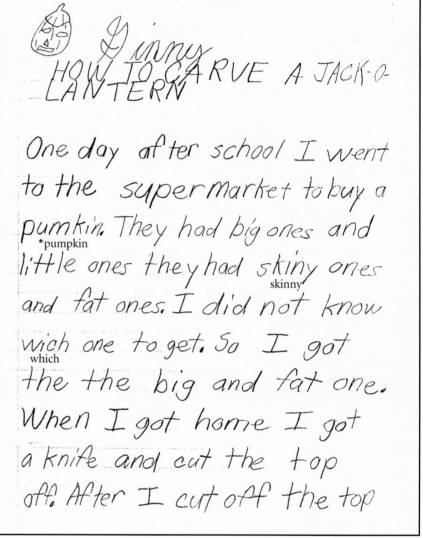

Second Grade

This is a good example of a second-grade student's ability to produce a narrative procedure. It provides a reader a clear sense of the steps involved in carving a jack-o'-lantern. It represents functional writing that meets the standard for second grade.

Ginny establishes a context for the piece ("One day after school") and sets a narrative frame for the procedure ("I went to the supermarket to buy a pumkin"). After identifying the topic in the title, she shows the steps in the procedure by using clear, straight-forward details ("big ones and little ones," "skiny ones and fat ones," "dug the seeds out," "two2 triagels") and appropriate transition words and phrases ("So," "When I got home," "After," "Then" and "Next"). The piece has an implied closure in the final step: the lighting of the candle in the pumpkin.

This piece meets the Language Use and Conventions Standard for second grade. Ginny uses sentences that are direct and explanatory, typical of proce-dural writing. Sentence patterns are typical of literary language ("They had big ones and little ones they had skiny ones and fat ones") as well as of oral language.

Ginny makes word choices that show a vocabulary large enough to exercise options ("supermarket" instead of *store*, "triagels" instead of *holes*). She uses words for numbers as well as showing the number ("two2 triagels") and uses shapes ("triagels," "squer," "banana" and "zigzags") to describe the pumpkin face.

*Translation of phonetically spelled words

Ginny correctly spells most words, especially high-frequency words. She also uses logic to spell unfamiliar words, writing "pumkin," an accurate repro-duction of the way many people pronounce the word *pumpkin*.

Ginny uses periods at the end of sentences and capitalizes correctly, beginning all sentences with a capital letter and consistently capitalizing the personal pronoun *I*.

This piece was written in October.

I got a pan and dug the
seeds out of the pumkin [pumpkin]
and put them in the pan.
Then I got a pencil and
drew two2 triagels [triangles] for the
eyes and a squer [square] for the
nose. And a banana for the
mouth and five5 zigzags for
the teeth. Next I cut
them all out and put the
candle in the middle of the
pumkin [pumpkin] and lit the candle.

▶▶

Third Grade: Revised Version

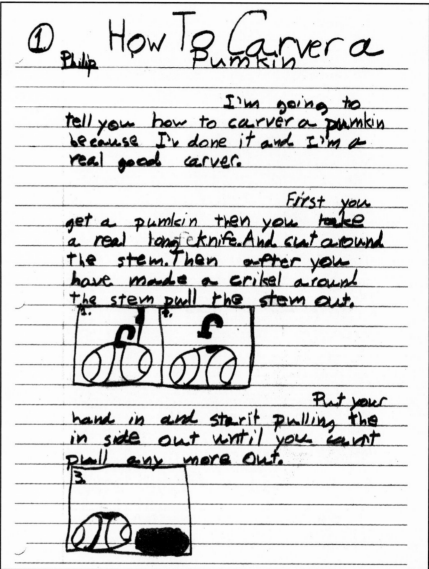

Third Grade

This piece provides a clear example of how a third grader can engage a reader's interest and show — with clear illustrations — the steps involved in an action. This sample takes apart the procedure of carving a pumpkin and shows the steps involved in some detail. It represents functional writing that meets the standard for third grade.

Both the title ("How To Carver a Pumkin") and the initial sentence ("I'm going to tell you how to carver a pumkin") establish a context and identify the topic of the piece. It is a clear guide to the process of carving a pumpkin and in clear, sequential language gives the reader suitable information for performing the task. This piece is particularly noteworthy because Philip has revised his illustrations and, by so doing, reveals his understanding of their importance to his piece. (He changes illustrations 2, 3 and 9 — see first draft, page 286.) By putting pictures into the text at critical junctures, Philip makes explicit what is being said; the pictures actually help the writer be more concrete.

This example has one complex sentence ("Put your hand in and starit pulling the in side out until you can't pull any more out"). In general, however, the sentence structure is straightforward and simple. Philip uses the expected transition words ("First," "Then" and "Now").

He uses everyday language but incorporates shape names ("crikel" and "triagals") to describe the procedure and the carving of the pumpkin. The revised piece contains a number of misspelled words ("pumkin," "I'v," "crikel," "starit" and "triagals") but not nearly so many as the first draft (there are 22 changes).

Philip consistently starts all sentences with capital letters and uses periods at the end of all sentences. In addition, he correctly uses apostrophes in all contractions ("I'm," "I'v" and "can't"); however, he misuses the apostrophe in one instance ("eye's").

This piece was written in February.

2.

Now you take a little knife and cut two little triagals eyes. Then you cut a mouth with triagals teeth.

4.   5.

Now you cut each little triagal hair in the middle for a nose.   6.

Now you place a candle inside then light it with a match or a lighter. Now put the top on.

7.   8.

3.

Now you can put the pumkin on your perch.

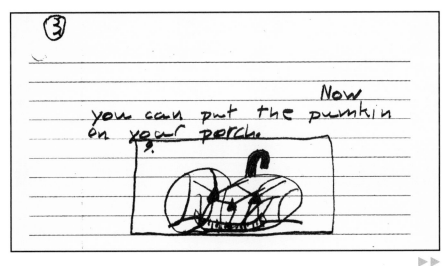

Third Grade: First Draft

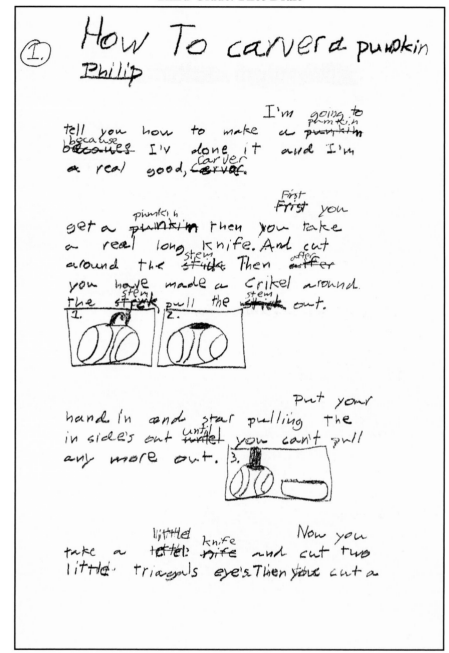

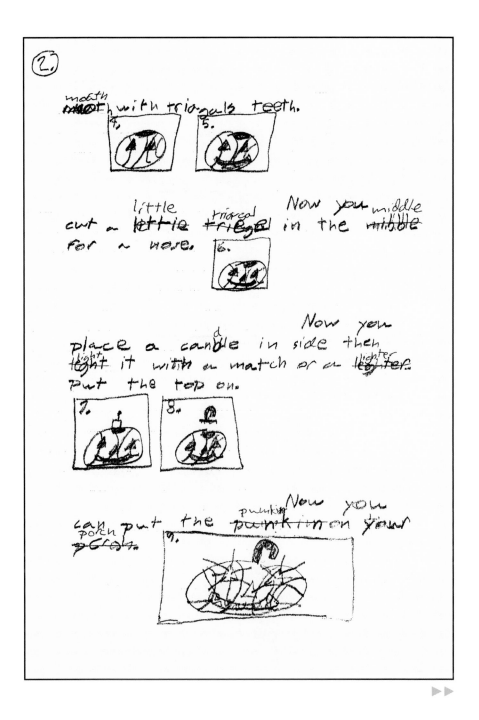

(2.)

mouth
mouth with triangals teeth.

cut a little triangal in the middle
for a nose.

Now you
place a candle in side then
light it with a match or a lighter
Put the top on.

Now you
can put the punkin on your
porch

▶▶

Third Grade

Catherine's sample represents the third-grade standard for functional writing. By changing the topic from how to carve a jack-o'-lantern to how to paint a jack-o'-lantern, Catherine is able to bring her own experience and expertise to the topic to provide a richly detailed explanation.

The piece engages the reader by establishing Catherine's credentials for writing the piece ("When I was 6"). It addresses the reader directly ("I want to teach you how"). The topic is identified clearly. The piece provides considerable detail in a step-by-step guide to painting a pumpkin. Clear, descriptive language is used throughout ("plump" and "orange not green"). Catherine gives explicit instructions about how to paint the nose ("a half triangle under the eyes"). She also includes illustrations at strategic points in the guide. The illustrations contribute to the functional purpose of the text rather than just decorate the page.

This sample is noteworthy for several other reasons. Catherine presents options to the reader ("you can put a hat on the pumkin if you want to," "if you want a smile" and "if you want a sad face"). The language is very precise ("about 1 inch down from the nose," "half triangle" and "quarter circle"). The illustrations provide an additional guide to actions. The small drawings demonstrate the addition of each feature — hair, hat, eyes, nose and mouth. Catherine consistently is aware of the reader: She accommodates the reader throughout the piece by referring to

"you" and anticipates possible errors ("Make sure you put the eyes right next to each other!").

The two drafts of the sample show that she made editing and syntax changes and chose to delete information. (See first draft, page 290.) She made a copying error from the first

draft to the final draft in the third paragraph. The meaning actually is more clear in the first draft ("put [the yarn] on top of the pumkin, or just on top of the stem").

Third Grade: Revised Version

How to paint a Jack-o-Lantern

When I was 6 my famliy and I painted a Jack-o-Lantern, so I want to teach you how.

First you go to your nearest grocey store and buy a plump pumkin, make sure the pumkin is orange not green so your pumkin will look good, also get yarn for the hair and diffrent color paints. If you want to you can buy a hat for your pumkin.

Next you make hair for your pumkin, you do this by using the yarn for hair, put it on top of the pumkin, or just on the top of the pumkin.

Then you can put a hat on the pumkin if you want to, but if you don't want to skip this step, all you do is get the hat and super glue it on the top of the hair.

Next you paint the eyes, do this buy putting a dot a little bit below the hair and hat, make surac you put the eyes right next to each other! If you want to you can paint the eyes any way you want to.

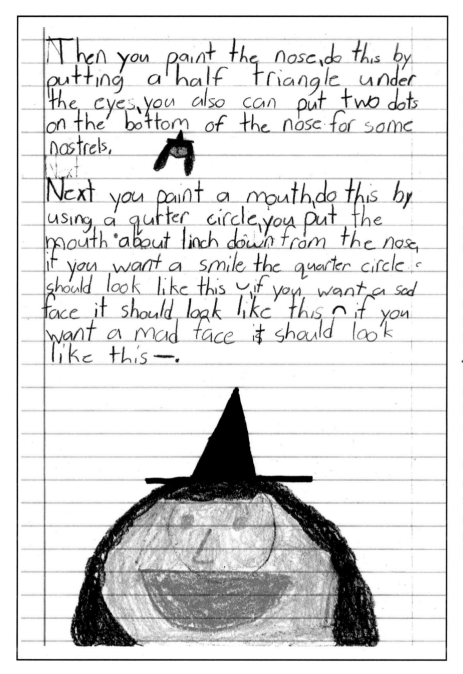

Then you paint the nose, do this by putting a half triangle under the eyes, you also can put two dots on the bottom of the nose for some nostrels,

Next you paint a mouth, do this by using a qurter circle, you put the mouth about 1inch down from the nose, if you want a smile the quarter circle should look like this ⌄ if you want a sad face it should look like this ⌒ if you want a mad face it should look like this —.

Syntactically, the piece is well written. The sentence structure is varied, with clear and appropriate coordination and subordination of ideas. Catherine repeats certain structures ("do this by") and produces parallel phrases with appropriate omission ("if you want a smile the quarter circle should look like this … if you want a sad face it should look like this … if you want a mad face … ").

Catherine uses precise language throughout and uses transition words appropriately. The spelling also is mostly correct. She misspells *pumpkin* throughout, misspells *nostrils* and *grocery,* and misspells *quarter* once and then spells it correctly another time. She also uses "buy" instead of *by* once, but the correct word is in the first draft, indicating another copying error.

Catherine uses complex sentence structures throughout the piece but does not have control of punctuation required by these constructions. Commas are not used correctly, producing run-on sentences. The use of capital letters to begin sentences is inconsistent.

This piece was written in February.

▶▶

Third Grade: First Draft

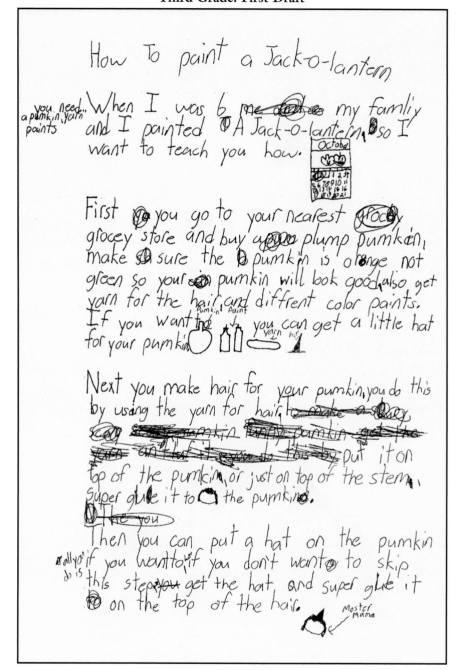

Next you paint the eyes, do this by puting a dot a little bit below the hair and hat, make sure you put the eyes right next to each other! If you want to you can paint the eyes any way you want to.

Then you paint the nose, do this by putting a half triangle under the eyes you also you can put two dots on the bottom of the nose for some nostrels.

Next you paint a mouth, do this by a qarter of a circle, you put the mouth under the nose about 1 inch down from the nose, if you want a smile the qarter circle should look like this if you want a sad face it should look like this if you want a mad face it should look like this.

Appendix

Standard 1: Print-Sound Code

By the end of the first grade, we expect students to know the regular letter-sound correspondences and use them to recognize or figure out regularly spelled one- and two-syllable words. The chart that follows lists the elements of the print-sound code we expect first-grade students to be able to put together to read meaningful texts.

Letter-Sound Correspondences

Most beginning consonants	*b-, c-, d-, f-, g-, h-, j-, k-, l-, m-, n-, p-, r-, s-, t-, v-, w-, y-, z-*
Ending consonants	*-b, -d, -g, -m, -n, -p, -t, -x, -ff, -ll, -ss, -zz*
Two-consonant beginning blends	*br-, cr-, dr-, fr-, gr-, pr-, tr-, sc-, sk-, sl-, sm-, sn-, st-, sw-*
Ending blends	*-mp, -nd, -nk, -ng, -ft, -lt, -nt, -st, -lf*
Digraphs	*ch, sh, th*
Short vowels	*a, e, i, o, u*
Long vowels with silent *e* at end of word	*a+e, e+e, i+e, o+e, u+e* (+ = consonant)
Vowel digraphs	*ai, ee, oa, ea*
Word families ending in frequent rimes	e.g., *-in, -at, -ent, -ill, -or, -un, -op, -ing*
Common grammatical endings	*-s, -ed, -ing* without dropping *e*

Vocabulary

150 high-frequency words	e.g., *the, of, and, here, one, some, what*

Some new vocabulary related to setting or topic of the text

Regularly spelled words in oral vocabulary (see above)

Selected Committee Bibliography

Members of the New Standards Primary Literacy Committee were asked to recommend their publications for readers interested in further research on primary literacy. Here is a selection of their choices.

Marilyn Jager Adams

Adams, Marilyn Jager. *Beginning To Read: Thinking and Learning About Print.* Cambridge, MA: MIT UP, 1990.

—. "The Great Debate: Then and Now." *Annals of Dyslexia* 47 (1997): 265–76.

—. "Modeling the Connections Between Word Recognition and Reading." *Theoretical Models and Processes of Reading.* 4th ed. Eds. Robert B. Ruddell, Martha R. Ruddell, and Harry Singer. Newark, DE: International Reading Association, 1994, 838–63.

—. "Reading." *The MIT Encyclopedia of the Cognitive Sciences.* Eds. Frank C. Keil and Robert A. Wilson. Cambridge, MA: MIT UP, 1999.

—. "The Science and Politics of Beginning Reading Practices." *Reading Development and the Teaching of Reading: A Psychological Perspective.* Eds. Jane Oakhill and Roger Beard. London: Blackwell, 1999.

—. "Thinking Skills Curricula: Their Promise and Progress." *Educational Psychologist* 24 (1989): 22–77.

—. "The Three-Cueing System." *Literacy For All: Issues In Teaching And Learning.* Eds. Jean Osborn and Fran Lehr. New York: Guilford, 1998, 73–99.

Adams, Marilyn Jager, and Maggie Bruck. "Resolving the 'Great Debate.'" *American Educator* 19.2 (Summer 1995): 7–20.

Adams, Marilyn Jager, and Marcia K. Henry. "Myths and Realities About Words and Literacy." *School Psychology Review* 26.3 (1987): 425–36.

Adams, Marilyn Jager, Rebecca Treiman, and Michael Pressley. "Reading, Writing, and Literacy." *Mussens' Handbook of Child Psychology. Child Psychology in Practice, Vol. 4.* Eds. William Damon, Irving E. Sigel, and K. Ann Renninger. New York: Wiley, 1998, 225–56.

Adams, Marilyn Jager, et al. *Phonemic Awareness in Young Children: A Classroom Curriculum.* Baltimore, MD: Brookes, 1998.

Blanchard, Jay, and Lyndon Searfross. "An Interview with Marilyn Jager Adams on *Beginning to Read." Journal of Reading Behavior* 23 (1991): 126–33.

Rosalinda B. Barrera

Barrera, Rosalinda B. "Bilingual Reading in the Primary Grades: Some Questions About Questionable Views and Practices." *Early Childhood Bilingual Education: A Hispanic Perspective.* Ed. Theresa H. Escobedo. New York: Teachers College Press, 1983, 164–84.

—. "The Cultural Gap in Literature-based Literacy Instruction." *Education and Urban Society* 24.2 (Feb 1992).

—. "Reading in Spanish: Insights from Children's Miscues." *Learning to Read in Different Languages.* Ed. Sarah Hudelson. Washington, DC: Center for Applied Linguistics, 1981, 1–9.

Barrera, Rosalinda B., and Oralia Garza de Cortés. "Mexican American Children's Literature in the 1990s. Toward Authenticity." *Using Multiethnic Literature in the K–8 Classroom.* Ed. Violet J. Harris. Norwood, MA: Christopher-Gordon, 1997.

Barrera, Rosalinda B., Olga Liguori, and Loretta Salas. "Ideas a Literature Can Grow On: Key Insights for Enriching and Expanding Children's Literature About the Mexican American Experience." *Teaching Multicultural Literature in Grades K–8.* Ed. Violet J. Harris. Norwood, MA: Christopher-Gordon, 1993.

Barrera, Rosalinda B., R. E. Quiroa, and C. West-Williams. (in press). "Poco a Poco: The Continuing Development of Mexican American Children's Literature in the 1990s." *The New Advocate* 12.3 (Fall 1999).

Barrera, Rosalinda B., Verlinda D. Thompson, and Mark Dressman, eds. *Kaleidoscope: A Multicultural Booklist for Grades K–8.* 2nd ed. Urbana, IL: National Council of Teachers of English, 1997.

Barrera, Rosalinda B., G. Valdés, and M. Cárdenas. "Analyzing the Recall of Students Across Different Language-reading Categories: A Study of Third-graders' Spanish-L1, English-L1, and English-L2 Comprehension." *Solving Problems in Literacy: Learners, Teachers, and Researchers.* Eds. Jerome A. Niles and Rosary V. Lalik. Rochester, NY: National Reading Conference, 1986.

Hudelson, Sarah, and Rosalinda B. Barrera. "Bilingual/Second Language Learners and Reading." *Helping Children Learn to Read.* Eds. Lyndon W. Searfoss and John E. Readence. Englewood Cliffs, NJ: Prentice-Hall, 1985.

Jimenez, R. T., et al. "Conversations: Latina and Latino Researchers Interact on Issues Related to Literacy Learning." *Reading Research Quarterly* 34.2 (1999): 217–30.

Lucy Calkins

Calkins, Lucy McCormick. *The Art of Teaching Writing.* Portsmouth, NH: Heinemann, 1986.

—. *Lessons from a Child.* Portsmouth, NH: Heinemann, 1983.

Calkins, Lucy McCormick, and Shelley Harwayne. *Living Between the Lines.* Portsmouth, NH: Heinemann, 1991.

—. *The Writing Workshop: A World of Difference.* Portsmouth, NH: Heinemann, 1987.

Calkins, Lucy McCormick, Shelley Harwayne, and Alex Mitchell. *The Writing Workshop: A World of Difference* [video]. Portsmouth, NH: Heinemann, 1987.

Calkins, Lucy McCormick, et al. *A Teacher's Guide to Standardized Reading Tests: Knowledge is Power.* Portsmouth, NH: Heinemann, 1998.

Courtney B. Cazden

Cazden, Courtney B. "The Acquisition of Noun and Verb Inflections." *Child Development* 39 (1968): 433–48.

—. "Can Ethnographic Research Go Beyond the Status Quo?" *Anthropology and Education Quarterly* 14.1 (Spring 1983): 33–41.

—. *Child Language and Education.* New York: Holt, Rinehart, & Winston, 1972.

—. "Classroom Discourse." *Handbook of Research on Teaching.* 3rd ed. Ed. Merlin C. Wittrock. New York: Macmillan, 1986, 432–63.

—. *Classroom Discourse: The Language of Teaching and Learning.* Portsmouth, NH: Heinemann, 1988.

—. "Concentrated Versus Contrived Encounters: Suggestions for Language Assessment in Early Childhood Education." *Language and Learning in Early Childhood.* Ed. Alan Davies. London: Heinemann, 1977, 40–54.

—. "Environmental Assistance Revisited: Variation and Functional Equivalence." *The Development of Language and Language Researchers.* Ed. Frank S. Kessel. Hillsdale, NJ: Erlbaum, 1988, 281–97.

—. "Hypercorrection in Test Responses." *Theory into Practice* 14.5 (Dec 1975): 343–6.

—. *Language in Early Childhood Education.* revised ed. Washington, DC: National Association for the Education of Young Children, 1981.

—. "Problems for Education: Language as Curriculum Content and Learning Environment." *Language as a Human Problem.* Eds. Einar I. Haugen and Morton W. Bloomfield. New York: Norton, 1973, 137–50.

—. *Whole Language Plus: Essays on Literacy in the United States and New Zealand.* New York: Teachers College Press, 1992.

Cazden, Courtney B., Vera P. John, and Dell H. Hymes, eds. *Functions of Language in the Classroom.* Prospect Heights, IL: Waveland, 1985.

Barbara R. Foorman

Adams, Marilyn Jager, et al. *Phonemic Awareness in Young Children: A Classroom Curriculum.* Baltimore, MD: Brookes, 1998.

Foorman, Barbara R. "The Relevance of a Connectionist Model of Reading for 'The Great Debate.'" *Educational Psychology Review* 6.1 (1994): 25–47.

—. "Research on 'The Great Debate': Code-oriented Versus Whole-language Approaches to Reading Instruction." *School Psychology Review* 24.3 (1995): 376–92.

Foorman, Barbara R., Jack M. Fletcher, and David J. Francis. "Preventing Reading Failure by Ensuring Effective Reading Instruction." *The Keys to Literacy*. Eds. Susannah Patton and Madelyn Holmes. Washington, DC: Council for Basic Education, 1998.

Foorman, Barbara R., L. Jenkins, and David J. Francis. "Links Among Segmenting, Spelling, and Reading Words in First and Second Grades." *Reading and Writing* 5 (1993): 1–17.

Foorman, Barbara R., and Alexander W. Siegel. *Acquisition of Reading Skills: Cultural Constraints and Cognitive Universals*. Mahwah, NJ: Erlbaum, 1986.

Foorman, Barbara R., et al. "The Case for Early Reading Interventions." *Foundations of Reading Acquisition and Dyslexia: Implications for Early Intervention*. Mahwah, NJ: Erlbaum, 1997, 243–64.

Foorman, Barbara R., et al. "Early Interventions for Children with Reading Problems." *Scientific Studies of Reading* 1.3 (1997): 255–76.

Foorman, Barbara R., et al. "How Letter-sound Instruction Mediates Progress in First-grade Reading and Spelling." *Journal of Educational Psychology* 83 (1991): 456–69.

Foorman, Barbara R., et al. "Relation of Phonological and Orthographic Processing to Early Reading: Comparing Two Approaches to Regression-based, Reading-level-match Designs." *Journal of Educational Psychology* 88.4 (1996): 639–52.

Foorman, Barbara R., et al. "The Role of Instruction in Learning to Read: Preventing Reading Failure in At-risk Children." *Journal of Educational Psychology* 90.1 (1998): 37–55.

Sally Hampton

Hampton, Sally. "Children Doing the Business of School." *The Reading Teacher* 48.4 (Dec–Jan 1994–95): 350–53.

—. "The Education of At-Risk Students." *Theory and Practice in the Teaching of Writing: Rethinking the Discipline*. Ed. Lee Odell. Carbondale, IL: Southern Illinois UP, 1993, 186–212.

—. "Restructuring Curriculum for 'Real-World' Experiences." *Educational Horizons* 74.4 (Summer 1996): 187–91.

—. "Strategies for Increasing Achievement in Writing." *Educating Everybody's Children: Diverse Teaching Strategies for Diverse Learners*. Ed. Robert W. Cole. Alexandria, VA: Association for Supervision and Curriculum Development, 1995, 99–120.

—. "Teacher Change: Overthrowing the Myth of One Teacher, One Classroom." *Teachers Thinking, Teachers Knowing*. Ed. Timothy Shanahan. Urbana, IL: National Council of Teachers of English, 1994, 122–42.

Odell, Lee, and Sally Hampton. "Writing Assessment, Writing Instruction, and Teacher Professionalism." *A Rhetoric of Doing*. Carbondale, IL: Southern Illinois UP, 1992, 276–90.

Angela M. Jaggar

Cullinan Bernice, E. Greene, and Angela M. Jaggar. "Books, Babies, and Libraries: The Librarian's Role in Literacy Development." *Language Arts* 67.7 (Nov 1990): 750–55.

Jaggar, Angela M. "New Views of Language Learning." *Language Arts* 60.1 (Jan 1990): 130.

—. "Teacher As Learner: Implications for Staff Development." *Teachers and Research: Language Learning in the Classroom*. Eds. Gay Su Pinnell and Myna L. Matlin. Newark, DE: International Reading Association, 1989, 66–80.

—. "What is Whole Language and Where Does Emergent Literacy Fit?" *Pre-K Today* 3 (1989): 23–4.

Jaggar, Angela M., D. H. Carrara, and S. E. Weiss. "Research Currents: The Influence of Reading on Children's Narrative Writing (and Vice Versa)." *Language Arts* 63.3 (Mar 1986): 292–300.

Jaggar, Angela M., and M. Trika Smith-Burke. "Implementing Reading Recovery in New York: Insights From the First Two Years." *Getting Reading Right From the Start: Effective Early Literacy Interventions*. Eds. Elfreida H. Heibert and Barbara M. Taylor. Boston: Allyn and Bacon, 1994.

—. *Observing the Language Learner.* Newark, DE: International Reading Association and National Council of Teachers of English, 1985.

—. *The Reading Recovery Program in New York City: A Five Year Summary Report, 1989-1994.* New York: New York UP, 1995.

Pinnell, Gay Su, and Angela M. Jaggar. "Oral Language: Speaking and Listening in the Classroom." *Handbook of Research on Teaching the English Language Arts.* Eds. James Flood, et al. New York: Macmillan, 1991, 691–720.

Smith-Burke, M. Trika, Dorothy H. Deegan, and Angela M. Jaggar. "Whole Language: A Viable Approach for Special and Remedial Education." *Topics in Language Disorders* 11 (1991): 58–68.

P. David Pearson

Barr, Rebecca, et al., eds. *Handbook of Reading Research, Volume 2.* New York: Longman, 1991.

Diez, Mary E., Virginia Richardson, and P. David Pearson. *Setting Standards and Educating Teachers: A National Conversation.* Washington, DC: American Association of Colleges for Teacher Education, 1994.

Fielding, Linda G., and P. David Pearson. "Reading Comprehension: What Works." *Educational Leadership* 51.5 (Feb 1994): 62–7.

Garcia, G. E., and P. David Pearson. "Assessment and Diversity." *Review of Research in Education, Volume 20.* Ed. Linda Darling-Hammond. Washington, DC: American Educational Research Association, 1994, 337–92.

Pearson, P. David. "Reclaiming the Center." *The First R: Every Child's Right to Read.* Eds. Michael F. Graves, Paulus W. van den Broek, and Barbara M. Taylor. New York: Teachers College Press, 1996, 259–74.

—. "Six Ideas in Search of a Champion: What Policymakers Should Know About the Teaching and Learning of Literacy in Our Schools." *Journal of Literacy Research* 28.2 (1996): 302–09.

—. "Teaching and Learning Reading: A Research Perspective." *Language Arts* 70.6 (Oct 1993): 502–11.

Pearson, P. David, and Anne C. Stallman. "Resistance, Complacency and Reform in Reading Assessment." *Reading, Language, and Literacy: Instruction for the Twenty-first Century.* Eds. Jean Osborn and Fran Lehr. Hillsdale, NJ: Erlbaum, 1994, 239–51.

Pearson, P. David, and D. Stephens. "Learning About Literacy: A 30-year Journey." *Elementary Reading: Process and Practice.* Eds. Christine J. Gordon, George D. Labercane, and William R. McEachern. Boston: Ginn, 1993, 4–18.

Pearson, P. David, et al., eds. *Handbook of Reading Research.* New York: Longman, 1984.

Taylor, Barbara M., Larry Allen Harris, and P. David Pearson. *Reading Difficulties: Instruction and Assessment.* New York: Random House, 1988.

Taylor, Barbara M., et al. *Reading Difficulties: Instruction and Assessment.* 2nd ed. New York: McGraw-Hill, 1995.

Charles Perfetti

Perfetti, Charles A. "Cognitive Research Can Inform Reading Education." *Journal of Research in Reading* 18.2 (Sept 1995): 106–15.

—. "The Psycholinguistics of Spelling and Reading." *Learning to Spell: Research, Theory, and Practice Across Languages.* Eds. Charles A. Perfetti, Laurence Rieben, and Michel Fayol. Mahwah, NJ: Erlbaum, 1997, 21–38.

—. *Reading Ability.* New York: Oxford UP, 1985.

—. "Reading Acquisition and Beyond: Decoding Includes Cognition." *American Journal of Education* 93 (1984): 40–60.

—. "The Representation Problem in Reading Acquisition." *Reading Acquisition.* Eds. Philip B. Gough, Linnea C. Ehri, and Rebecca Treiman. Hillsdale, NJ: Erlbaum, 1992, 145–74.

—. "Representations and Awareness in the Acquisition of Reading Competence." *Learning to Read: Basic Research and Its Implications.* Eds. Laurence Rieben and Charles A. Perfetti. Hillsdale, NJ: Erlbaum, 1991, 33–44.

—. "Two Basic Questions About Reading and Learning to Read." *Problems and Interventions in Literacy Development.* Eds. Pieter Reitsma and Ludo Verhoeven. London: Kluwer, 1998, 15–57.

Perfetti, Charles A., and M. A. Marron. "Learning to Read: Literacy Acquisition by Children and Adults." *Advances in Adult Literacy Research and Development.* Ed. D. A. Wagner. Hampton, 1998.

Perfetti, Charles A., and Deborah McCutchen. "Schooled Language Competence: Linguistic Abilities in Reading and Writing." *Advances in Applied Psycholinguistics: Reading, Writing and Language Learning, Vol. 2.* Ed. Sheldon Rosenberg. New York: Cambridge UP, 1987, 105–41.

Perfetti, Charles A., Laurence Rieben, and Michel Fayol, eds. *Learning to Spell: Research, Theory, and Practice Across Languages.* Mahwah, NJ: Erlbaum, 1997.

Perfetti, Charles A., and Sulan Zhang. "What It Means to Learn to Read." *The First R: Every Child's Right to Read.* Eds. Michael F. Graves, Paulus W. van den Broek, and Barbara M. Taylor. New York: Teachers College Press, 1996, 37–61.

Rieben, Laurence, and Charles A. Perfetti, eds. *Learning to Read: Basic Research and Its Implications.* Hillsdale, NJ: Erlbaum, 1991.

Gay Su Pinnell

Fountas, Irene C., and Gay Su Pinnell. *Guided Reading: Good First Teaching for All Children.* Portsmouth, NH: Heinemann, 1996.

Lyons, Carol A., Gay Su Pinnell, and Diane E. DeFord. *Partners in Learning: Teachers and Children in Reading Recovery.* New York: Teachers College Press, 1993.

Pinnell, Gay Su. "Reading Recovery: Helping At-risk Children Learn to Read." *The Elementary School Journal* 90.2 (1989): 161–83. (Winner of the Albert J. Harris Award.)

—. "Success for Low Achievers Through Reading Recovery." *Educational Leadership* 48.1 (1990): 17–21.

—. "Teaching for Problem Solving in Reading." *Reading and Writing Quarterly* 9.4 (1993): 289–306.

Pinnell, Gay Su, and Irene C. Fountas. *Help America Read: A Handbook for Volunteers.* Portsmouth, NH: Heinemann, 1997.

—. *Word Matters: Teaching Phonics and Spelling in the Reading-Writing Classroom.* Portsmouth, NH: Heinemann, 1998.

Pinnell, Gay Su, Mary D. Fried, and Rose Mary Estice. "Reading Recovery: Learning How to Make a Difference." *The Reading Teacher* 43.4 (1990): 282–95.

Pinnell, Gay Su, and Angela M. Jaggar. "Oral Language: Speaking and Listening in the Classroom." *Handbook of Research on Teaching English Language Arts.* Eds. James Flood, et al. New York: Macmillan, 1991, 691–720.

Pinnell, Gay Su, et al. "Comparing Instructional Models for the Literacy Education of High Risk First Graders." *Reading Research Quarterly* 29.1 (1994): 9–38.

Lauren B. Resnick

Resnick, Lauren B. "Literacy in School and Out." *Daedalus* 119.2 (Spring 1990): 169–85.

—. *Education and Learning to Think.* Washington, DC: National Academy Press, 1987.

Resnick, Lauren B., A. Collins, and James G. Greeno. "Learning Environments." *International Encyclopedia of Education.* 2nd ed. Eds. Torsten Husen and T. Neville Postlethwaite. New York: Pergamon, 1994, 3, 297–302.

Resnick, Lauren B., and Megan Williams Hall. "Learning Organizations for Sustainable Education Reform." *Daedalus* 127.4 (Winter 1998): 89–118.

Resnick, Lauren B., and Sharon Nelson-Le Gall. "Socializing Intelligence." *Piaget, Vygotsky and Beyond: Future Issues for Developmental Psychology and Education.* Eds. Leslie Smith, Julie Dockrell, and Peter Tomlinson. New York: Routledge, 1997, 145–58.

Resnick, Lauren B., and Daniel P. Resnick. "Assessing the Thinking Curriculum: New Tools for Educational Reform." *Changing Assessments: Alternative Views of Aptitude, Achievement and Instruction.* Eds. Bernard R. Gifford and Mary Catherine O'Connor. Boston: Kluwer, 1992, 37–75.

Resnick, Lauren B., et al. *Children's Early Text Construction.* Mahwah, NJ: Erlbaum, 1996.

Resnick, Lauren B., et al. "Reasoning in Conversation." *Cognition and Instruction* 11.3–4 (1993): 347–64.

Dorothy S. Strickland

Galda, Lee, Bernice E. Cullinan, and Dorothy S. Strickland. *Language, Literacy, and the Child*. 2nd ed. Fort Worth, TX: Harcourt, 1997.

Strickland, Dorothy S. "The Learner Develops: Language Development in the Elementary School Years." *Handbook of Research on Teaching the English Language Arts*. revised edition. Eds. James Flood, et al. New York: Macmillan, 1999.

—. "Planning the Writing Curriculum (K-2)." *Handbook of Writing Research*. Eds. James R. Squire and R. Indrisano. New York: Macmillan, 1999.

—. "Reinventing our Literacy Programs: Books, Basics, Balance." *The Reading Teacher* 48.4 (Dec–Jan 1994–95): 294–303.

—. *Teaching Phonics Today: A Primer for Educators*. Newark, DE: International Reading Association, 1998.

—. "What's Basic in Reading? Finding Common Ground." *Educational Leadership* 55 (Mar 1998): 7–10.

Strickland, Dorothy S., and E. Kulliseid. *Literature, Literacy, and Learning*. Chicago: American Library Association, 1990.

Strickland, Dorothy S., and Lesley Mandel Morrow, eds. *Emerging Literacy: Young Children Learn to Read and Write*. Newark, DE: International Reading Association, 1989.

Wepner, Shelley B., Joan T. Feeley, and Dorothy S. Strickland. *The Administration and Supervision of Reading Programs*. 2nd ed. New York: Teachers College Press, 1995.

Elizabeth Sulzby

Committee on the Prevention of Reading Difficulties in Young Children. *Preventing Reading Difficulties in Young Children*. Eds. Catherine E. Snow, M. Susan Burns, and Peg Griffin. Washington, DC: National Academy Press, 1998.

Sulzby, Elizabeth. "Assessment of Emergent Literacy: Storybook Reading." *The Reading Teacher* 44.7 (Mar 1991): 498–500.

—. "The Development of the Young Child and the Emergence of Literacy." *Handbook of Research on Teaching the English Language Arts*. Eds. James Flood, et al. New York: Macmillan, 1991, 273–85.

—. "Kindergartners as Writers and Readers." *Advances in Writing Research, Vol. I. Children's Early Writing Development*. Ed. Marcia Farr. Norwood, NJ: Ablex, 1985, 127–99.

—. "Literacy's Future for All Our Children: Where is Research in Reading Comprehension Leading Us?" *Reading Research into the Year 2000*. Eds. Anne P. Sweet and Judith I. Anderson. Hillsdale, NJ: Erlbaum, 1993, 37–64.

—. "Roles of Oral and Written Language in Children Approaching Conventional Literacy." *Children's Early Text Construction*. Eds. Clotilde Pontecorvo, et al. Mahwah, NJ: Erlbaum, 1996, 25–46.

—. "Transitions From Emergent to Conventional Writing: Research Directions." *Language Arts* 69.4 (Apr 1992): 50–7.

—. "Writing and Reading: Signs of Oral and Written Language Organization in the Young Child." *Emergent Literacy: Writing and Reading*. Eds. William H. Teale and Elizabeth Sulzby. Norwood, NJ: Ablex, 1986, 50–89.

Sulzby, Elizabeth, and P. A. Edwards. "The Role of Parents in Supporting Literacy Development of Young Children." *Language and Literacy in Early Childhood Education*. Eds. Bernard Spodek and Olivia N. Saracho. New York: Teachers College Press, 1993, 156–77.

Sulzby, Elizabeth, and William H. Teale. "Emergent Literacy." *Handbook of Reading Research, Volume II*. Eds. Rebecca Barr, et al. New York: Longman, 1991, 727–57.

—. "Writing Development in Early Childhood." *Educational Horizons* 64.1 (Fall 1985): 8–12.

Teale, William H., and Elizabeth Sulzby, eds. *Emergent Literacy: Writing and Reading*. Norwood, NJ: Ablex, 1986.

Sharon Taberski

Taberski, Sharon. *A Close-Up Look at Teaching Reading: Focusing on Children and Our Goals* [video series]. Portsmouth, NH: Heinemann, 1996.

—. "From Fake to Fiction: Young Children Learn About Writing Fiction." *Language Arts* 64.6 (Oct 1987): 586–96.

—. "Motivating Readers." *Instructor Magazine* 107.2 (Sept 1997): 34–6.

—. "Motivating Readers." *Instructor Magazine* 107.3 (Oct 1997): 83–5.

—. "Motivating Readers: Give Shared Reading the Attention It Deserves." *Instructor Magazine* 107.7 (Apr 1998): 32, 35.

—. "Motivating Readers: How Skillful Are You at Matching Kids and Books?" *Instructor Magazine* 107.4 (Nov–Dec 1997): 53–5.

—. "Motivating Readers. How to Make the Most of Your Time During Independent Reading." *Instructor Magazine* 107.5 (Jan–Feb 1998): 32–4.

—. "Motivating Readers. Make Guided Reading Groups Flexible and Independent." *Instructor Magazine* 107.6 (Mar 1998): 83–4.

Taberski, Sharon, et al. *Reading Instruction: What's It All About?* [video]. National Council of Teachers of English and Whole Language Umbrella, 1997.

William Teale

Boardman, A. (Producer), and William H. Teale. *Parents, Kids & Books: The Joys of Reading Together* [video]. Dallas, TX: KERA, 1993.

Center for the Study of Reading (Producer), and William H. Teale. *Emergent Literacy* [video]. *Teaching Reading: Strategies from Successful Classrooms, A Six-part National Teacher Training Video Series.* Champaign, IL: Center for the Study of Reading/University of Illinois, 1991.

Labbo, Linda D., and William H. Teale. "Emergent Literacy as a Model of Reading Instruction." *Instructional Models in Reading.* Eds. Steven A. Stahl and David A. Hayes. Mahwah, NJ: Erlbaum, 1997, 249–81.

Martinez, Miriam G., Markay Cheyney, and William H. Teale. "Classroom Context and Kindergartners' Dramatic Story Reenactments." *Play and Early Literacy Development.* Ed. James F. Christie. Albany, NY: State University of New York Press, 1991, 119–40.

Martinez, Miriam G., and William H. Teale. "Teacher Storybook Reading Style: A Comparison of Six Teachers." *Research in the Teaching of English* 27.2 (May 1993): 175–99.

Sulzby, Elizabeth, and William H. Teale. "Emergent Literacy." *Handbook of Reading Research, Volume II.* Eds. Rebecca Barr, et al. New York: Longman, 1991, 727–57.

Teale, William H. "Reading to Young Children: Its Significance in the Process of Literacy Development." *Awakening to Literacy.* Eds. Hillel Goelman, Antoinette A. Oberg, and Frank Smith. Exeter, NH: Heinemann, 1984, 110–21.

—. "Toward a Theory of How Children Learn to Read and Write Naturally." *Language Arts* 59.6 (Sept 1982): 555–70.

—. "Young Children and Reading: Trends Across the 20th Century." *Journal of Education* 177.3 (1995): 95–125.

Teale, William H., and Miriam G. Martinez. "Getting on the Right Road to Reading: Bringing Children and Books Together in the Classroom." *Young Children* 44.1 (Nov 1988): 10–5.

Teale, William H., and Elizabeth Sulzby. "Emergent Literacy: New Perspectives on Young Children's Reading and Writing Development." *Emerging Literacy: Young Children Learn to Read and Write.* Eds. Dorothy Strickland and Lesley Mandel Morrow. Newark, DE: International Reading Association, 1989, 1–15.

Teale, William H., and Elizabeth Sulzby, eds. *Emergent Literacy: Writing and Reading.* Norwood, NJ: Ablex, 1986.

Josefina Tinajero

Gonzalez, Maria Louisa, Ana Huerta-Macias, and Josefina Villamil Tinajero, eds. *Educating Latino Students: A Guide to Successful Practice.* Lancaster, PA: Technomic, 1998.

Tinajero, Josefina Villamil, and Alma Flor Ada, eds. *The Power of Two Languages: Literacy and Biliteracy for Spanish Speaking Students.* New York: Macmillan, 1993.

Tinajero, Josefina Villamil, Maria Louisa Gonzales, and Florence Dick. *Raising Career Aspirations of Hispanic Girls. Fastback 320.* Bloomington, IN: Phi Delta Kappa Educational Foundation, 1991.

Tinajero, Josefina Villamil, and Ana Huerta-Macias, eds. *Special Issue: Parental Involvement. Journal of Educational Issues of Language Minority Students* 16 (Summer 1996).

Tinajero, Josefina Villamil, and Ana Huerta-Macias. "Teacher Preparation in the Language Arts: A Synthesis." *Handbook of Research on Teaching Literacy Through the Communicative and Visual Arts.* Eds. James Flood, et al. New York: Macmillan, 1997, 428–36.

Tinajero, Josefina Villamil, and Sandra Rollins Hurley. "Literacy Instruction for Students Acquiring English: Moving Beyond the Immersion Debate." *The Reading Teacher* 50.4 (Dec–Jan 1996–97): 356–59.

Tinajero, Josefina Villamil, Sandra Rollins Hurley, and Elizabeth Varela Lozano. "Developing Language and Literacy in Bilingual Classrooms." *The Education of Latino Students: A Guide to Successful Practice.* Eds. Maria Louisa Gonzalez, Ana Huerta-Macias, and Josefina Villamil Tinajero. Lancaster, PA: Technomic, 1998.

Tinajero, Josefina Villamil, and M. A. Maier. *Creating a Hope and a Future: The Mother-Daughter Program.* El Paso, TX: The University of Texas Office of News and Publications, 1995.

Gordon Wells

Gutfreund, Mary, Maureen Harrison, and C. Gordon Wells. *The Bristol Language Development Scales.* Windsor, UK: NFER-Nelson, 1989.

Wells, C. Gordon. *Dialogic Inquiry: Towards a Sociocultural Practice and Theory of Education.* New York: Cambridge UP, 1999.

—. *Language Development in the Pre-school Years. Language at Home and at School, Vol 2.* Cambridge: Cambridge UP, 1985.

—. *Language, Learning and Education: Selected Papers from the Bristol Study, Language at Home and at School.* Philadelphia, PA: NFER-Nelson, 1985.

—. *Learning Through Interaction: The Study of Language Development. Language at Home and at School, Vol 1.* Cambridge: Cambridge UP, 1981.

—. *The Meaning Makers: Children Learning Language and Using Language to Learn.* Portsmouth, NH: Heinemann, 1986.

—. "Some Questions About Direct Instruction: Why? To Whom? How? and When?" *Language Arts* 76.1 (Jan 1998): 27–35.

—. "Talk About Text: Where Literacy is Learned and Taught." *Curriculum Inquiry* 20.4 (1990): 369–405.

Wells, C. Gordon, and Gen Ling Chang-Wells. *Constructing Knowledge Together: Classrooms as Centers of Inquiry and Literacy.* Portsmouth, NH: Heinemann, 1992.

Wells, C. Gordon, et al. *Changing Schools from Within: Creating Communities of Inquiry.* Portsmouth, NH: Heinemann, 1994.

Other Bibliography

To learn more about running records, refer to the following text:

Clay, Marie M. *An Observation Survey of Early Literacy Achievement.* Portsmouth, NH: Heinemann, 1993.

To learn more about research referred to in **Research Perspectives,** refer to the following texts:

Hayes, D. P., and M. G. Ahrens. "Vocabulary simplification for children: A special case of 'motherese'?" *Journal of Child Language* 15.2 (1988): 395–410.

Robbins, C., and L. C. Ehri. "Reading storybooks to kindergartners helps them learn new vocabulary words." *Journal of Educational Psychology* 86.1 (1994): 54–64.

Acknowledgments

As co-chairs of the New Standards Primary Literacy Committee, we wish to acknowledge the many people whose contributions to the work of the committee and the preparation of this publication and companion CD-ROMs have been invaluable. Their specific contributions are noted below.

Phil Daro

Sally Hampton

Lauren Resnick

Sally Mentor Hay, director of product development, National Center on Education and the Economy, for managing the production of this publication, the companion CD-ROMs, video production and the writing of the commentary for the student reading performances. Without her leadership and management skills, this book would not have been possible.

Megan Williams Hall, research associate, University of Pittsburgh, Learning Research and Development Center, for serving as the staff writer who wrote the standards and became the project's valued historian.

Donna DiPrima Bickel, University of Pittsburgh, Institute for Learning, Learning Research and Development Center, for significant contributions to the development of the reading standards, the collection, video production, and the selection and writing of the commentary for student reading performances.

Martha Vockley, for writing, editing and project management; **Judith Lang,** for art direction and graphic design; **Kathy Ames,** for copyediting and production management; and their colleagues at KSA Group, all of whom transformed the manuscript and student work samples into this engaging publication.

Bonnie Dickinson, Susan Fitzgerald, Amy Heckathorn, Linda Lewis, Jennifer Regen and **Faye Richardson,** English Language Arts Unit, National Center on Education and the Economy; and **Lucille Davidson,** Fort Worth Independent School District, Fort Worth, Texas, for their significant support of the committee's work and in the preparation of this publication.

Fran Claggett, Sebastopol, Calif.; **Virginia Lockwood,** Public School 116, New York, N.Y.; **Susan Radley,** Houston, Texas; **Halah Shaheen Young,** Linden Academy, Pittsburgh Public Schools, Pittsburgh, Pa.; **Leslie Zachman,** Public School 59, New York, N.Y.; and **Maria Lamb,** principal, and **Lori Bolling, Nancy Box, Elizabeth Donaldson, Gracie Escovedo** and **Charlotte Sassman,** teachers, Alice Carlson Applied Learning Center, Fort Worth Independent School District, Fort Worth, Texas, for their assistance with collecting, selecting and advising on student performances in writing.

Donna Micheaux and **Kathleen Young** for their comments on early draft standards, and other **Research**

Fellows at the University of Pittsburgh's Institute for Learning for their support of this work.

Nancy Artz, Manjula Duckett, Pat Stanton and Eliza Tweedy, University of Pittsburgh, Learning Research and Development Center, for their support in the preparation of this publication.

Judy Codding, vice president of the National Center on Education and the Economy, for her active support of this project, and the following staff members: Andrea Chalmers, Marc Collien, Susan Dean, Judith Curtis, Andy Plattner, Suzie Sullivan, Pat Whiteaker and Tom Wilkins, for their contributions to the preparation of this publication and the companion CD-ROMs.

Ann Bowers, Noyce Foundation; Isabel Beck, University of Pittsburgh, Learning Research and Development Center; Bill Honig, California State University at San Francisco; Samuel J. Meisels, School of Education, University of Michigan; Fritz Mosher, Carnegie Corporation of New York; and Peter Heany, Board of Education of the City of New York, for consultation on issues related to the development of the Primary Literacy Standards.

Marge Cappo, Kathy Darling, Mike Fish, Lara Meyer, Lisa Paul and Devin Wilson, Learning in Motion, Inc., Santa Cruz, Calif., for design and development of the companion CD-ROMs.

Ron Bricker, Gallina-Bricker, Washington, D.C.; Kathy Darling, Learning in Motion, Inc., Santa Cruz, Calif.; Emil Gallina, Gallina-Bricker, Washington, D.C.; and Dave Kent, Pittsburgh, Pa., for video production and editing.

Student performances in reading were collected from urban schools around the country with strong reading programs that prepare students to meet high standards of performance. For their assistance in producing videos of students demonstrating performances related to the grade-by-grade reading standards, we thank the following teachers, administrators and staff:

Gary Rader, principal, and Kate Bartley, Ida Patacca and Wendy Wexler, Highland Elementary School, Columbus Public Schools; and Polly Lipkin, Ohio State University, Columbus, Ohio.

Elba Diana Carrion, principal, and Anthi Egglezos, Joyce Halam, Dorothy Johnson, Bettye Miller, Mireya Ortiz, Christine Roberts and Adriana Salazar, Martinez Elementary School; and Phyllis Hunter, manager, reading department, Houston Public Schools, Houston, Texas.

Susan Feinberg, principal, and Tracy Bellmar, Carla Jones, Barbara Kimber, Lisa Petersen and Angela Susnjar, Grant Elementary School; Ruth Perez, principal, and Theresa Cooper, Linda Smith and Louise Wright, International Elementary School; and Cecelia Osborn, literacy coordinator, Long Beach Unified School District, Long Beach, Calif.

Shelley Harwayne, principal, and Joanne Hindley Salch, Amy Mandel, Pamela Mayer and Sharon Taberski, Manhattan New School; Leslie Zackman, principal, and Neva Amo, Susan Dillon and Jennifer Karson, teachers, Public School 59; and Anna Switzer, principal, and Jacqui Getz, Jennifer Purdy and Dana Ostrowsky, Public School 234, Community School District 2, New York, N.Y.

Richard Goldstein, assistant principal in charge; Liz Phillips, early childhood coordinator; and Phyllis Allen, Bill Fulbrecht, Hannah Schneewind and Pascale Pradel, teachers, Public School 321, Community School District 15, New York, N.Y.

Students and teachers from the GAMS Tech Magnet School of the Newburgh Enlarged City School District in Newburgh, N.Y., worked patiently and diligently to assist the artist in posing for the illustrations in this book. For their assistance, we thank the following staff, administrators and students:

Teachers Martha Alexander, Janet Carlson, Liza Coopersmith, Rosana Lopez, Carole Marchese, Goncalo Pinheiro, Alicia Ramos and Brenda Underhill, for assisting the artist with their time and care both by posing as models and by helping with the students. Carole Mineo, principal, and José Carrión, assistant principal, for their organizational skills and support.

—

Lauren Resnick and Phil Daro wish to acknowledge the special contribution of their colleague and co-chair, Sally Hampton, who drafted the Learning to Write chapter, selected and analyzed the student writing samples, and wrote the commentary.

About New Standards

New Standards is a joint project of the Learning Research and Development Center (LRDC) at the University of Pittsburgh and the National Center on Education and the Economy (NCEE). Since it began in 1991, New Standards has led the nation in standards-based reform efforts. New Standards, heading a consortium of 26 states and six school districts, developed the New Standards® Performance Standards, a set of internationally competitive performance standards in English language arts, mathematics, science and applied learning in fourth, eighth and 10th grades.

New Standards also pioneered standards-based performance assessment, developing the New Standards® Reference Examinations and a portfolio assessment system to measure student achievement against the performance standards. With support from the U.S. Department of Education's Office of Educational Research and Improvement, New Standards is working on Speaking and Listening Performance Standards for kindergarten through third grade, a parent handbook, and various video and CD-ROM products to support implementation of the Primary Literacy Standards.